About this book

Biotechnology is already playing an increasing role in medicine and agriculture in the industrialized nations. But are these developments likely to bypass the majority of the world's population in the South? Do Southern societies lack the necessary financial resources and technological infrastructure to embark on long-term research and development in this area? Mila Avramovic addresses these questions against the background of how biotechnology has actually developed in the West.

The author highlights how human health care, rather than agriculture, has received most investment; how universities, multinationals and small specialized firms have all been involved; and the respective roles of the public and private sectors. She concludes that it is possible for some Third World countries to engage in those areas of biotechnology development of most relevance to them.

About the author

Mila Avramovic began her career as a microbiologist at the National Cancer Institute, National Institutes of Health, Maryland, USA, working on the development of recombinant DNA technology and research concerning RNA tumor viruses. She then went on to pursue her interests in health finance and management, particularly in regard to the Third World, studying at Johns Hopkins University, the London School of Economics, the Institute of Social Studies (The Hague) and the University of Amsterdam, where she recently received her Ph.D. Ms Avramovic has also worked for the World Health Organization's Department of Social and Economic Research. Her writings have appeared in *Social Science and Medicine* and *Genetic Engineering News*, as well as in several governmental publications, such as *The Developing Countries on the Eve of Cancun 1981* (UNCTAD, Geneva: 1981).

An Affordable Development?

Biotechnology, Economics and the Implications for the Third World

MILA AVRAMOVIC

ZED BOOKS
London & New Jersey

Dedicated to
my mother, my father,
Thanh-Binh and Thanh-Dam Truong,
Leo and Karen, Helga, Peter and Michael.
Special thanks to Professor Gerd Junne, Linda McPhee,
Renée Pittin, Joy Misa and Victor Vergeer.

An Affordable Development? was first published in 1996 by
Zed Books Ltd, 7 Cynthia Street, London N1 9JF, UK, and
165 First Avenue, Atlantic Highlands, New Jersey 07716, USA

Cover designed by Andrew Corbett
Typeset in Monotype Garamond by Lucy Morton, London SE12
Printed and bound in the United Kingdom
by Biddles Ltd, Guildford and King's Lynn

A catalogue record for this book is available from the British Library
US CIP data is available from the Library of Congress

ISBN 1 85649 333 4 (Hb)
ISBN 1 85649 334 2 (Pb)

Contents

List of Tables

Glossary

ANTIBODY (Ab) A specific protein produced by the immune system in humans and higher animals in response to exposure to a foreign substance. An antibody is characterized by its specific reactivity and its structural complementarity to the foreign substance, the antigen, which provoked its formation, and is thus capable of binding specifically to the foreign substance to neutralize it.

ANTIGEN A substance, usually a protein or carbohydrate, which when introduced in the body of a human or higher animal elicits from it an immune response which includes the stimulation of production of antibodies that will specifically react against the antigen.

ANTIGENIC DETERMINANT The structural portion of the antigen to which an antibody complementarily binds. Also termed EPITOPE.

ANTI-ID VACCINE A vaccine based on ANTI-IDIOTYPIC MONOCLONAL ANTIBODY technology, which serves to boost the immune systems of patients already afflicted with the disease in question.

ANTI-IDIOTYPIC MONOCLONAL ANTIBODY A monoclonal antibody which acts as a surrogate antigen. It is made by first producing a protective monoclonal antibody to the disease-causing antigen, and then making a second monoclonal antibody – which is the anti-idiotypic monoclonal antibody – to the initial protective monoclonal antibody.

ANTISERUM Blood serum containing antibodies that were present in the whole blood. See SERUM.

B CELLS *See* B LYMPHOCYTES.

B LYMPHOCYTES (B cells) A subset of white cells called lymphocytes, released from the bone marrow, which produce antibodies after challenge by an antigen.

BIOLOGICAL RESPONSE MODIFIER (BRM)   A generic term for immunoactive compounds, neuroactive compounds and hormones that act at a cellular level.

BIOLOGICAL THERAPY   A therapy for cancer which works by boosting the body's natural defensive tumor-killing mechanisms; also termed IMMUNO-THERAPY.

BIOPROCESS   A process in which living cells or components thereof are used to effect desired physical or chemical changes. A fermentation process, though often used to denote any bioprocess, strictly speaking refers only to an anaerobic bioprocess.

BIOTECHNOLOGY   In its broadest sense refers to a wide range of techniques which involve living organisms, or substances from those organisms, as a means of production. Biotechnology is an enabling technology, whose techniques are used to make or modify a product, to improve plants or animals, or to develop microorganisms for specific uses such as acting on the environment. In this study, biotechnology is used to mean "new" biotechnology, which includes only the use of modern, novel biological techniques – specifically, those techniques of recombinant DNA, monoclonal antibody technology, and/or novel bioprocessing techniques for commercial production.

CELL CULTURE   The growing of isolated cells from plants, animals or humans in the laboratory in an artificial medium that nourishes the cells and keeps them viable.

CELL FUSION   The joining of membranes of two different cell types (by use of electric shocks or chemicals), resulting in the creation of hybrid cells containing some or all of the genetic and nuclear material from both cell types and thus having properties of both the parent cells.

CHIMERIC MONOCLONAL ANTIBODY   A monoclonal antibody that is part human and part rodent.

CHROMOSOME(S)   The physical structure(s) within a cell's nucleus which contains genes, which store and transmit hereditary characteristics. Each species has a characteristic number of chromosomes.

CLONE   A group of identical genes, cells or organisms produced asexually from a common ancestor.

COMPLEMENTARITY   The relationship of the chemical bases on the two different strands of DNA. When the bases are paired properly – adenine (A) with thymine (T), and guanine (G) with cytosine (C) – the DNA strands are said to be complementary.

CROSS-REACTIVITY   An aspect of immunodiagnostic tests related to, yet different from, specificity. A cross-reaction occurs when the test correctly identifies the appropriate chemical entity, but that chemical happens to exist in a different organism than the one tested for, resulting in a false positive.

CYTOKINES Protein substances normally found in minute quantities in human blood which are necessary for coordinating, enhancing and amplifying an immune response.

DENATURATION When DNA is exposed to near-boiling temperatures and changes from its double-stranded normal state to two single strands.

DIAGNOSTIC PRODUCTS Products that recognize molecules associated with disease or other biological conditions to determine the presence or absence of the disease and/or to characterize the extent of disease.

DNA (deoxyribonucleic acid) The molecule which carries the genetic information found in all living organisms (with the exception of a few viruses). The information coded by the DNA determines the structure and function of the organism. Every inherited characteristic has its origin somewhere in the code of each individual's DNA.

DNA HYBRIDIZATION PROBE *See* DNA PROBE.

DNA PROBE A sequence of DNA that is used to detect the presence of a particular DNA SEQUENCE contained in a sample of DNA. Also termed DNA HYBRIDIZATION PROBE or GENE PROBE or PROBE.

DNA SEQUENCE The order of chemical bases in the DNA molecule, essential to the proper storage of genetic information.

ELISA (enzyme-linked immunoabsorbent assay) A type of IMMUNOASSAY where enzyme reactions are set in motion by the presence of a specific antibody–antigen binding, which produces an easy-to-spot color change.

ENZYME A protein that acts as a catalyst, speeding the rate at which a chemical reaction occurs, but not altering the reaction's nature or direction, and without the enzyme itself being destroyed.

EPITOPE *See* ANTIGENIC DETERMINANT.

EPO (erythropoietin) A genetically engineered drug which replicates the action of a hormone in the human kidney, triggering the production of red blood cells to correct chronic anemia (often found in kidney-impaired patients), thus obviating the need for frequent blood transfusions which could be contaminated with such things as the hepatitis B virus or the HIV virus (which causes AIDS).

FACTOR VIII A key blood-clotting protein missing from the blood of hemophiliacs, which causes them to suffer often from internal bleeding, and which prior to genetic engineering required infusions of the protein derived from human blood. Factor VIII is now produced as a drug through genetic engineering, avoiding possible contamination by such things as the HIV virus in infusions derived from human blood.

FALSE NEGATIVE   *See* SPECIFICITY.

FALSE POSITIVE   *See* SENSITIVITY.

FERMENTATION   An anaerobic process used for growing microorganisms (yeasts, fungi, molds and bacteria), which convert a raw material into various chemical or pharmaceutical compounds, food or drink. The microorganisms are normally incubated under specific conditions in the prescence of nutrients in large tanks called fermenters. The nutrients may consist of starches, sugars, vegetable oil, or even petroleum fractions, and the microorganisms may also need additional nitrogen, phosphorous, oxygen, vitamins, metals or other compounds to grow. Once the desired conversion by the microorganisms has taken place, the products of the reaction are removed from the fermenter, and the specific compound desired is separated from wastes and by-products and purified for use.

GENE   The fundamental physical and functional unit of heredity; an ordered sequence of chemical bases, comprising a segment of DNA, which encodes information for the production of a particular protein and the necessary signals for the production of that protein.

GENETIC ENGINEERING   Technologies (of which r-DNA technology is one of the most significant) used to isolate genes from an organism, manipulate them in the laboratory, and insert them stably in another organism. *See* RECOMBINANT DNA TECHNOLOGY.

GENE PROBE   *See* DNA PROBE.

GENOME   All the genetic material in the chromosomes of a particular organism.

HYBRID   An offspring resulting from a cross between two genetically unlike individuals.

HYBRIDIZATION   The binding together of complementary strands of DNA. Also called RENATURATION.

HYBRIDOMA   The cell resulting from the fusion of a particular type of immortal cell line (which divides continuously in cell culture and hence is "immortal"), a myeloma, with an antibody-producing B lymphocyte. The resulting fused cell is capable of continuous growth in cell culture, and produces the specific antibody produced by the parent lymphocyte, i.e. monoclonal antibodies.

IMMUNOASSAY   A diagnostic test where antibodies and antigens are used for the identification of each other.

IN VITRO Literally "in glass". Refers to a process, test or procedure in which something is measured, observed or produced outside a living organism after extraction from the organism. *In vitro* diagnostic products are products used to diagnose disease outside the body after a sample has been taken from that body.

IN VIVO Literally "in the living". Refers to a process taking place in a living organism. *In vivo* products are used within the body.

MONOCLONAL ANTIBODIES (MABs) Highly pure identical antibodies derived from a single clone of specialized cells which recognize a single, specific portion of an antigen.

MONOCLONAL ANTIBODY (MAB) *IN VIVO* IMAGING A diagnostic test to identify, localize and visualize the spread of disease within the body. MAbs are linked to radioisotopes and injected into the body, where the MAb transports the linked radioisotope to the disease site(s). The location of the disease site(s) is made visible outside the body with a special camera that can detect the radiation the radioisotopes emit.

MONOCLONAL ANTIBODY (MAB) KIT MAbs used in diagnostic tests are often sold commercially as a "kit", of which MAbs are the essential raw material. A kit refers to a complete packaged entity required to carry out the diagnostic test on the body's sample. In addition to the MAb, the kit would include such things as positive and negative controls, and other standard reagents needed for the test reaction, such as buffered salts to maintain the proper acidity, test tubes, etc.

NEW BIOTECHNOLOGY *See* BIOTECHNOLOGY.

PCR (polymerase chain reaction) An *in vitro* process in which repeated cycling of the reaction replicates a specific region of DNA exponentially, yielding millions of copies of that specific region of DNA.

PLANT VARIETY Cultivated plants that are clearly distinguishable from others by one or more characteristics, and that when reproduced retain those distinguishing characteristics.

POLYCLONAL ANTIBODIES The mixture of different antibodies produced in response to the various antigenic determinants on a particular antigen.

PROBE *See* DNA PROBE.

RECOMBINANT DNA (r-DNA) Hybrid DNA produced by joining pieces of DNA from different organisms together *in vitro*.

RECOMBINANT DNA TECHNOLOGY A broad range of techniques used to produce recombinant DNA. The term is often used synonymously with "genetic engineering", although the latter is sometimes distinguished by referring to a broader range of techniques involved in manipulating DNA. The two terms are used interchangeably in the text.

RENATURATION *See* HYBRIDIZATION.

RESTRICTION ENZYMES Certain naturally occurring bacterial enzymes which recognize specific short sequences of DNA and cut the DNA where these sites occur.

RESTRICTION FRAGMENT LENGTH POLYMORPHISMS (RFLPs) Variation in DNA fragment sizes cut by restriction enzymes.

SENSITIVITY Refers to the ability of a diagnostic test to detect a disease-producing agent or disease when it is present. A very sensitive test correctly identifies all infected individuals. A test in which the result is negative (i.e. indicating no disease present) on individuals who, in reality, actually do have the disease, is termed a FALSE NEGATIVE.

SERUM The clear liquid which separates in the clotting of blood and which contains the antibodies that were present in the whole blood.

SPECIES A taxonomic category that includes closely related, morphologically similar individuals that actually or potentially interbreed.

SPECIFICITY The ability of a test procedure correctly to determine that a disease-producing agent or disease is not present. A very specific test will correctly identify all uninfected individuals. Positive tests for individuals who do not have the disease are termed FALSE POSITIVES.

STRAIN A group of organisms of the same species having a distinctive characteristic or quality (pathogenic, biochemical or other) that can be differentiated, but that are not different enough to constitute a separate species.

SUBUNIT VACCINE A vaccine which contains only portions of an antigenic molecule of a pathogen.

THERAPEUTIC VACCINE A vaccine which boosts the immune systems of patients already afflicted with the disease in question.

TPA (tissue plasminogen activator) A genetically engineered protein drug that helps to dissolve blood clots.

TRANSFORMATION Change in the genetic structure of an organism by the incorporation of foreign DNA. After the organism has incorporated the foreign DNA in its genetic structure, it is referred to as "transformed".

Introduction

The revolutionary breakthroughs in the mid-1970s that characterized the new biotechnology – namely, recombinant DNA technology and monoclonal antibody technology, coupled with novel bioprocessing techniques – were greeted with tremendous hope and excitement as these technologies were seen as an important advance in the drive to solve some of the fundamental problems plaguing mankind, such as disease, hunger and pollution.

This study attempts to analyze the economic and financial experience of utilizing these techniques in the industrialized countries, where virtually all of the biotechnology research, development and commercialization has taken place. From this experience, the study draws implications for biotechnology policy in developing countries.

Two factors emerge as essential to the development of biotechnology: an adequate scientific/technical labor force, and finance to sustain the long gestation period – ten to twelve years – of most product development (with the notable exception of diagnostics). The two factors are in part interrelated. The main emphasis in this study is on the economics and finance of biotechnology – the most critical aspect of the experience of industrialized countries for biotechnology sustainability – although the wo/manpower aspect has not been neglected. Further work in both areas, and particularly on wo/manpower, is needed; such future research should be organized on a country-by-country basis, thereby furnishing the data for separate country studies.

The overwhelming majority of resources spent in biotechnology has been on pharmaceutical development, with agriculture ranking a distant second. In pharmaceuticals most of the resources have gone on research into key diseases in developed countries. Progress has been made in the development of new pharmaceuticals, but the advent of biotechnology has not changed the political economy of innovative drug research. The process of development of new drugs and the period of trials before products reach the market remain lengthy, with the result that most companies lose considerable sums of money over a number of years. This factor together with the setting of high profit targets, employment of highly qualified personnel, and payment of high salaries to top executives has resulted in the products marketed thus far being extremely expensive – beyond the reach of many people who need them in developed countries and prohibitively expensive for the vast majority of people in developing countries.

The major finding of the present study is that one product line of biotechnology, monoclonal-antibody-based diagnostics, is both relatively easy to develop and well-suited to the resources available in the developing countries for product development. Demands for these products are large and growing; capital requirements are relatively small and product development times relatively short. The fields of application are human health care and agriculture – cultivation of both animals and crops – as well as environmental monitoring. Furthermore, this product line can serve as a stepping stone and basis for the development of other biotechnology products in two ways. First, due to short product development times, it can generate relatively quickly the cash flow needed to help finance current operations and research requirements (thus reducing dependence on external capital). Second, it is an integral part of the vaccine development process, for which the demand in developing countries is enormous. Additionally, monoclonal antibodies offer possibilities for development into therapeutic drugs by enhancing the body's natural immune system or by serving as a "magic bullet" to deliver cell-killing agents to diseased cells and tissues.

Another way in which the developing countries may enter the field of biotechnology despite the high cost of development is by undertaking contract research for biotechnology firms and institutions and other users of biotechnology research data (for example, pharmaceutical firms) located mostly in developed countries. Contract research was undertaken on a substantial scale by existing biotechnology firms in industrial countries in the early phases of their development, enabling them to generate cash flow before they placed their products on the market. Such contract research is encountered in several developing countries, mainly under the control of institutions in developed countries.

A more recent development has been the establishment of bilateral arrangements between a developed and a developing country, under which cooperative and complementary biotechnology product ventures and sales have been organized and financed, such as the US–Thailand agreement of 1991. While it is too early to assess the impact of such arrangements, in principle they should lead to biotechnology development in developing countries growing faster than would otherwise be the case, provided that the interests of developing countries are fully protected.

Contract research and bilateral agreements may focus on diagnostics development. In such an approach, not only would cash be generated in the early phases of biotechnology, but skills and knowledge generated could, more directly and more quickly than in other biotechnology sectors, serve the broader policy objectives in developing countries of improving the health care of their populations and promoting agricultural growth by the domestic application of modern and cost-effective biotechnology techniques.

This study is divided into three parts. Part I traces historically the scientific underpinnings of the technologies comprising new biotechnology. Part II describes the biotechnology industry's organization, industrial structure and growth; it also examines the trends in industrialized countries, analyzing the business results of a sample group of companies over a decade and observing how these companies have financed their operations. Part III offers analysis and suggestions with regard to the way developing countries might pursue biotechnology given their financial and other constraints. The central point made here is that they should consider, as a highest priority in biotechnology, the development of diagnostic products, particularly monoclonal-antibody-based diagnostics.

Part I

Scientific Evolution and the Development of Biotechnology

Chapter 1

The History of Biotechnology and Its Applications

Biotechnology is a general term and in its broadest sense refers to a variety of techniques involving living organisms as a means of production. The evolution of biotechnology techniques has been characterized by three major phases or generations of biotechnology.

The first generation

The first generation or phase of biotechnology, based on empirical practice with minimum scientific or technological inputs, dates back to the Stone Age and uses biological organisms such as bacteria, yeasts, enzymes and traditional methods of fermentation to produce food and drink (such as bread and wine).

The second generation

The interwar period witnessed developments in fermentation technology using pure cell culture and sterile manufacturing facilities to yield new products (e.g. acetone, butanol, glycerol, vitamin B2, citric acid and lactic acid), but it was the discovery in 1928 of penicillin and its subsequent development which served to initiate the second generation or phase of biotechnology. This led to intense interest in the large-scale production of fermentation products for the pharmaceutical industry, and research efforts expanded rapidly, leading to new antibiotics such as cephalosporines, an increasing range of enzymes and vitamins, and steroids like hydrocortisone. By the late 1950s, increasing interest in and knowledge of biological processes led to their use in the preparation of amino acids (e.g. glutamate, used for food flavoring) and polysaccharides (used in stabilizing/filling agents in food manufacture). Another critical development in this period, beginning in the 1930s, was the use of hybrid crop varieties in the US corn belt, which resulted in dramatic yield increases.

These developments had a threefold significance. First, they led to an explosion of interest in microbiology – the properties and characteristics of microorganisms such as bacteria, yeasts and fungi and their range and functions in the environment. This in turn led to a second significant development: the successful use of mutation and selection of strains to achieve substantial improvement in yields and production efficiencies. Third, considerable refinements in fermentation technology were achieved, the most notable being the discovery of methods for immobilizing enzymes. This meant that enzyme catalysts that activate and accelerate the fermentation process, which were often isolated at considerable cost, could be reused over and over again rather than being discarded with each batch processed.

The third generation

The third generation or phase of biotechnology, also referred to as new or modern biotechnology, is the present one. A turning point occurred in 1953 with the discovery at Cambridge University (UK) of the structure of deoxyribonucleic acid (DNA) and with subsequent research linking the crucial components of DNA – four related chemicals called "bases" – and how these are lined up in specific sequences (the "DNA sequence") to contain instructions for the regulation and production of a particular protein. A gene is an ordered sequence of the chemical bases, each gene being defined as containing the information or coding for the composition of a particular protein and necessary signals for the production of that protein. Proteins, in turn, determine the traits, features, characteristics, abilities and functioning of cells within an organism. Thus, the set of instructions or code contained in the gene spells out, for instance, how a brain cell or a liver cell is to function, grow and reproduce. Simply stated, the individual segments along the DNA that determine heritable characteristics are called genes.

The structure, function and composition of DNA are virtually the same in all living organisms, from a snail to an elephant, a blade of grass to a redwood tree, and a single-cell bacterium to a human being. The DNA molecule, however, is made specific and meaningful through the extremely precise ordering of its chemical bases. A single molecule of DNA, containing many thousands of genes, is called a chromosome. Some authors/scientists refer to the DNA molecule as being located or lying on the chromosome (or chromosomes in the case of more than one DNA molecule) which is found in every cell. Thus each cell contains thousands of genes, the number of genes correlating with the complexity of the organism. It is the amount and huge variety of information the genes contain – due to the varying sequences of bases of the DNA – that result in the variety of living beings. A simple organism, such as a bacterium for example, has only one DNA molecule (chromosome) and that single chromosome contains some 5,000 genes. More complex organisms, such as plants and animals, have several chromosomes, each containing many thousands of different genes. It is estimated that a single plant may contain some 100,000 genes, whilst humans may have up to 300,000 genes.[1]

The code by which genetic information is translated into proteins is the same for all organisms. Hence, since all organisms contain DNA and all organisms interpret that DNA in the same manner, it follows that all organisms are related. This concept forms the basis for the industrial use of DNA.

Recombinant DNA technology or genetic engineering

Recombinant DNA (r-DNA) technology, or – a term that is often used interchangeably – genetic engineering,[2] one of the revolutionary breakthroughs characterizing new biotechnology, is founded on this understanding of DNA. R-DNA technology, first successfully carried out in 1973 by Stanford and University of California scientists, describes the techniques whereby the genetic information contained in the gene of a cell of one organism is isolated, taken out of that organism, and placed in the chromosome of a cell (or cells) of another organism. The resulting DNA in the recipient cell contains both its own original, naturally occurring genes and the new gene. If the process succeeds, the characteristic encoded in the foreign gene will be manifested, or "expressed", in the recipient cell or cells (and organism). The recipient organism which has the new DNA incorporated into its chromosome is said to be "transformed" by the arrival of the new genetic information. The technology relies in part on the basic principle that as each transformed cell multiplies, its descendent cells, and the chromosomes within each cell, will all contain the additional gene insertion. In theory, it is possible to incorporate genes from any source – microorganism, plant, animal or human – into the chromosomes of any other source.

For example, one could take a human gene, remove it from the human cell's chromosome and introduce that human gene into a bacterial chromosome. That bacterium will be able to recognize that gene as a set of instructions. The bacterium reads/decodes the human gene, with the result that it starts producing the human protein. If, for example, that gene was the gene coding for the protein interferon, bacterial cells containing the human interferon gene could be grown and multiplied relatively cheaply in large fermenters, resulting in millions and millions of bacteria, all of them now producing interferon (bacteria being used because of their easy and rapid multiplication). It is essential to note here that bacteria do not normally make interferon. The only way bacteria can make interferon is when the human gene has been put into them.

The reason one would want to make interferon would be to use it as a therapeutic drug. Interferon is part of the human body's natural defenses against disease, helping to fight off cancer and infections. Interferon cannot be made by chemists, due to its complexity. Until the advent of r-DNA technology, the only way to obtain interferon outside the body was to collect it from human blood. However, it would require approximately 1,000 liters of blood to produce an amount of interferon sufficient to try testing on only two or three people. The process would involve extremely expensive production and purification procedures, and consequently it would not be economically viable to make a drug in this way. By using r-DNA techniques, a quantity of interferon, enabling commercialization, can be made by simply isolating the gene (which can be done with a minute quantity of human blood) and putting it back into a bacterium; this, in effect, renders the transformed bacteria (with the additional human gene coding for the production of interferon) into a living factory producing (human) interferon.

Monoclonal antibodies

The second fundamental breakthrough, which occurred in the UK's Medical Research Council's laboratories in 1975, was the production of monoclonal antibodies (MAbs). MAbs are the result of techniques, classified under the heading of cell fusion, whereby two different types of cell are fused together, creating hybrid cells that have the properties of both parents.

Antibodies are complex proteins that can recognize and attach themselves to foreign proteins or substances in the body, collectively known as antigens, setting in motion a process that will eventually eliminate the antigen from the body. A monoclonal antibody results from the fusion of mammalian cells that produce a particular antibody (cells which have a limited lifetime to grow) with a cancer cell, which has the capacity to grow indefinitely in cell culture (in the laboratory). Thus chemically identical, pure antibodies could be produced on a large scale and indefinitely using this method. This could not have been done previously by conventional means, which produced mixtures of antibodies in an unreproducible manner.

Monoclonal antibodies, because of their unprecedented specificity for a particular antigen or foreign protein, can be used to identify the presence of disease-causing agents; they can be used in laboratory research for separating and purifying proteins, and to deliver drugs to a particular and precise location in the body. MAbs preferentially binding to pathogenic cells are also being investigated as therapies in themselves. Additionally, MAbs are being used in vaccine research and development – for example, to identify more precisely which components of an infective agent (for instance, a virus) are responsible for the induction of protective immunity or pathogenicity. Thus far the main use of MAbs has been in the diagnosis of disease and the purification/separation of proteins. Monoclonal antibodies, along with their uses and aspects of commercialization, are examined in greater detail in Chapters 9 and 10.

Novel bioprocessing techniques

The industrial application of these two advances – recombinant DNA and the production of monoclonal antibodies through cell fusion – necessitated advances in chemical engineering, to move from the laboratory to large-scale production of biotechnology-based products – drugs, enzymes, chemicals, food additives, and so on. Fermentation of large quantities of new types of inputs called for sophisticated processing equipment and an industry to produce it. Effort is being concentrated on such things as the automation of bioprocesses (the conversion of raw material substrate to a product using microbial fermentation or enzymes), and improved techniques for recovery of the desired product, its separation from the fermentation broth and its purification.

New or modern biotechnology (the reference of the term

biotechnology as used in this study) comprises those techniques and technologies that utilize r-DNA technology, monoclonal-antibody technology, and/or novel bioprocessing methodology.

Practical applications

New biotechnology is a set of enabling techniques that have the potential to increase industrial process efficiencies and to create new products and processes in a broad spectrum of industries. Biotechnology could potentially affect any current industrial biological process or any process in which a biological catalyst could replace a chemical one. The significance of this potential is underscored by the fact that 40 per cent of manufactured output worldwide is biological in origin,[3] ranging from paper and wood products to textiles, rubber, pharmaceuticals and agricultural products.

The advent of new biotechnology, based on advances in its underlying disciplines over the last few decades – including genetics, virology, biochemistry, microbiology, enzymology, molecular biology (the science of the ways physiological processes can be altered by changing the genetic make-up of the body) – has fundamentally altered the way biomedical research is conducted and what fruits can reasonably be expected from that research. New biotechnology comprises a set of research techniques that have altered in a basic way the capabilities of biomedical researchers to understand health and disease; in addition researchers have uncovered a wealth of new information about the way DNA functions and is organized in cells. It is biomedical research that has benefitted most immediately from the new techniques of biotechnology; and perhaps the most important application of these evolving techniques will be to facilitate further biomedical research.[4]

Notes

1. National Research Council, 1984, p. 27; and UNCTAD, 1991, p. 5.
2. These two terms are often used interchangeably. Some studies distinguish between the two, with genetic engineering being the broader term, encompassing a number of techniques to isolate, manipulate and transfer DNA from one organism to another, of which recombinant DNA technology is one of the most important. The two terms will be used interchangeably in this text.
3. Sharp, 1985, p. 21.
4. Olson, 1986, p. 2.

Part II

Salient Features of Biotechnology Growth
in Industrialized Countries

Chapter 2

The Application of Biotechnology by Sector

Overview

Distribution of sales and investments

The distribution of investments and sales in different economic sectors by US dedicated biotechnology firms (DBFs – those founded exclusively to exploit biotechnology commercially) in 1986 is shown in Table 2.1. Although precise data are not available, the USA accounts for the lion's share of worldwide commercial activity in biotechnology. As can be seen, the human health-care field – pharmaceuticals and diagnostics – accounts for some three-quarters of both investments and sales, with agriculture lagging far behind. Of particular note is that diagnostics, while taking only 10 per cent of investment, accounted for more than half of biotechnology industry sales.

Distribution of research efforts

The areas of research and development (R&D) concentration, as they appear in a 1987 survey of US-dedicated biotechnology firms and large diversified companies that devote part of their efforts to biotechnology commercialization, are shown in Table 2.2.[1] The survey was conducted by the Office of Technology Assessment (OTA) of the US Congress and included responses from about 75 per cent of DBFs and large diversified companies that the OTA had identified as being active in biotechnology in the USA.

The results confirm the dominance of human health care in the field of biotechnology: it accounts for the primary biotechnology work of 39 per cent of the DBFs and 37 per cent of large, diversified companies, with other applications lagging far behind.

Table 2.1 US dedicated biotechnology firms: investments compared to sales, by economic sector, 1986

Economic sector	Investments (%)	Sales (%)
Diagnostics	10	55
Human pharmaceuticals	65	20
Animal health/agriculture	10	5
Process/production supply	5	5
Specialty chemicals	5	< 1
Equipment supply	5	15
Consumer products/personal care	1	< 1

Source: Miller, 1987.

The above data refer to numbers of companies. Data available for 1990 refer to the distribution of industrial research investment funds in dollars – a more meaningful distribution. Included are expenditures made by both dedicated biotechnology firms (DBFs) and large diversified companies. As much as 77 per cent of industrial funds was spent on human health care, of which therapeutics accounted for 63 per cent and diagnostics 14 per cent; agriculture accounted for 15 per cent.[2] 1993 data referring exclusively to DBFs reveals that the therapeutics and diagnostics sector accounted for 53 per cent and 11 per cent, respectively; the agriculture and supply sectors accounted for 15 per cent each.[3]

Elsewhere, of the other regions in the world active in biotechnology (albeit to a much lesser extent than the USA), the majority, 42 per cent, of Western European DBFs in 1994 specialized in human health care; 22 per cent were in the supply sector and 16 per cent in agriculture.[4] In Japan, a 1985 Nikkei Biotechnology survey of 268 companies showed that 68 per cent of the companies were pursuing biotechnology research and development in pharmaceuticals and diagnostics.[5] In 1987, 67 per cent of company biotech R&D expenditures were in human health care.[6]

Trends

Aggregate sales and investment Estimates of sales by US firms of biotechnology products – mostly pharmaceuticals and diagnostics – are about $2 billion for 1990, $1.5 billion for 1989, $1 billion for 1988,

Table 2.2   Areas of primary focus of US biotechnology companies, 1987

Research area	Dedicated biotechnology firms		Large, diversified companies	
	Number	*(%)*	*Number*	*(%)*
Human therapeutics	63	(21)	14	(26)
Diagnostics	52	(18)	6	(11)
Reagents	34	(12)	2	(4)
Chemicals	20	(7)	11	(21)
Plant agriculture	24	(8)	7	(13)
Animal agriculture	19	(6)	4	(8)
Equipment	12	(4)	1	(2)
Cell culture	5	(2)	1	(2)
Waste disposal/treatment	3	(1)	1	(2)
Diversified	13	(4)	6	(11)
Other	51	(18)	0	(0)

Source: US Congress, 1988b, p. 79.

$600 million for 1987, and $350 million for 1986.[7] To convey a sense of scale, sales of biotechnology products in the agricultural sector are estimated at around only $50 million for 1989.[8]

Available data are not comprehensive enough to indicate how much investment it took to produce this level of output. However, one can make an approximation from several pieces of evidence. From 1983 to 1990, US federal investment in biotechnology research was approximately $20 billion.[9] *The Economist* estimated private investment through 1988 at $10 billion,[10] presumably mostly occurring in the 1980s. For 1989 and 1990 private investment can be estimated at $4 billion (in 1990 alone, investment was estimated at $2.3 billion[11]). This yields a total investment of some $34 billion in current dollars through 1990, implying a gross capital to output ratio of 17:1 – a very high figure on any reckoning.[12]

Human health care   In 1991, however, sales were forecast to more than double, to $4–5 billion, in the USA by 1995. This estimate appears to be based on specific information on promising products in the R&D pipeline. Human health-care products would dominate the market, followed far behind by products for animal and plant agriculture. This 1991 forecast proved accurate. Other industry categories are not likely to be significant until the turn of the century.[13]

In the 1980s just over ten new biotechnology drugs and vaccines were introduced on the US market, including vaccines against hepatitis B and influenza type B; tissue plasminogen activator (TPA) used to dissolve coronary artery blood clots, which trigger heart attacks; Factor VIII, a protein involved in blood-clot formation used by hemophiliacs; alpha interferon, used to treat hairy cell leukemia and Kaposi's sarcoma; human insulin; human growth hormone; and erythropoeitin, a protein growth factor that stimulates the production of red blood cells to treat anemia associated with kidney disease.[14] A large number of diagnostic kits for detection of disease were also introduced on the market.

A 1990 survey by the US Pharmaceutical Manufacturers' Association, however, showed that 104 biotechnology drugs and vaccines were in various stages of human testing and approval in the US regulatory process. Of these 104, 18 had completed clinical trials and were awaiting final approval by the US Food and Drugs Administration (FDA), the US regulatory authority (the FDA takes an average of two to three years to review and approve drugs at this stage). Another 14 genetically engineered medicines and 1 vaccine were in the final stages of clinical testing.[15]

Five years later, by March 1995, the number of biotech drugs and vaccines in various stages of clinical testing and approval in the USA had more than doubled to 234, up from 143 in August 1993. Of the 234, 14 approval applications were pending at the FDA and 49 were in the third and final stage of clinical testing. The number of biotech drugs and vaccines approved and introduced to the US market also more than doubled from 1990 to March 1995, rising from 11 in 1990 to 19 in 1993, and 24 in 1995.[16]

Agriculture Agriculture is one of the largest economic sectors worldwide, and market forecasts made in the early 1980s predicted that biotechnology sales within it would rival or exceed those of human pharmaceuticals and diagnostics. As mentioned previously, these predictions were exceedingly optimistic.

The possible applications of biotechnology in agriculture are in principle huge, having the potential to boost food production substantially by, for example, producing plants that are resistant to diseases, insects and herbicides; raising the nutritional value of crops, having them produce their own nitrogen fertilizer; and enabling them to withstand harsh environmental stress such as extremes in temperature and salinity. The plants themselves can be genetically engineered to introduce new traits, or microorganisms can be engineered and then applied to plants to effect the new traits. The application of biotechnology to animals includes the creation of new and improved diagnostic tests, drugs and vaccines; improvement in growth efficiency and nutritional content; and production of drugs in animals.

Despite the vast potential of agricultural biotechnology, the top ten ag-biotech companies had revenues of only $312 million in 1995;[17] in contrast, the top ten bio-drugs in 1993 commanded net sales of $4.3 billion.[18] The next section explains the huge gap, in terms of biotech R&D and commercialization, between agriculture and health care.

Factors influencing concentration on human health care and the relative neglect of agriculture

Greater basic knowledge in biomedical science

An enormous information base generated by university and public research provided the foundation for the sweeping advances in biomedical science; indeed, recombinant DNA and monoclonal antibody technologies were developed with public funds directed towards biomedical research during the past several decades. The first biotechnology products – insulin and MAb-based diagnostics – were a direct result of the biomedical nature of basic research that led to the new technologies. For example, the US government, the expenditure of which by far exceeds that of other national governments supporting biotechnology research, awarded over 80 per cent of its $3.5 billion 1991 biotechnology research budget to biomedical research.[19]

In contrast, comparable basic knowledge about plants and plant systems does not exist. The genetic origins of almost all agriculturally useful traits are not yet known and the basic biochemistry of plants and plant systems is poorly understood.[20]

By mid-1995, the genes which control the ripening process in tomatoes had been identified; it was also discovered how to make plants resistant to weedkiller. However, no one has yet pinpointed the genes which control most of a plant's other characteristics; although it is known that most of plants' more important traits, such as yield, are controlled by several genes operating together. The process by which genes are transferred to plants, to confer desirable traits, is complicated by the fact that, unlike in gene transfer to animals, scientists cannot control where on the plant's genome the foreign gene will be inserted. The transferred gene may end up next to a gene which turns it off or on at the wrong moment, with unexpected effects. The foremost challenge, however, is to find which sets of genes to put into a plant in the first place.[21]

Greater environmental concerns and regulatory uncertainties in agriculture

A second major reason for the lack of progress in agricultural biotechnology is regulatory uncertainty, exacerbated by varying degrees of public opposition. This uncertainty and opposition particularly concerns the deliberate release of genetically modified organisms into the environment. The difficulty stems primarily from the present insufficiency of the knowledge base that is required to predict adequately the ecological consequences of deliberate releases of genetically modified organisms (GMOs).

When the r-DNA technique was first developed, its novelty and tremendous power to manipulate characteristics of animals, plants and microorganisms raised concern about the potentially drastic consequences to human health and the environment that might follow from the creation and proliferation of organisms with unknown but potentially hazardous traits. As time and experience accumulated – with no serious incidents or 'accidents' having occurred – a consensus was reached among most experts that, for laboratory and factory work with r-DNA organisms, risks may be assessed generally in the same way as those associated with conventional organisms. Thus, work with r-DNA organisms could be regulated by standard laboratory and industrial practices.[22] This consensus, in turn, greatly facilitated research into, and the commercialization of, biotechnology applied to pharmaceuticals and diagnostics.

Risk assessment problems posed by agriculture No such broad degree of consensus exists to date concerning the risks entailed in releasing GMOs into the environment, upon which many applications of agricultural biotechnology depend. These applications include, for example, microorganisms to control insect pests, and to fix nitrogen, as well as animals and plants genetically engineered to enhance one or more desired characteristics. Such applications raise safety issues entirely different from laboratory or factory/industrial use of r-DNA organisms, where they are deliberately contained and often intentionally weakened. In the case of agricultural applications the organisms are engineered to survive in the environment, at least to the extent of performing their intended function.

Potential problems arising from releases of GMOs into the environment include: the creation or enhancement of pests or weeds; the possibility that GMOs will transfer the new bits of DNA to other organisms; unintended harm to nontarget species either directly or through competition for resources; the dispersal of GMOs to areas far from their intended sites; and changes in the basic biochemical processes that support the ecosystem, such as nutrient cycling.[23]

According to Martin Alexander, a widely quoted ecologist at Cornell University who testified before subcommittees of the US Congress in 1983, the probability of a genetically engineered organism having a detrimental effect is the product of five factors: release, survival, multiplication, dispersal and effect. If an unintended organism acquires foreign DNA from the recombinant organism, the last four factors must be calculated anew. The probabilities associated with one or more of these factors are likely to be small, and thus the overall probability of a harmful effect is likely to be very small. A small probability is, however, not a zero probability. And, as Dr Alexander points out, "the consequences of this low probability event may be enormous."[24]

There are uncertainties surrounding each of the risk factors, rendering it impossible to state precisely how small the risk is. Furthermore, the uncertainties will become larger as the kind and number of introduced genes grow, and as more organisms are altered and released into a wider range of environments. The reasons for these uncertainties are, first, that there is very little in the way of a historical or scientific database of the behavioral characteristics of genetically engineered organisms introduced into the environment; and, second, that there is no standard ecological methodology for predicting the outcome of such introductions.[25] However, the October 1991 Office of Technology Assessment study, *Biotechnology in a Global Economy,* states that a consensus does seem to exist that the vast majority of genetically modified organisms pose little or no risk if released; nevertheless, certain environmental introductions could warrant concern. In assessing risks to the environment, the amount of genetic alteration or type is less important than how that change affects the characteristics of the organism and the interaction of that organism with the environment. The report cites several studies that list risk criteria and attempts to weigh or prioritize them. These criteria include:

- familiarity with the parent organism and its modified derivatives;
- the likelihood of the organism competing successfully against other important organisms;
- the ease with which the organism can transfer its genetic material to other organisms;
- direct involvement of the organism in basic ecosystem processes (e.g. nutrient cycling and respiration);
- response of the organism to selective pressures in the new environment;
- the size and frequency of the releases, as greater size or frequency can increase the probability of long-term survival.[26]

Due to the scientific controversy surrounding the risks posed by the release of genetically engineered organisms and how those risks might be assessed, and because the characteristics of both the organism and the environment must be considered, national authorities in most industrialized countries are proceeding on a case-by-case review process. A stepwise progression of experiments – from the laboratory to the greenhouse, to the small-scale field test, and then to larger field tests – is performed, so that experience can be gained and safety evaluated at each step.[27] Rules, guidelines and regulations are being developed, instituted and amended as experience accumulates.

In the period 1987–93, some 38 per cent of total (1,022) worldwide field tests occurred in the USA (France ranked second with 16 per cent).[28] Routine progress in moving products from the laboratory and greenhouse to small- and larger-scale field tests has been slow in the past and hampered by regulatory delays due to controversy and confusion among federal regulatory agencies; this has led to uncertainty within the biotechnology research community and industry. This uncertainty has resulted in significant delays in field research on potential agricultural biotechnology products.[29]

Public attitudes   Mr Jeremy Rifkin, head of the Foundation for Economic Trends based in Washington, DC, has been largely credited with awakening citizens in industrialized countries in the mid-1980s to the risks of releasing recombinant organisms into the environment; he has done so by holding numerous lectures, conferences and meetings in a number of countries and lodging legal proceedings in the USA to try to prevent field testing of GMOs.[30] (Mr Rifkin has no objections to the use of biotechnology for the production of human therapeutics.[31]) It was he who was largely responsible for a four-year delay in the release of a genetically modified (bacterial) organism into the environment in the USA, which finally took place in California in 1987. Scientists heralded this as a historic experiment: it had come to symbolize the bitter debate over the wisdom of making new organisms and releasing them into nature.[32]

In this experiment, the bacterium known as "ice minus" had a gene removed which normally produces a frost-causing protein. Thus altered, ice-minus bacteria would be sprayed onto the plant surfaces to be protected from frost damage – in this case about 2,300 strawberry plants – in the hope they would colonize on the plants and replace the naturally occurring bacteria called "ice-plus". If the ice-minus bacteria do replace the ice-plus bacteria normally found on the plant, then the temperature at which ice forms on the plants should be lowered – that is, the plant would be better able to withstand lower temperatures. Agricultural losses due to frost damage, although they vary from year to year, are substantial. Some estimates place the average annual loss at $1.6 billion in the USA alone, and $14 billion worldwide.[33]

Mr Rifkin and his allies exposed inadequacies in federal regulation of the release of genetically altered organisms into the environment and maintained that more studies needed to be done to determine whether or not airborne ice-minus bacteria would disrupt the climate by interfering with the natural condensation of moisture in the atmosphere.[34] Even when permission for the field test had been granted by the US Environmental Protection Agency (EPA), local protesters uprooted the strawberries, which had to be replanted.[35] A field test of the spraying of ice-minus bacteria on potatoes in another city in California suffered a similar fate: local protesters and the Foundation for Economic Trends filed suit; there was a court-imposed delay, and even after permission had been granted in 1987, about half the plants were physically damaged and uprooted by activists. There was a further local protest in Missouri in 1986 against the release of a microbial pesticide designed to protect the roots of corn plants against black worm, with subsequent court proceedings and delays.[36]

Although general opposition has since dissipated, several states have introduced, and in some cases enacted, legislation regulating planned introductions. This is due to the perception of gaps in federal legislation and to oversight; to the fact that federal agencies do not require the notification of local officials or citizens in the area of test sites; and to a belief that federal agencies are not attuned to local needs.[37]

Elsewhere, opposition was also mounting. For example, there was a storm of protest from the Green Party at Germany's first deliberate release in May 1990, and in the Netherlands field tests were physically uprooted by activists in June 1989 and August 1991. Chicco Testa, an Italian deputy with a particular interest in the environment, proposed a bill in 1990 which called for a moratorium on the deliberate release of genetically engineered plants and animals, and a ban on the release of microorganisms.[38]

There also exists reluctance on the part of consumers in industrialized countries to eat genetically engineered foods. For example, the first genetically engineered plant product to be marketed in the USA in 1993 – a tomato designed to retard rotting, which can therefore be picked when redder and better-tasting than its counterpart: pale, picked when green and artificially ripened – is creating much controversy in the USA. Some consumers and environmental activists, with the support of a number of grocers and restaurateurs, suggest that the tomato's biotech origins make it inherently unsafe, despite the fact that it has passed all the safety tests. The Campbell Soup Company financed the development of genetically engineered tomatoes at two US DBFs, in return for marketing rights to such genetically engineered fresh tomatoes outside the USA and processed tomatoes worldwide. In response to consumer opposition, however, Campbell announced in January 1993 that it had no immediate plans to market genetically engineered food products.[39]

In Europe, the largest biotechnology companies, concerned about their public image, are planning a major advertising campaign designed to persuade consumers that genetically engineered food products are good for your health, modern and economically sound. Britain's Agricultural and Food Research Council has sought some £100,000 for a three-year study of consumer attitudes to biotechnology and food, and of the factors that influence consumers as they form these attitudes.[40] Meanwhile, a survey carried out by the Dutch Institute for Consumer Research in 1990–91 on 870 people showed that most are unwilling to accept food that is produced by biotechnology or genetic engineering. On a scale of acceptability ranging from 1 (totally unacceptable) to 38 (totally acceptable), people gave genetically engineered foods a rating of just 5.6, in part due to apprehension concerning their safety.[41]

The effect of agricultural slump

The 1980s, when the biotechnology industry was maturing, were years of low profitability for farming both in the USA and throughout the rest of the world. In the USA, thanks to price supports, the prices received by farmers rose marginally, by 3 per cent, between 1980 and 1988; but the prices paid by farmers rose 23 per cent, and their terms of trade deteriorated by almost 20 per cent. This was reflected in the behavior of farm assets. The average value of land per acre in the USA fell from \$737 in 1980 to \$564 in 1988 – a decline of 23.5 per cent.[42] Average prices of farm assets are not available for areas outside the USA, but the behavior of product prices is known. Export prices of foodstuffs in developing countries fell by 34 per cent, and that of other agricultural products by 18 per cent, between 1980 and 1987.[43] As the import prices of developing countries continued to rise in this period, the deterioration in their terms of trade has been even larger than these figures indicate.

In contrast to these movements, prices of prescription drugs in the USA rose by 79 per cent between 1980 and 1986.[44] As the general US GNP deflator price index rose much less steeply, by 33 per cent in the same period, the improvement in the terms of trade of the US pharmaceutical industry was remarkable. The drugs industry has consistently been among the most profitable sectors in the US economy, a situation mirrored in many other industrialized countries. The ratio of profits to stockholders' equity in the USA was 19.6 per cent in 1980–86, almost double the 11.5 per cent average for all US manufacturing corporations.[45]

No significant recovery in world prices of agricultural commodities was expected. The Organization for Economic Cooperation and Development (OECD) predicted an exportable surplus by OECD countries by 1995 of some 20 million tons of wheat, of 30 million tons of barley and maize, as well as a doubling of the sugar surplus, a tripling of bovine meat production, and a 10 per cent increase in dairy products.[46]

The strong demand for drugs to treat chronic and fatal diseases

In sharp contrast to the widespread controversy, consumer reluctance and skepticism that surrounds agricultural biotechnology products generally in developed countries, there is an enormous demand for breakthrough drugs to treat fatal and chronic diseases such as AIDS, heart disease, cancer, arthritis and Alzheimer's disease.

AIDS

Virtually all aspects of AIDS research have been strongly dependent on the methods of biotechnology. Such research ranges from the study of the life cycle of the AIDS-causing virus, HIV; to the way it attacks its victims and causes AIDS and other symptoms; to efforts aimed at developing a vaccine against HIV and drugs either to cure the infection, arrest its spread or alleviate its symptoms.

Had the disease struck a mere ten years earlier, it would most likely have remained a terrifying plague of unknown origin. Instead, the interval from the first outbreak of AIDS in the USA to the discovery of its cause was less than three years, and the second stage of advance to large-scale antibody testing to allow assessment of the epidemic (and development of control strategies) was accomplished in less than one year. It is claimed that never in human history have researchers and science moved from recognition of a major medical problem to comprehensive understanding so rapidly as with AIDS.[47]

At the beginning of 1991, the World Health Organization (WHO) estimated that 1.2 million cases of AIDS had occurred since the pandemic began a decade earlier.[48] By mid-1995 WHO estimated that 4.5 million people had AIDS, and the number of people infected with the virus but not yet showing symptoms of the full-scale disease was about 19.5 million and likely to be 30 to 40 million by the year 2000.[49]

The first generally approved drug (and the only one until 1992) directed against the actual virus that causes AIDS – AZT – was introduced in 1987 by the UK pharmaceutical company Wellcome. AZT disrupts an enzyme (called reverse transcriptase) that the virus uses to reproduce itself. AZT arrests the progress of the disease but does not cure it; and because the drug also interferes with human DNA replication it causes a variety of side-effects, including cases of severe anemia which can require frequent blood transfusions.[50] Almost half of AIDS patients find they are forced to give up AZT, often after only a few months, because it damages their bone marrow.[51]

Several chemical cousins of AZT, which also disrupt the virus's reverse transcriptase, were approved in the USA in 1992, but they suffer from the same drawbacks as AZT: not curing the disease and eliciting severe side-effects.[52] By November 1995, twenty-nine drugs for the treatment of AIDS-related diseases (such as pneumocystis carinii pneumonia, a severe lung infection found in nearly 80 per cent of AIDS patients at some time during the course of the disease) were approved in the USA, four of which (14 per cent) are biotech-based.[53]

Given the huge demand, a number of biotechnology companies are working on AIDS. According to 1995 surveys by the US Pharmaceutical Research and Manufacturers of America, about one-third (34 out of 110) drugs and vaccines being developed in the USA to treat AIDS and AIDS-related disorders are biotechnology-based, including 11 of the 14 vaccines undergoing clinical trials.[54]

Heart disease

Heart disease is the leading killer in the USA and Europe, responsible for about 45 per cent of all US deaths, or nearly one million lives each year. It is also a leading cause of death around the world, responsible for some 12 million fatalities annually.[55] Sales of drugs to treat cardiovascular diseases reached £7.4 billion in 1986 – about a tenth of the world drug market. From January to September 1995, sales of these drugs through pharmacies for the world's top ten markets reached $18.6 billion – 18 per cent of total sales ($102.7 billion).[57]

One of the most successful new drug launches in history, with first-year sales of $150 million (November 1987–November 1988) was Genentech's (a leading US biotechnology company) tissue plasminogen activator (TPA).[58] TPA (a human protein found in minute quantities in the blood) is a recombinant protein drug used to dissolve blood clots – that is, a thrombolytic, for the treatment of heart attacks.

Greater sales growth potential is indicated by the fact that, in the USA alone, about 1.5 million people per year suffer heart attacks. Between 400,000 and 600,000 of them are considered candidates for treatment with a clot-dissolving drug, but only 20 per cent of those receive treatment. Genentech's TPA captured about two-thirds of those 20 per cent receiving treatment. Studies have shown that prompt treatment of heart-attack patients with a combination of aspirin and a clot-dissolving drug reduces their risk of dying by almost half.[59]

TPA will, however, face competition from other thrombolytics. For example, Genentech's dominant position was jolted in 1991 by large clinical studies involving 46,000 patients in twenty countries showing that streptokinase, a thrombolytic on the US market since 1977 and made by Kabi Pharmacia of Sweden and Hoechst of Germany, reduced mortality among the patients as effectively as TPA; streptokinase costs about one-tenth the price of TPA.[60]

Cancer

The second leading cause of death in the USA and UK, accounting for between one-quarter and one-fifth of deaths, is cancer.[61] A WHO publication states (1989) that the number of cancer deaths worldwide has been calculated to be about 4 million each year, while over 6 million new cases are diagnosed annually.[62] A more recent estimate (1991) by Sweden's Karolinska Institute estimates the number of people dying worldwide from cancer at 4.9 million, of which 2.2 million deaths occur in developed countries. New diagnoses of cancer in developed countries were estimated at 4 million. The incidence and number of deaths from cancer is expected to increase in the future.[63]

Sales of cancer drugs worldwide in 1986 were some $500 million, reaching in excess of $1 billion by the end of 1988.[64] Chemotherapy is used in about half of all cases of cancer, and by 1994 the world market for anti-cancer drugs had risen to an estimated $7.8 billion.[65] This figure could substantially increase if more effective drugs with less severe side-effects became available. For example, in 1994, when British Bio-technology reported promising results from early clinical trials of their drug candidate to treat ovarian cancer, analysts at James Capel, a London stockbroker, estimated the drug's potential market for this cancer alone at up to $6 billion.[66] In 1994, sales of US pharmaceuticals to treat cancer and cardiovascular disease shared the top position, each capturing $1.7 billion (34 per cent) of total US pharmaceutical sales ($5 billion).[67]

New biotechnology is providing the foundations for "biological therapy", or, as it is sometimes called, "immunotherapy" – a fourth major method for treating cancer, alongside surgery, radiation and chemotherapy. Biological therapy works by boosting the body's natural defensive tumor-killing mechanisms. For example, cytokines are protein substances normally found in minute quantities in human blood and are necessary for coordinating, enhancing and amplifying an immune response. Recombinant DNA technology has enabled large-scale production of some pure cytokines for further research and possible use as anti-cancer drugs. An example of this is the drug Interleukin-2, which is a growth stimulant for white cells known as T-lymphocytes, which play a key role in the immune system. Cytokines have also been termed 'biological response modifiers' (BRMs).

As biotechnology has provided the means to prepare commercial quantities of the proteins which regulate the human immune system, medical attention has focused on these BRMs and their potential role in the treatment of cancer. One particularly promising BRM was called the T-cell Growth Factor when it was discovered in 1976, and subsequently renamed Interleukin-2. In Europe, EuroCetus has used recombinant DNA technology to produce large quantities of Interleukin-2 in the form of its first commercial product, Proleukin. After completing medical trials, EuroCetus won marketing approval in the UK in March 1992 for Proleukin, which has proved effective in the treatment of renal cell carcinomas, the most common cancer of the kidney. The cancer is notoriously difficult to treat and was relatively insensitive to prior existing forms of chemotherapy and radiotherapy. Proleukin appears to work indirectly by stimulating the immune system rather than by direct attack on cancer cells, and researchers hope that it may also prove effective in treating other cancers.[68]

A fifth method for treating cancer, also being developed and researched with new biotechnology, is "immunotoxin" therapy in which a tumor-killing toxin is attached to a monoclonal antibody that can recognize and stick to cancer cells. When injected into the body the antibodies carry the poison specifically to the cancer cells and kill them. The monoclonal antibody thus acts as a vehicle to deliver the poison selectively. Monoclonal antibodies that preferentially bind to tumor cells are also being investigated as cancer therapies in themselves (see Chapter 10).

Anti-inflammatory drugs

Extensive efforts have been made in recent years to develop anti-inflammatory drugs based upon new advances in biotechnology and research into the body's immune system. The market for such drugs is huge: in 1990, 37 million Americans suffered from arthritis alone and spent approximately $5 billion a year on treatments.[69] About 1 per cent of the world's population suffers from rheumatoid arthritis.[70] Better treatments are also needed for other conditions involving inflammation, such as allergies, dermatitis, chronic bowel disease, lupus and multiple sclerosis.

Alzheimer's disease

Other diseases that affect the elderly are attracting biotechnology investment as that market is increasing. The demand for drugs for diseases of the elderly will rise as the population ages; moreover, there is a higher incidence of chronic disease and illness in old age. As a consequence, in the USA, for example, the elderly purchase 30 per cent of all drugs, although they only account for 12 per cent of the population. The US Census Bureau predicted that from 1985 to 1995 the number of Americans aged 65 and over would increase by more than 10 per cent, to 34 million;[71] it is estimated that by the year 2020, some 17 to 20 per cent of the population will be 65 or older.[72]

More generally, low birth rates and longer life spans are increasing the proportion of elderly people in most OECD countries. Across the OECD as a whole, the proportion of the population aged 65 and over is projected to increase from its average of just over 12 per cent in 1980 to 20.5 per cent in 2030. The most rapidly increasing population group in many OECD countries is the very old – those aged 80 and over. Current projections indicate that the proportion of very old people in OECD countries could rise from 3 per cent at the end of the 1980s to between 6 and 9 per cent by the middle of the next century.[73] In the developing countries, according to projections by the United Nations, life expectancy will reach at least the age of 60 by the year 2000 in virtually all the countries of the Third World.[74]

In Japan, pharmaceutical applications dominate biotechnology R&D efforts. Japan is the world's second largest pharmaceutical market (after the USA) and is the fastest ageing country in the world. Japan is facing the prospect that 23 per cent of its population will be older than 65 in the year 2020. The leading cause of death is cancer, and its incidence is increasing. These factors have stimulated a great emphasis on research for drugs and diagnostics against cancer, cardiovascular disease, immunological disorders and Alzheimer's disease.[75]

Few diseases are more dreaded than Alzheimer's, the progressively degenerative brain disorder that causes ever-increasing memory loss and confusion. It is believed to affect 5–10 per cent of people over 65 and to be the main reason for long-term admissions to nursing homes.[76] In the USA alone, some 3 million people suffer from the affliction, and in the UK 500,000; worldwide the figure is in excess of 10 million.[77] In 1990, Alzheimer's disease killed 100,000 Americans, making it the fourth leading cause of adult death.[78] As of 1995, the exact cause(s) of the disease are still unknown, and no definitive biological diagnostic test exists. The magnitude of Alzheimer's, coupled with rapid advances in biotechnology, motivated the formation of at least eighteen biotechnology companies in a two-year period (1987–89) in the USA committed to research into the disease.[79]

In sum, biotechnology applied to the development of new pharmaceuticals and diagnostic products has not faced as many basic science hurdles as agriculture, not to mention the thorny ethical, environmental and regulatory issues confronting agricultural biotechnology. Additionally, pharmaceuticals are generally high-value-added products and can be priced to recover costs incurred in R&D. In developed countries the demand for many new pharmaceutical products is highly price-inelastic (see Chapter 5), and demand in a number of therapeutic areas is sure to increase.

It should be noted that concomitant with the incidence of the diseases mentioned, as well as a host of others, there is a demand for proper diagnosis. Biotechnology-based diagnostics have been and are being developed where biologically based diagnostics had not previously been available, such as in the case of Alzheimer's disease, or for unprecedentedly early detection of disease and accuracy in locating its spread – such as with various cancers and heart disease. Thus, novel biotechnology-based therapeutics and diagnostics are reinforcing each other's demand in the case of a number of diseases.

Notes

1. Conceptually, research expenditures are a part of investment and therefore are implicitly included in Table 2.1 (investments vs. sales). It is not clear, however, whether they are in fact included, and in any case the years referred to in the two tables differ.
2. US DOC, 1991, p. 18-3.
3. Burrill and Lee, 1994, p. 76.
4. Lucas, 1995, p. 9.
5. Fujimura, 1988, p. 150.
6. Fukui, 1990, p. 11.
7. US DOC, 1991, p. 18-3.
8. Sercovich, and Leopold, 1991, p. 15.
9. United States, 1991, p. 6.
10. *The Economist*, 1989, pp. 69–70.

11. US DOC, 1991, p. 18-3.

12. An adjustment for constant prices would further raise the capital output ratio. However, some of the physical capital invested in the early part of the period may already have been withdrawn, which works in the opposite direction.

13. US DOC, 1991, p. 18-5. Many forecasts had been made by various sources previously, but did not seem to have a strong basis in specific well-founded estimates. Sales expectations were borne out. In 1994, sales of human bio-pharmaceuticals – $5 billion – represented more than 70 per cent of total US biotechnology product sales. Again, based on specific biopharmaceutical products in the pipeline, US sales are projected to grow at an average annual rate of about 12 per cent, from $5 billion in 1994 to almost $16 billion in 2004. (Keough and Sharmel, 1995, p. 6.)

14. PMA, 1990a.

15. *Ibid.*

16. PhRMA, 1995; and PMA, 1993.

17. Burrill and Lee, 1995, p. 16.

18. Burrill and Lee, 1994, p. 14.

19. United States, 1991, p. 6.

20. *The Economist,* 1995d.

21. *Ibid.*

22. UNIDO, 1990, pp. 6, 24; OECD, 1989, p. 59.

23. US Congress, 1991, p. 178; *The Economist,* 1988a, p. 15; Schoon, 1996.

24. UNIDO, 1990, p. 33; Olson, 1986, pp. 56, 61.

25. UNIDO, 1990, p. 34.

26. US Congress, 1991, p. 178.

27. *Ibid.*, p. 194.

28. Goy and Duesing, 1995, p. 455.

29. US Congress, 1988b, p. 210.

30. *The Economist,* 1988a, p. 15; Fowler et al., 1988a, p. 213.

31. Van Kleef and Scholtens, 1988.

32. Schneider, 1987, p. 1.

33. US Congress, 1988a, p. 94.

34. *The Economist,* 1988a, p. 16.

35. Schneider, 1987, p. 16.

36. US Congress, 1988a, p. 52.

37. US Congress, 1991, p. 188.

38. Mackenzie, 1990; *Volkskrant,* 1991: 17; Hodgson, 1990, pp. 25, 26.

39. Hamilton, Ellis, 1992, p. 99; Fisher, 1993b, p. D4.

40. Watts, 1990, p. 25.

41. Coghlan, 1991b, p. 9.

42. US Bureau of the Census, 1990, pp. 644, 653.

43. United Nations, 1989, p. 170.

44. Daily press reports.

45. US Bureau of the Census, 1988.

46. World prices of agricultural commodities have, in fact, improved steadily since 1992, mainly as a result of supply shocks such as poor weather and voluntary production cuts, rather than higher demand. The World Bank projects that its

index of primary commodities will, in real terms, be 8 per cent below March 1995's peak by the year 2000, and then stagnate for five years. The index had risen 8.6 per cent in nominal terms in 1995 (Jonquières 1996). In 1995, share prices of the world's pharmaceuticals companies rose 47 per cent, their best performance since 1986. They outperformed global stock markets by an impressive 26 per cent (Green, 1996).

47. Baum, 1987, p. 12; Osborn, 1986, pp. 46, 49.
48. Cookson, 1991.
49. WHO, 1995.
50. Marsh, 1987a.
51. Cookson, 1991.
52. Waldholz, 1992, p. A11; *Le Monde*, 24 June 1992.
53. PhRMA, 1995, 1995a.
54. *Ibid.*
55. Bristol-Myers Squibb Company, 1990, p. 19.
56. P. Marsh, 1988.
57. Green, 1995.
58. Gebhart, 1989, p. 1.
59. Okie, 1991; *The Economist*, 1991a.
60. *Financial Times*, 1991, p. 3; and Okie, 1991. Genentech's share of the US thrombolytic market dropped from two-thirds to one-half in the following two years after the 1991 study. However, Genentech's TPA regained the market share it had lost in September 1993 within three months after results from a subsequent large-scale study were published in April 1993. In this study, 41,000 heart-attack patients around the world were given either streptokinase or TPA, and it was shown that TPA treatment saves an additional 1 per cent of lives over streptokinase (Chase, 1993).
61. Reuben and Wittcoff, 1989, p. 46.
62. Whelan, 1989, p. 25.
63. Maurice, 1991.
64. *Chemical Marketing Reporter*, 1988, p. 7.
65. *Xenova Group PLC,* 1994, p. 11 (Xenova Group is a DBF based in the UK).
66. Green, 1994b.
67. Keough and Sharmel, 1995.
68. *Financial Times*, 1992.
69. Waldholz, 1991.
70. Houlder, 1995.
71. Freudenheim, 1988a.
72. Hinden, 1992.
73. Maguire, 1987, p. 5.
74. Ozorio, 1988, p. 26.
75. Martin, 1989, p. 10.
76. *The Economist*, 1986b, p. 89.
77. Cookson, 1996.
78. *Wall Street Journal Europe*, 1991a, p. 6.
79. Fisher, 1989.

Chapter 3

Organization of the Industry

Two distinct types of firm, in addition to universities, have been and presently are involved in the commercialization of biotechnology: the smaller, specialized, new or "start-up" biotechnology firms, specifically founded to commercialize innovations in biotechnology, the technical term for which, "dedicated biotechnology firms" (DBFs), will be used in this study; and the larger, established multiproduct companies in such sectors as pharmaceuticals, chemicals, agriculture, energy and food processing.

The relationship between university and industry

Commercial biotechnology has its roots in academia, which continues to play a vital role. Researchers in universities and biomedical research institutes, largely funded by the government, carried out nearly all the basic research (in disciplines such as microbiology, biochemistry, enzymology, the molecular basis of genetics, botany, plant pathology, biochemical engineering and fermentation technology) from which biotechnology techniques and processes were developed.

> More perhaps than any other technology except nuclear fusion, biotechnology derives from university science. To date [1985] all the seminal discoveries have come from universities or research institutions, not large firms, and this is where the centre of gravity of the technology remains. The diffusion of technology therefore demands close linkages to be established with academic science.[1]

In turn, the first experts in the field were primarily university research professors, and they were among the first to recognize the commercial potential of the new techniques. The founders of many DBFs also recognized early that most developments in biotechnology would flow from basic research carried out in academic institutions. For these reasons many DBFs were formed around a core of talented university scientists, many of whom were also among the founders and first employees of the new biotechnology companies.

Most analysts trace the birth of the industry to San Francisco, in 1976, when B. Swanson, a venture capitalist, and H. Boyer, a well-recognized University of California bacteriologist, formed Genentech, the first company established to devote itself exclusively to commercializing biotechnology. Several DBFs (for example, Genentech, Centocor, Genetic Systems) got started by placing R&D contracts with academic researchers for the commercial development of a laboratory discovery.[2]

In addition to university researchers being among the founders of many DBFs, a wide-ranging scale of alliances between the biotechnology industry (both DBFs and large firms) and universities has been and continues to be established, both nationally and internationally. The Office of Technology Assessment (OTA) of the US Congress identifies five broad types of university–industry arrangements in biotechnology: consulting arrangements, industrial associate programs, research contracts, research partnerships, and private corporations.[3]

The processes of university–industry technology transfer and the industrial sponsorship of university research are not new. What distinguishes biotechnology is that, in the USA, where such links are perhaps most numerous, the proportion of university research in biotechnology supported by industry is between 16 and 24 per cent – some four to five times higher then the average of 4 to 5 per cent spent on overall industry-sponsored research; and that, per dollar spent, company-supported university research in biotechnology generates four times as many patent applications as does industrial support of other university research.[4]

Nearly one-half of US biotechnology companies support research in universities, and this is expected to continue. A 1988 OTA study states:

Although an increasing number of biotechnology companies are strengthening their in-house research capabilities, available evidence suggests that the private sector will continue to seek the cutting edge research and technical breakthroughs provided by the Nation's universities. Direct industry support for all campus research has increased in constant dollar terms every year since 1970. Between 1981 and 1984, this increase was 8.5 percent annually.[5]

In 1984 biotechnology companies in the USA spent approximately $120.7 million in grants and contracts to universities.[6] Even with the increases noted above, industry funding remains small compared to government support of biotechnology research at the university level.

Evidence suggests that large capital inflows for long-term basic research – such as the $70 million agreement of 1980 whereby the German chemical firm Hoechst would create and provide support over a ten-year period for a department of molecular biology at Harvard University's teaching hospital; or the $23.5 million five-year agreement made in 1982 between the US chemical firm Monsanto and Washington University, with 30 per cent of funds going towards fundamental research – are the exception rather than the rule. In 1984, 60 per cent of industrially funded biotechnology projects at universities were funded at less than $50,000; 20 per cent were funded at between $50,000 and $100,000; and the remaining 20 per cent were funded for over $100,000.[7]

Furthermore, according to the 1988 study, an increasing number of industry–university arrangements in biotechnology are developing as consulting and contract research rather than long-term research partnerships, with industrial expectations of university research requiring more pragmatic collaborative arrangements than in the past. Also, in an April 1987 OTA workshop, industry representatives predicted that few companies will be prepared to invest large sums in university research for long periods, as in the Monsanto–Washington University agreement.[8] This prediction proved accurate up to 1996.

Dedicated biotechnology firms and their concentration

Of the three major categories of institution involved in the commercialization of biotechnology, those that showed by far the most rapid growth in the early 1980s were the smaller specialized dedicated biotechnology firms (DBFs). The vast majority of DBFs are in the USA and the boom years for their founding was 1980–84, when about 250 firms were established.[9] This boom was made possible largely by the availability of venture capital in the USA, which provided the initial start-up financing, in combination with the willingness of scientists to pursue commercial gain through small, newly formed entrepreneurial companies.

As of January 1988 the OTA identified 403 DBFs in the USA. The dedicated biotechnology firm industry is, however, dominated by a small number of companies. One analyst placed total private investment at over $4 billion by the end of 1985, of which 63 per cent was accounted for by ten companies.[10] Katherine Behrens, a biotechnology analyst with the California investment banking firm Robertson, Colman and Stephans is referred to by the OTA as saying (in 1987) that in fact 80 per cent of the funds were invested in ten companies.[11] Analyst L. Miller poignantly refers to US DBF concentration attained through 1986 and early 1987:

> Most pronounced is the dominance of one company – Genentech. Genentech possesses: 30% of industry revenues; 50% of market capitalization; and 30% of property, plant and equipment invested in by the independent firms. The top ten companies ranked by market capitalization represent: 80% of industry revenues; 90% of industry market capitalization and 80% of property, plant and equipment.[12]

Concentration and stratification of US DBFs has continued through the fall of 1990, as indicated by Ernst & Young's fifth annual survey of business and financial trends in US commercial biotechnology. S. Burrill, who directed the survey of biotechnology executive and financial officers, states (September 1990): "You're seeing the large companies pull away from the pack and become the dominant part of the industry."[13] Indeed, the survey showed that over 80 per cent of drugs entering clinical trials are produced by the top 3 per cent of companies.[14]

The terms "top tier", "second tier" "and lower tier" are used to describe the stratification of the companies followed on Wall Street by a number of biotechnology analysts. "The lower tier is in 'biotech purgatory'", says analyst D. Gilbert. "They'll either move up or out."[15] In contrast, the upper crust will move up as their products move closer to the market. Gilbert's top-tier list includes the DBFs Amgen, Genetics Institute, Immunex and Xoma. Gilbert says that among second-tier companies there is an "upper crust" that stand the best chance of obtaining financing; this layer includes Cytogen, Synergen, Repligen and California Biotechnology.

Veteran biotechnology stockbroker R. Bock, referring to Ernst & Young's survey, states (January 1990):

> An interesting and somewhat disturbing fact is that only 10 per cent of the industry,[16] or approximately 16 companies, received over 70 per cent of all financing during 1989. While substantial amounts of capital are periodically available to the biotech industry, depending on investor's moods, it is definitely going to fewer and fewer companies, thereby causing increased stratification of the industry. The financial disparity between the leading companies and

the smaller second tier firms is becoming more and more pronounced every day…[17]

Bock prefaced this observation with his opinion that, "The single most important problem facing the biotech industry during the 1990s continues to be its ability to raise vast amounts of capital…"[18]

In 1991, the number of US DBFs was about 1,100, and the DBF Amgen (of California) ascended to the number one position after winning a four-year legal battle with Genetics Institute (see Annex 1), giving Amgen exclusive rights to the sale and production of erythropoietin (EPO) in the USA. EPO, which stimulates the bone marrow to produce red blood cells and is used to treat anemia, had first-year (1989) sales in excess of $190 million, setting an industry record.[19] Amgen's lead was further strengthened by the company's obtaining marketing approval, also in 1991, for Neupogen, a drug which also works by stimulating the bone marrow, but this time to produce infection-fighting white blood cells. It is used in the chemotherapy treatment of cancer patients, as chemotherapy, in addition to killing cancerous cells, damages the bone marrow, and with it the body's defense mechanisms. (Chemotherapy agents kill cancers by destroying cells that are dividing, such as stem cells, contained in the bone marrow. Stem cells divide and develop into a range of blood cells – red, white, and the platelets which cause blood clotting. Hair cells are also dividing cells, which is why cancer patients often lose their hair.)

Neupogen and EPO are, respectively, the industry's number one and number two top-selling drugs.[20] In 1992 Amgen became the first biotech company to achieve in excess of $1 billion in annual product sales (Neupogen – $544 million; EPO – $506 million). Since then, sales of these two top-selling biotech drugs have steadily increased: sales in 1993 totaled $719 million for Neupogen and $587 million for EPO; in 1994 Neupogen reached $829 million and EPO $721 million.[21] According to analysts at stockbroker Lehman Brothers, Amgen's success will continue into the next century, as it predicts that by 2000 Amgen's EPO will be the world's best selling drug, with Neupogen close behind in third place. Their combined sales will be in excess of $5 billion a year.[22]

By 1995 Amgen had come to be considered the world's most successful biotechnology firm. At the end of February 1995 *The Economist* stated that, "In America, where it [the biotechnology industry] first started, and which remains the world's leader, the sector is steadfastly losing money, $1 billion or so last year. Only 1% of the biotech companies [about 1,300] make a profit. Of those that do, one company, Amgen of Thousand Oaks, California, makes more than all of its leading competitors put together…"[23] Amgen's pre-eminence is also reflected in its market capitalization (MC). Between 8 March 1991 and 5 May 1995 Amgen's MC more than doubled, from close to $4.5 billion to a staggering $10.3 billion, 61 per cent higher than its rival Genentech at $6.3 billion (5 May 1995) and well ahead of other top DBFs, such as the third- and fourth-ranked biotech companies by MC (5 May 1995) – Chiron at $1.9 billion and Biogen at $1.57 billion.[24]

Large multiproduct firms and their collaboration with DBFs

The financing needs of the DBFs is one of the critical factors contributing to their complex and evolving relationship with the third category of pivotal institutions involved in the commercialization of biotechnology: the large established multiproduct companies. These companies were established on the market before the advent of new biotechnology in sectors such as pharmaceuticals, chemicals, food processing and energy. Most, if not all, of these companies are transnational corporations (TNCs) based largely in the USA, Japan and Western Europe.

When biotechnology first began to receive commercial attention (prompted by the DBF formation in the USA), the vast majority of TNCs did not possess any major in-house biotechnology programs and viewed genetic engineering with ambivalence: the techniques themselves were new, the problem of scale-up untackled, and the issues of patent and safety/ethical controls a big unknown. Many large companies thus elected to gain in-house expertise and hedge against the market threat posed by the DBFs by obtaining technology through research contracts with DBFs or universities, and concluding licensing agreements, marketing agreements, joint ventures or equity purchase of DBFs. These collaborative ventures between companies, or "strategic alliances" as they are often termed, are associations between separate business entities that fall short of a formal merger, but that commit and unite certain agreed-upon resources of each entity for a limited purpose.[25] In this way the TNCs could gain access to the technology but with a limited commitment – letting the DBF function as a "litmus test" for the new technologies and giving the TNCs time to see where biotechnology was going before expanding internally.

This large-firm strategy was facilitated by the considerable expenditures in time and money required to research, develop and market biotechnology-based products. Although a number of DBFs aim eventually to become fully integrated pharmaceutical or chemical houses, they were founded to exploit innovations in biotechnology and initially concentrated their activities and efforts in research. Consequently, as a rule, the DBFs had limited financial resources with which to fund production scale-up activities beyond the pilot plant stage, let alone the financing and expertise required for regulatory approval and marketing, should their biotechnology research activities yield pharmaceuticals, and to a lesser extent, animal drugs, food additives, chemicals, or microorganisms for deliberate release into the environment.[26]

Many of the large established multiproduct companies were at a disadvantage vis-à-vis DBFs with respect to the possession of technical expertise in biotechnology. The TNCs, on the other hand, were well-versed in dealing with government regulators and had established market access, including mature distribution systems and marketing know-how (factors critical to success in medical biotechnology), not to mention the TNCs' considerable financial strength. These strategic alliances reflected a shared search on the part of the DBFs and large established companies for complementary skills and resources.

With the exception of a handful of pharmaceutical and chemical TNCs such as Merck, Hoffmann-La Roche, Monsanto, Du Pont and Eli Lilly, which had biotechnology research efforts underway since about 1978, most established US (and foreign) TNCs did not begin in-house biotechnology until after 1981.[27] Despite the TNCs increasingly investing large sums in their own in-house biotechnology programs, the number of collaborative ventures with DBFs and universities has been rising.[28]

In January 1987, *The Economist* stated that "Big drug companies now devote about 30 per cent of their R&D budget to biotechnology, usually in a 'hands-off' way."[29] Du Pont's chief of biotechnology research, D. Jackson, in an interview in mid-1987, stated, that "The big companies are probably three to five years behind [the DBFs], because they didn't get started as soon, and they go slower."[30] Jackson's interviewer, reporting in *Fortune*, states: "As the search for the next generation of products begins [such as erythropoeitin, interleukins, epidermal growth factors], neither start-ups nor large companies can do without each other's talent and resources."[31]

A 1987 survey of major US corporations with significant investments in biotechnology, conducted by the OTA (with 53 out of 70 identified corporations participating), showed that while nearly all (96 per cent) respondents indicated that at least some of this R&D was conducted in house, over four-fifths (83 per cent) indicated that some of the research was conducted by outside firms and universities.[32]

The degree of collaborative effort prompted analyst L. Miller to say (fall 1987) that there has been almost a "de facto consolidation" in the biotechnology industry. This trend is illustrated, she says, by the joint research marketing and distribution relationships that small biotechnology companies have been forging with the chemical and pharmaceutical giants, not only in the USA, but abroad as well.[33] The US Department of Commerce assessment of the US biotechnology industry, based on 1988 data, states:

> Most biotechnology firms are not profitable and rely more on contract R&D rather than product sales for revenues. Until more products reach the market, which is not likely to happen on a large scale until the 1990s, their survival as independent companies rests on being able to raise sufficient funds to conduct research... Funding from large companies has grown in importance, as firms have had difficulty raising money from the stock market especially since October 1987.[34]

By 1990, virtually every major biotech company had significant stategic alliances in place. The convergence of interests between large established companies and DBFs persisted through 1995, and is set to continue for the foreseeable future. In 1993, alliances forged totaled $1.8 billion; 1994 saw 152 alliances formed, totaling $1.3 billion; and in 1995, 246 alliances were struck.[35]

The changing nature of collaboration

The nature of the alliances between leading DBFs and the large firms has been evolving with time. The 1984 OTA study *Commercial Biotechnology – An International Analysis* describes agreements occurring just after DBFs were formed:

> Many of the first DBFs (e.g., Genentech, Genex, Cetus) financed their own proprietary research by providing large established US and foreign companies with research services for initial product development or by entering into licensing agreements with such companies that would result in future product royalty income. Product development contracts between DBFs and established

companies provide for periodic cash payments from the established company to the DBF during the stages of research and early product development and for additional payments to the DBF (royalties income) following product sales. Following early product development by the DBF, the established company is generally responsible for obtaining the necessary regulatory approvals, manufacturing and marketing of the products.[36]

During the early 1980s many of the larger DBFs began shifting away from developing products for larger companies and put a new emphasis on their own product development. One of the primary reasons for this was that profit margins from licensing technology to established companies were low and generally not providing DBFs with adequate financing for growth and expansion.[37]

> In the early days, almost every biotech firm struck licensing deals for the big drug companies to develop and market their products. The reality is that many have sold their inheritance... Of course, most firms couldn't have managed any other way. A royalty-bearing agreement at least allowed them to raise further funds for research.[38]

By the fall of 1988 new biotechnology was starting to establish itself, with products in the pipeline, and the DBFs still largely maintained their technical edge over the large firms. The DBFs – at least the larger ones – began to possess the clout to forge more lucrative and favorable alliances with the TNCs.

> In the belief that the biotechnology industry is about to become a major source of important new drugs, the big pharmaceutical companies are racing to strengthen their ties to the industry's most promising members. Both the number and relatively generous terms of the deals struck in the last few months [prior to October 1988] demonstrate that the big drug companies – including Pfizer Inc., SmithKline Beckman Corporation and F. Hoffmann-La Roche & Company – think the biotechnology industry will soon introduce a slew of products that could be blockbusters. In striking the deals, the big drug concerns are also acknowledging that the small companies are well ahead of their own efforts in biotechnology... The terms of the deals are a significant departure from the ones biotechnology companies have had to strike when their technology was less proven. In the past they often have resorted to selling or licensing rights to crucial technology, manufacturing and marketing in order to obtain vital capital. Now, the strongest biotechnology companies are being treated as equals in potentially lucrative deals with the big drug companies.[39]

It must be emphasized, however, that the DBF negotiating power was associated with having products in the pipeline.

While the big drug companies are eager to enter into alliances with bio-technology companies, they are typically interested only in the stronger ones whose products are nearing the market. By contrast, the scores of bio-technology start-ups are still struggling and often have to mortgage their future to survive.[40]

Mergers and acquisitions

Strategic alliances also include acquisitions. Since the early 1980s a number of analysts have predicted a shakeout among the DBFs consist-ing of a wave of bankruptcies, mergers, and acquisitions. By the end of 1990, a number of acquisitions and mergers had taken place, but a shakeout had not occurred; it still had not by 1995.[41]

The year 1985 marked the first two major acquisitions of bio-technology companies. Eli Lilly (Indianapolis) bought Hybritech (San Diego), the largest firm at the time in the business of making diagnostic kits based on monoclonal antibodies, for about $400 million, and Bristol Myers bought Seattle's Genetic Systems for some $250–300 million. These acquisitions allowed investors to measure valuation of bio-technology companies and provided a confirmation of biotechnology's value by a major corporation.

Genentech, the San Francisco superstar and leader of the bio-technology industry, was top of virtually everyone's list to become a fully integrated, independent multinational pharmaceutical company. The last company to develop into a major drug company on the basis of a technological advance was Syntex Corporation, which developed the birth-control pill in the 1950s.[42] Genentech made a historic public offering in 1980, when its stock underwent the most rapid price increase in Wall Street's history, rising from $35 to $89 a share in the first twenty minutes of trading,[43] although since then its price has fluctuated sub-stantially. In January 1989, analyst S. Weisbrod of Prudential Bache security firm (New York) stated that "it [Genentech] is the only thera-peutic biotechnology company in our universe that has a first-line sales force. Additionally, Genentech probably has the best biotech R&D capability in the world."[44]

By the end of 1989, Genentech was one of only two US DBFs to clear technical and regulatory obstacles to putting its own genetically engineered drugs on the market, and for the year made a net profit of $44 million on sales of $401 million. Additionally, a number of prom-ising products were in the pipeline. Biotech analyst D. Gilbert was quoted in February 1990 as saying: "They [Genentech] have huge potential; I can identify 14 products in clinical trials or development."[45]

The merger, which captured biotechnology business headlines, occurred on 2 February 1990, when Swiss pharmaceutical giant Hoffmann-La Roche purchased a 60 per cent controlling interest in Genentech to gain access to its undisputed R&D prowess. La Roche paid $2.1 billion, which represented a 65 per cent premium over the stock's closing price the day before. La Roche also had the option to buy the remaining 40 per cent at an agreed-upon progressively scaled price of up to an additional $2.5 billion by the end of the five-year period. Thus, if La Roche were to buy all of Genentech, the purchase price could exceed an amazing one hundred times Genentech's 1989 earnings.[46]

Genentech's managers said they could no longer afford the huge development and marketing costs required by their promising products. "Genentech just didn't have the critical mass in terms of cash [to become an independent drugs firm]," said J. Hirshberg, a corporate development specialist with International Divestitures Inc. (New York), "and now it also gets Roche's marketing, sales, promotion and production expertise too."[47] According to G. Buck, former head and CEO of Cambridge Bioscience (Cambridge, Mass.), the most compelling reason behind Genentech's search for a buyer was the "tyranny of Wall Street." It was reported that founder, former chairman and now president of Genentech, Robert Swanson, became weary of soliciting increasingly skeptical investors for new money every time a promising new product was identified in the laboratory. In Gilbert's words, "Genentech has a huge R&D pipeline. It needed to focus on some products, and the company was reluctant to make a decision. So, to raise capital and become independent of the [Wall] Street, it made the deal."[48]

The merger ended Genentech's dream of becoming a fully integrated independent pharmaceutical company. To many, the dream that biotechnology would produce an entrepreneurial success to rival the out-of-nowhere rise of companies like Apple in the electronics industry was over. Despite this, the terms of the deal represented a stunning reaffirmation of biotechnology's promise, or at least Genentech's. However, some other large DBFs were also commanding premium prices for equity stakes by established TNCs. For example, the first equity investment in a DBF by Ciba Geigy (another leading Swiss pharmaceutical TNC) was in November 1988, when it purchased a 7.9 per cent stake in Chiron (California) at a 51 per cent premium over the market price.[49] In May 1989, Hoffmann-La Roche bought a 4 per cent stake in Cetus, paying a 50 per cent premium.[50]

Analysts were divided about whether the Genentech–Roche deal would herald a wave of takeovers in the biotechnology industry. By the end of 1995 such a wave had not occurred. Among the reasons stated by analysts Gebhart and Burrill for the unlikelihood of such a wave occurring was the fact that many corporate linkages were already in place between the biotechnology firms and larger pharmaceutical, energy and food companies. This, in effect, represented a shield against large-scale takeover, as large companies would not feel comfortable buying into firms that often have not only licensed their product rights to other large firms but are also involved in an array of joint ventures and marketing arrangements with them.[51]

Ernst & Young's 1995 survey states: "A paradigm shift in the bio-pharmaceutical industry from drug production to disease management (drugs plus services) provides the opportunity for a renewing body of smaller niche-oriented players to successfully co-exist with, and indeed continually revitalize, the bigger players."[52]

Small firms and innovation

One factor favoring the continued existence of small firms in bio-technology is their continued importance in innovation. On the role of small teams in innovation, S. Crooke – who left a position at the pharmaceutical giant Smith-Kline and French to found a biotechnology company to produce a new type of pharmaceutical (based on recent advances in biotechnology) known as "anti-sense" drugs – had these comments: "While the research budgets of large organizations sound enormous, they're committed. Even for the largest company to carve out a new program of 30 to 50 people is very hard; I couldn't have done it at Smith Kline."[53]

Analysts D. Ernst and D. Mackie of Mckinsey and Company, an international management-consultancy firm based in New York, refer to research by Mckinsey and Company and Harvard University which suggests that biopharmaceutical research productivity – as measured by biotechnology patent applications per $10 million of R&D spending – is more than four times higher at small biotechnology companies than at established pharmaceutical leaders.[54] Peter Marsh of the *Financial Times* underscores the importance of small teams in pharmaceutical innovation:

> Against this argument [that mergers in the sector showed how companies should be able to bring down costs significantly by merging] is the opposing idea that small teams often appear to work better in the drug industry in the vital area of drug discovery – the part of the business on which future growth in the sector depends more than anything else. Analysts can trot out innumerable case studies relating how many of the most successful drugs have been produced by small groups of people working with limited resources rather than by large R&D combines. That proves, some believe, that the smaller company in the pharmaceuticals business will continue to have a big role to play in terms of coming up with new products. This does not mean that the smaller outfit may not need the help of some of the larger groups when it comes to developing the selling muscle needed to ramp up revenues from the products once they have been placed on the market.[55]

An example of the marketing muscle that large firms can offer is shown in the Genentech–Roche deal. Analysts figure that Roche has 1,200 US sales representatives, out of 3,500 worldwide. That compares with Genentech's total sales force of 278.[56]

The analysis of this chapter leads to three considerations for developing countries: first, if they try to enter the biotechnology-based therapeutics market, they face formidable problems in raising needed capital and overcoming technical and regulatory hurdles; second, movement into therapeutics calls for collaboration with transnational corporations; third, developing countries are well-advised, at least initially, to focus their efforts on an area which would be less demanding on capital and skills, and where regulations are less stringent – namely, the field of diagnostics (See Chapters 5 and 9). Collaboration with experienced firms in developed countries will be needed in this field as well, but the duration and magnitude of such collaboration will be on a considerably smaller scale than in the attempts to develop therapeutic product lines.

Notes

1. Sharp, 1985, p. 120.
2. US Congress, 1984, p. 92.
3. *Ibid.*, p. 416.
4. US Congress, 1988b, pp. 113, 120.
5. *Ibid.*, p. 113.
6. *Ibid.*
7. *Ibid.*, p. 118.

8. *Ibid.*, p. 113.

9. *Ibid.*, p. 79.

10. Murray, 1986.

11. US Congress, 1988b, p. 82.

12. Miller, 1987.

13. Newman, 1990. The survey referred to is the San Francisco accounting firm's fifth annual survey of US DBFs, conducted in 1990 with 422 companies responding. Survey results were published by Ernst & Young under the title of *Biotech 91: A Changing Environment.* S. Burrill is national director of manufacturing/high technology industry services for Ernst & Young.

14. De Palma, 1990, p. 56.

15. As quoted by Newman, 1990. D. Gilbert is a biotechnology analyst for County Nat West Securities, San Francisco.

16. This presumably refers to the part of the industry that is publicly held.

17. Bock, 1991. Mr Bock is senior vice president of Sutro & Co's Biosciences Group in Los Angeles.

18. *Ibid.*

19. Zagor, 1991.

20. *The Economist*, 1995a, pp. 4, 8.

21. Amgen, 1995, pp. 4–5.

22. Green, 1994a, p. 12.

23. *The Economist*, 1995a, p. 4.

24. *The Economist*, 1995c; Zagor, 1991.

25. US Congress, 1988b, p. 87.

26. US Congress, 1984, p. 103.

27. Gannes, 1987, p. 48; and US Congress, 1988b, p. 99.

28. Graff and Winton, 1987, p. 22; *Wall Street Journal Europe*, 1989; Freudenheim, 1988b; and US Congress, 1988b, pp. 76, 88, 89.

29. *The Economist*, 1987a, p. 79.

30. Quoted by Gannes, 1987, p. 49.

31. *Ibid.*, p. 49.

32. US Congress, 1988b, p. 81.

33. Quoted by Graff and Winton, 1987, p. 20.

34. US DOC, 1989, pp. 19-2, 19-3.

35. De Palma, 1990, p. 56; Burrill and Lee, 1994, p. 33; Burrill and Lee, 1995, p. 29.

36. US Congress, 1984, pp. 92–3.

37. *Ibid.*, p. 107.

38. Furgusun, 1988, p. 57.

39. Freudenheim, 1988b, p. D1.

40. *Ibid.*, p. D2.

41. Gebhart, 1990, pp. 23, 30; and Burrill, 1990, p. 917.

42. Pollack, 1985, p. D1.

43. US Congress, 1988b, p. 85.

44. Quoted by Gebhart, 1989, p. 15.

45. Quoted by Lowenstein, 1990.

46. Chase and Lublin, 1990.
47. Quoted by Gebhart, 1990.
48. *Ibid.*
49. Schlender, 1988.
50. Gebhart, 1990, p. 22. In July 1991, Cetus agreed a merger with another Californian DBF, Chiron, in which Cetus would become a subsidiary of Chiron. The surviving company would be called Chiron Corporation (Chase, 1991b: 3). Chiron's acquisition of Cetus was completed in December 1991 (Chiron News Release, 10 August 1992). At the end of 1994 Ciba increased its stake in Chiron to 49.9 per cent, with an option after five years to increase its stake to a maximum of 55 per cent (Alper, 1995: 10–11). "Ciba Geigy is reckoned to have paid a 96 per cent premium for its 49.9 per cent shareholding in Chiron" (Brummer, 1995: 11).
51. *Ibid.*, p. 30.
52. Burrill and Lee, 1995, p. 52.
53. Fisher, 1990.
54. Ernst and Mackie, 1988, p. 499.
55. Marsh, 1989. David Thompson, vice president of business development at drug giant Eli Lilly, supports Marsh's analysis: "The biotech industry has proven that it can do innovative, leading-edge discovery quicker and faster than the big companies can." By April 1994, Lilly had forged between fifteen and twenty strategic alliances with US DBFs, and was seeking to form additional ones, according to Mr Thompson (Rundle, 1994).
56. Chase and Lublin, 1990.

Chapter 4

Geographical Distribution of Biotechnology Activity

Limitations of data

International competitiveness is often defined as the relative ability of firms based in one country to develop, produce and market equivalent goods or services at lower costs than firms in other countries. Standard analyses of competitiveness would thus examine the marketing of products. In biotechnology, by 1995, such assessments were still largely precluded, as relatively few products had yet been marketed. Furthermore, the biotechnology products that had reached the market by this time were not necessarily accurate indicators of the potential commercial success of the much larger number of biotechnology products and processes still in the R&D stages. Thus, in the early 1990s, assessments of geographic location were for the most part necessarily restricted to commercial biotechnology's potential, by examining such factors as the geographical distribution of biotechnology firms and R&D investment, the availability of and ability to attract and maintain qualified personnel. Even the numbers of firms and R&D investment in a given geographical area are often not known precisely. One can, however, gain an insight into relative degrees of geographic concentration and strength in biotechnology, which is the aim of this chapter.

It is difficult for a number of reasons to give an accurate indication of numbers and values. For example, various biotechnology directories and sources yield different firm numbers for the same area; more traditional companies may be conducting important research in biotechnology but not consider their work to be such; TNCs, with their subsidiaries and lack of exclusive effort in biotechnology endeavor, render exhaustive identification of programs and budgets difficult;

information given for a particular period of time can sometimes refer to previous periods (i.e. data is not thoroughly updated); sometimes it is unclear whether old or new biotechnology is being referred to, or what exactly constitutes a biotechnology firm or criterion for firm inclusion, or when and from what sources data was gathered.

The high concentration of biotechnology firms in the USA

Notwithstanding the reservations stated above, three regions of the industrialized world clearly lead efforts in biotechnology research, development and commercialization. Among the three regions, the USA, where the biotechnology industry started up with the foundation of the Californian DBF Genentech in 1976, has been and remains – at least through 1995 – the world's undisputed leader. Some considerable way behind the USA is Western Europe; even further behind is Japan.

The proliferation of small firms exclusively dedicated to commercializing biotechnology is basically and overwhelmingly a US phenomenon. Commercialization in Japan, on the other hand, is almost entirely being carried out by large established corporations, representing various industrial sectors (food and beverages, pharmaceuticals, steel, chemicals, etc.).[1]

Although differences exist among European countries, it can be generally said that small specialized firms have been established on a rather limited scale. By the mid-1980s the formation of small firms was largely confined to the UK, which had between 25 and 50 DBFs.[2] According to European biotech analyst Karl Simpson, by 1990 the geographical situation had changed, with France showing more biotechnology start-ups than anywhere else in Europe.[3] At the beginning of the 1990s, however, European DBF activity still remained small relative to that of the USA. For example, by the end of 1980 about 100 new biotechnology firms had been established in the US with a total market capitalization of over $1 billion. Western Europe, in contrast, by 1990 – nearly a decade on – could count a total market capitalization for biotechnology firms of less than half the US amount for 1980.[4] Chemical giants such as BASF, Bayer and Hoechst (Germany), Ciba Geigy, Hoffmann-La Roche and Sandoz (Switzerland), Zeneca (UK) and Rhone Poulenc (France), as well as a few UK DBFs, dominate European biotechnology efforts.

The US lead in public spending

The USA's world-leading position in biotechnology is founded upon its fast-moving intellectual base, which has been able rapidly to translate itself to the commercial marketplace. As with micro-electronics in an earlier period, its strength probably stemmed form the catalyst provided by federal funding, not in this instance for military and space research but for medical and biological research, and above all for cancer research.[5]

The US government has historically had the largest official commitment to basic research in biological sciences worldwide, both in absolute dollar amounts and as a percentage of its research budget.[6] The USA supports its basic research in biosciences to a greater extent than do all the other OECD countries taken together. This has been helpful in providing a basis for the new biotechnology companies, both in terms of exploitable research and high-quality skilled researchers able to move product and process development.[7]

In 1987, for example, the US government spent approximately $2,700 million supporting biotechnology research, whereas the combined Western European and Japanese official support for biotechnology was less than half that amount – some $1,200–1,300 million (about $800 million Western European and $400–500 million Japanese expenditure).[8] Similar proportions of expenditure were recorded in earlier years. No complete comparative data are available for recent years but it is likely that US official assistance will continue to predominate (in 1991 the US government budget for biotechnology research was $3.5 billion[9]).

Foreign corporate alliances with US-dedicated biotechnology firms

Another major reason for the US lead in commercialization of biotechnology is the unique dynamism and complementarity that exists between DBFs and established US companies in developing biotechnology for wider commercialization. It is not, however, just the US established companies that have formed strategic alliances with the US DBFs. Biotechnology is also being commercialized by other world biotechnology powers, overwhelmingly by the large established corporations. These foreign corporations, similar to their US counterparts, were technologically inferior to the US DBFs and did not begin in-house biotechnology R&D until after 1981.[10] Thus, although the vast majority of firms established exclusively for commercializing biotechnology are physically located in the USA, this does not mean that the US DBFs are exclusively US-financed. Precise figures for foreign established corporation investment in US DBFs are not available. Most evidence, however, indicates a substantial amount of foreign corporate investment and collaboration with US DBFs, motivated by the same considerations as US established companies (described in the previous chapter), with the additional purpose of enlarging corporate presence in the US market.

Biotech analyst L. Miller categorized the history of commercialization of US biotechnology up until 1987 into four time periods. Two of the attributes characterizing one of these periods, that of 1983–86, was that,

> The corporate alliance became ever more important as alternative sources of funds were diminished. Wall Street began to rely on these alliances as indicators of value. Globalization of biotechnology was accelerated. Many corporate partners were European and Japanese. This accelerated the development of a highly competitive environment on all commercial fronts.[11]

A 1984 study by the Office of Technology Assessment (OTA) of the US Congress, *Commercial Biotechnology – An International Analysis*, also refers to foreign corporate involvement with US DBFs:

> Reflecting the strong technological position of some US companies [DBFs] is the increasing number of established foreign companies that are seeking R&D contracts with the DBFs. Between 1981 and 1982, for example, the DBF Biogen experienced a 984 percent increase – $520,000 to $5.5 million – in R&D fees from Japanese companies, while Genentech experienced a 504 percent increase – $2.6 million to $15.7 million.[12]

Likewise, a 1985 OECD report on trade-related issues of the pharmaceutical industry refers to the international nature of collaboration:

> Major pharmaceutical, petrochemical and chemical firms have helped to set up, or increase the capital of, the specialized genetic engineering firms, and have either signed research contracts or established more elaborate forms of industrial cooperation for the development and production of given products... Many of these agreements are international. Japanese firms have been particularly interested in establishing ties with the specialized US genetic engineering enterprises.[13]

In 1985, M. Dibner (at the time a neurobiologist with Du Pont) created a database of recorded pharmaceutical-related interactions between US biotechnology firms and large companies, both US and

Table 4.1 Number of agreements between US DBFs and West European and Japanese corporations, 1981–1986

	1981	1982	1983	1984	1985	1986[a]	Total
Western Europe	6	22	26	41	61	17	173
Japan	16	36	23	28	29	9	141
Total	22	58	49	69	90	26	314

Note: [a] 1st quarter only.

Source: Based on data compiled by Rachel Schiller. Office of Basic Industries. International Trade Administration. US Department of Commerce, as quoted by Yuan, 1987, p. 20.

Japanese, in order to assess the extent of their relative collaboration with US DBFs. From 1981 to 1985, 72 joint or contractual interactions between US biotechnology firms and US large companies were recorded, whilst 43 such interactions were recorded between US biotechnology firms and Japanese large companies, i.e, 60 per cent as many as with US companies. "It is clear," states Dibner, "that Japanese companies, like large US companies, are relying on contractual agreements with small US firms to provide basic research or newly developed products."[14]

By 1985, European investment in American biotechnology firms was also growing steadily, and the globalization of US biotechnology continued further, in terms of both the US DBFs' sources of capital and their own business arrangements. "Nowadays [fall 1987], nearly every [biotechnology] equity deal we work out involves a large chunk of stock from overseas investors, particularly those in Europe and Japan," stated P. Drake, a biotechnology analyst at the brokerage firm Kidder Peabody of New York.[15] Analyst L. Miller adds: "You have a lot of small, innovative US companies that can stay in business only by licensing to Japanese or European companies."[16]

Table 4.1, compiled by the US Department of Commerce (DOC), shows the increasing number of contracts (with the exception of Japan in 1983) between US biotechnology companies and Japanese and Western European corporations for the period 1981 through the first quarter of 1986.

Table 4.2 classifies these contracts by type of agreement. The most common type of agreement with corporations in both Western Europe and Japan is that of distribution/marketing, with licensing for production

Table 4.2   International biotechnology agreements with US DBFs, 1981–86[a]

	A	B	C	D	E	F	G	H[b]	I
Belgium	1	1	1	3	–	1	2	9	9
Denmark	–	1	2	2	1	1	1	8	7
Finland	–	–	1	–	1	3	–	5	3
France	4	1	6	3	4	6	5	29	21
Germany	1	1	7	6	14	18	3	50	31
Italy	–	3	1	3	2	1	1	11	10
Netherlands	2	3	–	2	–	2	1	10	9
Norway	–	1	–	–	–	–	–	1	1
Spain	–	1	–	1	–	–	1	3	2
Sweden	3	3	5	4	5	6	3	29	19
Switzerland	1	2	11	4	5	6	5	34	26
UK	4	11	4	5	4	5	5	38	35
Total Europe	16	28	38	33	36	49	27	227	173
Japan	2	24	30	24	40	59	24	203	141

A	=	Acquisition
B	=	Venture capital/equity investment
C	=	Contract R&D
D	=	Joint R&D
E	=	License/production
F	=	Distribution/marketing
G	=	Joint production/marketing distribution/establishment of new firms
H	=	Total types of agreements
I	=	Total number of contracts

Notes: [a] 1st quarter only.
[b] Some contracts may involve more than one type of agreement.

Source: As Table 4.1.

and contract R&D the second most common. The table indicates that the significant difference between Europe and Japan is that the Western Europeans were much more active in acquiring US DBFs than their Japanese counterparts.

It appears that by the early 1980s, on the basis of publicly available R&D joint-venture agreements, the USA was a net exporter of technical know-how.[17] In fact, by the mid-1980s the influx of foreign capital in the US biotechnology industry began to worry ranking officials at the

US DOC, the National Science Foundation and the Office of Science and Technology Policy. They feared that further in the future the USA could be left as a giant research center for overseas manufacturers, who ultimately would capture the enhanced value of finished products.[18] By the end of 1989 some 40 per cent of total US biotechnology strategic alliances were with foreign investors, primarily Western European and Japanese.[19] In 1993 and 1994, 37 per cent and 35 per cent, respectively, of strategic alliances were with foreign investors. Europe accounted for 24 per cent in both years, Japan 11 per cent and 8 per cent, respectively.[20]

According to Raucon Biotechnology Consultants (based in Dielheim), by fall 1988 strict environmental controls and local opposition had largely accounted for the fact that over 50 per cent of biotechnology research by West German firms was being conducted abroad, notably in the USA and Japan.[21] Karl Simpson, European editor of *Genetic Engineering News*, also refers to substantial investment by German firms in the USA: "The government [FRG] has not been particularly helpful to the industry and, consequently, major biotech investments are being made in other countries, usually the US. Hoechst, Bayer and most recently BASF have all made investments of the order of $60 million in US R&D facilities."[22]

Even South Korean firms have invested in US biotechnology. Their economy is dominated by chaebols, or industrial conglomerates. The five major chaebols had total annual sales in 1985–86 of some $50 billion, accounting for about half the country's GNP. Two of these, Cheil Foods and Chemicals (part of Samsung, which began moving into pharmaceuticals in the 1970s and established a genetic engineering group in 1981) and Lucky-Goldstar are involved with biotechnology, primarily in pharmaceuticals. By 1994 South Korea emerged as the world's twelfth largest drug market, with annual sales at the time of about $2.8 billion.[23]

Both Lucky-Goldstar and Cheil were concerned about the slow progress of their efforts in biotechnology and the inadequacies of bio-technology R&D generally in South Korea, and sought to overcome this by establishing biotechnology companies in the USA. Lucky-Goldstar established Lucky Biotech in collaboration with the top-tier US DBF Chiron, which initially provided the technology and training; but by 1987 the company was operating as a fully owned subsidiary of Lucky-Goldstar, with a staff of ten scientists, about half of whom are rotated from the parent firm in South Korea. Aside from its research

Table 4.3 Genetic engineering patents registered in the USA by region of patent holder: 1986, 1988, 1989 (% distribution)

Origin	1986	1988	1989
USA	84	82	78
Total non-US origin	16	18	22
of which:			
Japan		9	10
EC		6	6
Rest of world		3	6

Sources: Copmann, 1989 and 1990.

projects the subsidiary also acts as a training facility and a window on the substantial biotechnology industry in the San Francisco area. In 1983, Cheil & Co. established Eugenentech in New Jersey with an initial investment of $3 million and a staff of twenty, mostly scientists of Korean origin.[24]

Regional distribution of patents

An indicator of the international distribution of industrial research activity in biotechnology is the granting of US patents. Although this is not a totally accurate reflection, as it probably overstates the US position vis-à-vis other countries, it is nevertheless a rough measure of the relative distribution of activity among other countries, as the USA is an important world market for biotechnology products. Caution should also be exercised in interpreting the data since variations in patenting practice between firms (and between countries) distort the picture to some degree. Variations partially reflect the propensity for the US DBFs and the Japanese to patent developments, whereas the major pharmaceutical and chemical companies often prefer to keep in-house activity as secret as possible, for the longest period possible (thus delaying the disclosure of information publicly via patenting.)[25] In this respect, patent data underrepresent European activity, where large firms predominate in biotechnology.

Lastly, in reviewing the patent activity data in Tables 4.3 and 4.4, it should be noted that patent applications were submitted to the US

Table 4.4 Genetic engineering patents applied to pharmaceuticals/health care registered in the USA, by region of patent holder: 1990, 1992, 1994 (% distribution)

Origin	1990	1992	1994
USA	82	79	78
Total non-US origin	18	21	22
of which:			
Japan	11	9	7
EC	5	8	11
Rest of world	2	4	4

Sources: Copmann, 1990; PMA, 1993, p. 12; PhRMA, 1995, p. 24.

Patent Office typically years before they were approved. For example, the average time of pendency (that is, the time needed by the Patent Office to review the patent application) for biotechnology patents was 25.6 months in 1990.[26] The figures, therefore, provide an indication of competitiveness at a time prior to the stated dates.

Of a total of 575 patents in genetic engineering registered in the USA between 1973 and 1986, 390 or 68 per cent were of US origin. Japan ranked a distant second with 13 per cent, while all other countries accounted for 19 per cent of registrations.[27] Data available through 1989 showed the USA continuing to be the origin of the vast majority of US genetic engineering patents issued, with Japan continuing to rank a distant second.

Of the US-registered genetic engineering patents, about half were applied to pharmaceuticals/health care during the period 1990–92, dropping to 38 per cent in 1994. Finally, the USA accounted for over four-fifths of the US patents awarded for R&D activity in the application of genetic engineering techniques to the pharmaceutical/ health care field during 1986–89, and almost three-quarters (an average of 71 per cent) during 1990–94.[28]

Despite the imprecision of some of the data presented in this chapter, it nevertheless unequivocally indicates worldwide US pre-eminence in the commercialization of biotechnology. The US lead has been grounded in extensive public funding of biomedical research. It has also benefitted from foreign resource inflow – both financially, as discussed in this chapter, and in the form of qualified personnel, as discussed in Chapter 5. Because so much of the world's biotechnology activity is concentrated in the USA, an examination of the performance of US firms provides insight into commercialization aspects that are applicable to the industry as a whole. Such an analysis is contained in Chapter 5.

Notes

1. *The Economist*, 1995e; UNCTC, 1988, p. 5; Fowler et al., 1988b, p. 186; and Wysocki, Jr., 1988, p. 1.
2. Sharp, 1985, p. 86; Fowler et al., 1988b, p. 188; and *The Economist*, 1985.
3. Simpson, 1990, p. 10.
4. *Ibid.*
5. Sharp, 1985, p. 41.
6. US Congress, 1988b, p. 35.
7. OECD, 1988, p. 92.
8. US Congress, 1988, p. 37; Fujimora, 1988, p. 146; Yuan, 1987; Rodger, 1989.
9. United States, 1991, p. 6.
10. US Congress, 1984, p. 98.
11. Miller, 1987, p. 3.
12. US Congress, 1984, p. 108.
13. OECD, 1985, p. 30.
14. Dibner, 1985, p. 1233.
15. Quoted in Graff and Winton, 1987, p. 20.
16. *Ibid.*
17. US Congress, 1984, p. 108.
18. Crawford, 1986, p. 14. A decade later, this fear had not been realized.
19. De Palma (1990, p. 56) states that over one-third of all US DBF partnerships were with foreign firms, mostly Western European; while Burrill (1990, p. 917) states that nearly half of all US DBF alliances were with foreign partners.
20. Burrill and Lee, 1994, p. 33.
21. UNIDO, 1988, p. 12.
22. Simpson, 1989, p. 7.
23. Yuan, 1988, p. B2; Yuan, 1995.
24. Yuan, 1988, p. B19.
25. Sharp, 1985, p. 40.
26. PMA, 1991, p. 15.
27. UNCTC, 1988, pp. 39–40.
28. PMA, 1991, p. 14; PMA, 1993, p. 12; PMA, 1995, p. 24; Copmann, 1989 and 1990.

Chapter 5

Business Performance, Costs and Prices

Causes of delay and high costs in the biotechnology industry have been of two kinds: those inherent to the industry and the general economic circumstances under which it operates, and those resulting from specific institutional constraints. The former include high research and development costs, high marketing costs, high skill requirements, high processing and environmental costs, long periods of testing and trials, and high capital costs. Causes of an institutional nature include, first, periods of waiting for approval by national government authorities of new biotechnology products and processes, influenced by concerns for their ultimate effects on public health; and, second, the delays in production and sales resulting from legal disputes among individual producing firms concerning patents on new products and processes. (For a discussion of patents and intellectual property rights in biotechnology and related disputes, see Annex 1.)

Business results

Business accounts of thirty-one US dedicated biotechnology firms were examined from the beginning of their operations. In most cases the period covered was the decade of the 1980s. The sample includes fourteen so-called top-tier firms (Amgen, Biogen, Centocor, Cetus, Chiron, Cytogen, Damon Bio-tech, Diagnostic Products, Genentech, Genetics Institute, Immunex, Life Technologies, Nova and Xoma) and seventeen others (Bio-Technology General, Biotech Research Laboratories, California Bio-Technology, Collaborative Research, Enzo Biochem, Genex, Immunomedics, Imreg, Integrated Genetics, Leeco Diagnostics, Molecular Genetics, Monoclonal Antibodies, NeoRx, Praxis Biologics,

Table 5.1 Top twenty firms in R&D as a percentage of sales, 1990

	USA		Non-USA
Genetics Institute	**112.4**	Sextant Avionique	25.9
Centocor	**71.0**	Synthelebo	18.2
Chiron	**40.7**	Astra	16.7
Continuum	37.3	Chugai Pharmaceutical	16.3
Genentech	**36.0**	Standard Elektrik Lorenz	16.0
Telematics International	31.0	CAE Industries	15.8
On-Line Software International	26.7	Finanziaria Ernesto Breda	15.7
International Microelectronic Products	26.4	Philips Kommunikations Industrie	15.4
Integrated Device Technology	25.6	Wellcome	15.1
Cypress Semiconductor	24.7	Roche Holding	14.9

Source: Buderi, 1991, p. 81.

Repligen, T-Cell Sciences and Techniclone International). These thirty-one companies had annual aggregate revenue in excess of US$1.1 billion, equivalent to almost three-quarters of total US biotechnology shipments, estimated at US$1.5 billion in 1989.[1]

The key finding which emerges is that the bulk of the industry has been operating at a substantial loss for most of the time. Aggregate net losses in the 1980s amounted to US$1.04 billion for the thirty-one firms as a group. Out of 244 business years for which records had been published for these firms, deficits show in 184 (75 per cent) of the years. Taking the entire life of individual firms in the 1980s, only three firms have shown net profit for the period as a whole. Another two companies have shown net profits in recent years.

The performance of British firms specializing in biotechnology has been marginally better. Data are available for nine companies with aggregate sales of £50 million; of these, three were profitable at the end of the 1980s. A British securities research firm concluded in 1988 that its report "demonstrates the paradox that potential markets are growing faster than actual markets. There is rapid progress in research leading to new possibilities, applications and processes. There is, however, frustratingly slow progress both in scaling up from laboratory to commercial production and in obtaining approval for use from the regulatory authorities."[2]

Of the thirty-one US biotechnology companies reviewed, only one – Diagnostic Products – has been distributing dividends. More generally, according to a 1991 analysis,

> diagnostics are one of the fastest growing applications of biotechnology. Recent breakthroughs in amplifying minute amounts of genetic material into larger quantities that can be analyzed is revolutionizing the speed and accuracy of testing. A new technique for producing monoclonal antibodies will make more varieties available for research at lower cost, and provide monoclonal antibodies (MAbs) more compatible with the human immune system. Most MAbs are used for *in vitro* (test-tube) diagnostic tests, but industry is also developing MAbs for *in vivo* (inside the body) imaging to detect cancers, and therapeutic MAbs linked to toxins as drug delivery agents. Researchers are also trying to determine whether MAbs can predict the remission, relapse and outcome of drug therapies in cancer patients.[3]

Research and development spending

Commenting on the results of a consulting firm's survey of US biotechnology companies in the late 1980s, a specialist noted that

> the biotechnology industry, as before, remains a big research and development spender... Overall, the industry spends 43% of product sales on R&D. Agricultural companies lead the way, with R&D expenditures at 116% of product sales, followed closely by therapeutic companies at 104% of sales. Diagnostic and supplier companies spend 35% and 13% of sales on R&D, respectively. As these figures show, companies that are more commercially mature – and hence have greater product sales – spend a smaller percentage of sales on R&D.[4]

For the sample firm Diagnostic Products, the proportion was 13 per cent. For comparative purposes, the pharmaceutical industry, which is a leading R&D performer, spends about 14 per cent of sales on R&D.[5]

For fourteen US biotechnology firms in the top-tier group, R&D expenditures as a proportion of revenue ranged from 9 per cent to more than 300 per cent in 1986–88.[6] The median value is 80 per cent. All non-profitable companies have R&D ratios above the median value. In the UK's largest biotechnology company, Celltech, R&D expenditure was equivalent to 48 per cent of sales in 1988. Research and development spending by US firms is continuing at a rapid rate. "According to the

Table 5.2   Pharmaceutical company expenditures as percentage of sales

Operating profit	28
Manufacturing	25
Marketing	24
Research and development	13
Other	10

Source: BZW research estimates, *The Economist*, 1990, p. 76.

US National Science Foundation, industry spent about US$2.3 billion in biotechnology R&D in 1990, an increase of 19 per cent a year over US$1.4 billion spent in 1987."[7] A 1990 international survey of firms cutting across industries showed that among the twenty firms in the world which lead in R&D spending as a percentage of sales, the first, second, third and fifth spenders were US biotechnology firms (see Table 5.1). A 1994 survey of US firm leaders in R&D expenses as a percentage of sales showed that seven of the top ten were biotech companies.[8]

Marketing costs

Marketing costs are among the highest expenditure items for pharmaceutical companies. According to one authority, these companies spend three to four times as much per dollar of sales on selling, marketing and distribution as they do on research – 25 per cent to 35 per cent of sales.[9] According to another estimate, marketing costs (1990) absorb 24 per cent of firms' revenues – about double the percentage a decade ago and well beyond the 13 per cent spent on R&D (see Table 5.2). In 1994, the world's drug companies spent about one-quarter of their sales revenues on marketing – more than twice as much as they devote to R&D, according to analysis by the stockbroker Lehman Brothers.[10]

As the bulk of the biotechnology industry is aimed at producing drugs and related items, it inevitably faces marketing problems and costs similar to those of the pharmaceutical companies, once it starts producing *en masse*. The difference is that the pharmaceutical firms already have a marketing and distribution network, and most of the biotechnology industry does not.

Once they get regulatory approval for new technology based products, the big old-line chemical and drug companies with their established sales and distribution networks will face few fiscal constraints in the marketing department. Yet marketing looms as by far the biggest single challenge to the small biotechnology outfits. "It's quite costly to send a sales force", writes Mark Skaletsky, president and chief operating officer at Biogen (Cambridge, Massachusetts). He estimates that it may cost US$80–90,000/year to keep a pharmaceutical sales representative on the road.[11]

As discussed in Chapter 3, a solution is sought in negotiating licensing or distribution agreements with large drug and chemical organizations, thereby tapping the established sales forces while getting a share of the profits. Biotechnology companies are also establishing limited sales staffs of their own for selected products. Finally, there are mergers – for example specialized biotechnology companies being absorbed by pharmaceutical giants.

Confirmation of the trend of rising marketing costs in the biotechnology industry comes in a review of the industry projections put forward in 1988–89:

> [An] indication of the industry's commercialization is the growing number of employees who work on production, marketing and sales – as opposed to research and development. As frequently noted, R&D is the core around which successful biotechnology companies are built. It is not surprising, therefore, that a substantial fraction (28 percent) of the projected personnel mix in 1990 is in R&D. However, the greatest projected personnel increases are in downstream functions. Marketing and sales, as well as production and operations, are each projected to double between 1988 and 1993.[12]

No comprehensive data on the marketing costs of pharmaceutical companies in developing countries are readily available. One would expect that they are lower, on average, than in developed countries: in most, or at least many, developing countries, medicines are in relatively short supply and the need for product-promotional advertisements and salespersons may be less than for countries with saturated markets; labor costs would presumably be lower, as the cost of living, on average, is less in developing countries than in industrialized countries. On the other hand, a significant proportion of legally authorized prescribers (and/or dispensers) of (non-traditional) medicines in developing countries – that is, physicians and/or other institutionally trained health professionals in pharmacology – are located in rural, remote areas of the country in question. These health professionals do not have the same high degree of access to medical journals and literature as

Table 5.3 Qualifications of personnel in US biotechnology industry

Company	Year	Total employees	Science staff	Science staff as % of total employees	Comments
Amgen California	1982–83	100	45	45.0	Ph.D.s
Biotechnology	1982–83	44	21	47.7	Ph.D.s
Chiron	1982–83	67	44	65.7	Ph.D.s
Collaborative Research	1982–83	125	25	20.0	Ph.D.s
Genex	1982–83	219	54	24.7	Ph.D.s
Integrated Genetics	1982–83	125	25	20.0	Ph.D.s
Genentech	1986–88	1,459	558	38.2	n.a.
Nova	1987*	150	46	30.6	Ph.D.s
Biogen	end-1987	228	34	14.9	Ph.D.s and M.D.s
Techniclone International Corporation	mid-1989	19	6	31.6	Ph.D.s
Biotech Research Laboratories	1988	215	129	60.0	21 Ph.D.s and 108 graduate researchers
Genetics Institute	1986	250	62	24.8	Ph.D.s

Sources: Daly, 1985, p. 16, for Amgen, California Biotechnology, Chiron, Collaborative Research, Genex and Integrated Genetics; annual reports for Genentech, Nova, Biogen, and Biotech Research Labs; report of the Securities and Exchange Commission, 1989, for Techniclone International; Schmergel, 1986, p. 233 for Genetics Institute.

physicians in developed countries, literature which announces and describes recent innovative drugs available to the market; distribution costs would also be presumably higher for remote areas and areas with poor/inadequate transportation infrastructure. Hence, the need for highly trained and qualified salespersons to visit these prescribers/dispensers in remote areas is essential, and perhaps to a greater degree than the need to contact and inform physicians who are located in developed countries about new, innovative drugs.

Furthermore, there probably are developing countries where the income distribution is so skewed as to produce a low effective demand for innovative drugs, the category of drugs to which all biotechnology-derived medicines belong. For this group of developing countries, despite the fact that unsatisfied human need for medicines is enormous – as most of the population is too poor to be in the market of buyers – promotional literature and information would still be an essential component of the successful launch of an innovative drug. Additionally, for this group of countries, although the physicians having high-income patients under their care are likely to be located in metropolitan (that is, non-"remote") areas, it nevertheless is likely that these physicians do not have equal access to the panoply of medical/pharmacological literature available to their counterparts in industrialized countries.

An examination of evidence on marketing and distribution costs in a properly stratified/categorized group of developing countries (for example, by income, income distribution, number of legally qualified prescribers per population, geographical size, proportion of the population living in urban as opposed to rural areas, adequacy of transportation infrastructure) would be of considerable interest for potential producers and investors in the pharmaceutical industry, including that of biotechnology-derived products.

High-skill requirements

Two categories of highly skilled manpower are needed in the biotechnology industry: (i) for basic research, it is necessary to have access to laboratory scientists engaged in molecular biology, genetics and immunology; and (ii) for scale-up and commercialization, there must be sufficient manpower in bio-process engineering.[13] Data are available for a number of US firms showing in many cases very high proportions of highly qualified personnel to total staff (see Table 5.3).

The technical talent working in the US biotechnology industry has partly been recruited abroad. Comprehensive data are not available. According to the president of Genetics Institute, one of the top-tier companies:

> We have created a technological jewel in one of the few industries where the United States still retains an edge. I think we are a real asset, not only to our investors, of course, but also to the community we live in – Cambridge, Massachusetts – as well as to the United States. It is, however, an undeniable fact that Genetics Institute would not be what it is today without its international connections. At best, we would be a small, struggling research boutique, rather than one of the powerhouses of the industry. In our company's case, a large percentage of our key scientific and managerial people are foreign-born. We have said from Day One that we will get the best talent wherever it is, and not worry about the costs of bringing them to Cambridge. Our people are a polyglot collection of former Englishmen, Frenchmen, Hungarians, South Africans, Chinese, Indians, Vietnamese, Koreans and Danes. We even have a few Americans![14]

A counterpart of the movement of high-level skills to US biotechnology has been the brain drain elsewhere. Even such an advanced and well-equipped biotechnology industry and educational system as the UK's has been experiencing brain drain, exacerbated by the reduction of government support for research.

> The number of university scientists under 35 years old is declining at a rate of 2 percent a year; out of 15 Ph.D.s graduated since 1981, only 3 are still working in the UK, while 10 have gone to the US... Staffing problems are beginning to appear in the recruitment of senior scientific staff (i.e., institute directors, department chairmen) with international reputations, since the salaries are not competitive with those paid in other countries and the work environment is deteriorating. This will become more acute as young researchers go abroad, make their careers in foreign countries and stay away permanently.[15]

A 1988 report by D.J. Bennett on *Manpower, Education and Training in Biotechnology* in the UK exposed both intermediate and long-term concerns about whether the supply of suitable recruits will keep pace with the demand. Already in short supply are protein chemists, immunologists, plant scientists and fermentation specialists at both graduate and doctoral levels. And the commercial exploitation of protein engineering is likely to create an unfulfilled demand for protein chemists, enzymologists and biochemical engineers, according to the survey.[16]

Remuneration levels in the US biotechnology industry are not known in detail. The president of Genetics Institute estimated in 1986 that "it costs US$170,000 a year on a fully loaded basis to keep a scientist working"; this includes, in addition to his/her pay, "expenses, supplies, overhead and equipment depreciation."[17] A 1988 survey of the US bio-technology industry showed the average R&D expense per person employed as US$26,000, which surprisingly is below the figure for the pharmaceutical industry of US$28,000 per employee. "Therapeutic companies lead the biotechnology industry, with R&D expenditures per employee of $48,000, followed by agricultural companies at $32,000, diagnostic companies at $20,000 and suppliers at $11,000."[18] These figures presumably cover all employees, unskilled as well as highly skilled; and it is not clear whether they include all costs. The impression of informed observers is that at least the highly skilled personnel in the US are well off:

> The most challenging aspect of managing biotech companies is the human one. While the industry faces obstacles at every turn, the people in it remain undeterred. Most firms have staffs of 100–300 employees with an average age of about 30. Typically, these are bright, dedicated people, inspired by their work and prepared to invest hard and long hours. Many of them work in beautiful offices so typical of American venture capital-funded companies. In almost every company the large majority of staff are directly involved in research and for many the job is just like the university research, but the pay and perks are better.[19]

Top-level managerial staff in the US biotechnology industry are much better paid than in other US industries. A survey by the Boston-based human-resource-management consulting firm William M. Mercer Inc.

> [in 1990] found that chief executives at 26 biotechnology concerns received an average of $608,300, including stock bonuses and options. By comparison, chief executives at similar-sized high-technology concerns received $355,300, including stock incentives. The average compensation for chief executives at similar sized firms in all industries was $284,000, according to Mercer.[20]

Bioprocessing costs

Manufacturing costs in biotechnology are influenced by environmental concerns to a higher degree than in industrial activities in general. The manufacturing regulations for biotechnology are perhaps the strictest in the world.

> Computers control the concentration of oxygen, carbon dioxide, acidity, temperature, and, most important of all sterility... Any microbes that escape

Table 5.4 Estimated time (in years) for launching new biotechnology products (other than *in vitro* diagnostics)

Estimates by	Discovery time	Testing and trials	Development and approval time	Total	Comments
US Department of Commerce			7–10		Biotech drug
Fildes and Fishlock			10		n.a.
Imreg Co.		4			Biotech drug
The Economist, based on Genentech experience		2	6–8		Biotech drug
Marsh				12	Agricultural chemicals
World Bank				10	Biotech for agriculture
T-Cell Science				12	Biotech drug
Stewart	3		9½	12½	Biotech drug
Godown			7–9		Biotech drug

Sources: US DOC, 1991; Dr R. Fildes, CEO of Cetus Corporation, quoted in Fishlock, *Financial Times*, 12 May 1989, p. 1; Imreg Co., 1987 Annual Report, p. 7; *The Economist*, 21 November 1987; Peter Marsh, *Financial Times*, 21 July 1990; World Bank, 1989, p. 16; (for T-Cell Science) J. Grant, quoted in Ferguson, 1988, p. 57; Stewart, 1988, p. 59; R. Godown, of the US Industrial Biotechnology Association, *New York Times*, 23 June 1987.

from a processing plant could rapidly spread. Even in a "small" fermenter containment becomes almost unmanageable. It is not enough to claim, as some biotechnologists have, that a heavily modified microbe will not survive outside a specific laboratory environment. All liquor leaving the fermenter must be cleared and sterilized to ensure that it is free of micro-organisms. It is a tremendous task to treat even 1,000 liters routinely. To comply with recommendations that grew out of the debate on safety, companies invested millions of dollars in special equipment facilities to prevent microbes from escaping into the environment.[21]

Yanchinski estimated that "downstream processing after fermentation accounts for at least 70 per cent of production costs in biotechnology."[22] However, the key category, production costs, is not qualified – perhaps it refers to manufacturing only, rather than to total costs; and the basis of the estimate is not known. Stewart has estimated "manufacturing start-up" costs at 54 per cent of total costs for a new drug. The two other major cost components are "development and testing" (24 per cent) and "sales and marketing start-up" (22 per cent). The "manufacturing start-up" proportion of costs is based on the investment experience of the two largest US biotechnology companies with their best known drugs: TPA, a blood clot dissolving drug (produced by Genentech) and EPO, a red blood cell production stimulator (produced by Amgen).[23] A larger sample of cases, along with knowledge of production costs as well as investment costs, would be needed for meaningful quantitative generalizations.

Gestation period

There is broad general agreement that it takes ten to twelve years to get new biotechnology products – therapeutic drugs and agricultural applications – to the market. This is in marked contrast to *in vitro* diagnostic products, which require only one-fourth to one-third of that time. In the case of therapeutic drugs, much of this time is accounted for by the requirements of the regulatory process for obtaining marketing approval for drugs, which involves their undergoing years of testing on animals and clinical trials with humans in order to establish safety, set dosage levels and confirm efficacy. This is followed by the drug agency's review of test results.

The regulatory component of the human therapeutic development process is perceived, by both large and small firms, as the major factor influencing the time required to develop a pharmaceutical product.[24]

Table 5.5 Estimated cost of developing new biotechnology drugs ($ million)

	Cost up to clinical trials	Cost of clinical trials	Start-up (investment) & manufacturing	Start-up (investment) sales & marketing	Imputed cost of capital during development &/or regulatory approval	Allowance for risk	Total
Imreg Co, 1987 Annual Report	10–12		n.a.	n.a.	n.a.	n.a.	80
Stewart, Peat Marwick RMK analyst, 1988	13.3		30.0	12.0	a	<43.0	<93.3b
US Dept. of Commerce, Industrial Outlook 1991				100	a	a	n.a.
The Economist, 1989, p. 70	30	70	n.a.	n.a.	a	a	n.a.
Professor Wiggins, 1987		65		n.a.	60c	a	125d
Clarke, 1995	n.a.	n.a.	n.a.	n.a.	n.a.	n.a.	200
Wallich, 1995	93	n.a.	n.a.	n.a.	46	a	n.a.

Notes: [a] Presumably included in other items; [b] Outlay to get a product to the launch point, i.e. excludes negative cash flow to reach break-even volumes which may take 2–3 years (Stewart, 1988, p. 61); [c] Range 38–77; [d] Range 103–142.

The time and expense involved in getting a drug through the regulatory process has been a significant contributing factor to the formation of strategic alliances between smaller, dedicated biotechnology firms and large, established multinational companies, as discussed in Chapter 3 (see Table 5.4).

A gestation period as long as ten to twelve years leads to a substantial increase in the capital cost because of earnings foregone during the period. The specific size of the increase will depend on the expected rate of return on alternative investments.

Cost of capital and profit expectations

A number of estimates of the total cost of developing a new drug have been put forward. According to Stewart, classical wisdom in the pharmaceutical industry states that "it takes US$100 million to develop a product." A *Fortune* article raises the ante in referring to Genentech's TPA [a biotechnology product]: "Security analysts estimate that Genentech has sunk US$200 million into TPA."[25] In support of the view that the cost exceeds $100 million and may approach $200 million, Professor Wiggins has pointed out that,

> A cursory examination of the data on research expenditures and drug approvals illustrates dramatic changes in the cost of dug development. Of the 47 new chemical entities[26] approved in a typical year in the late 1950s, the majority came from industrial laboratories. During the same period, industry research expenditures averaged roughly $176 million per year. By the late 1960s, new approvals fell to roughly 13 new products per year, while research expenditures rose to $525 million. By the early 1980s, approvals rebounded to about 19 new products per year, while annual expenditures jumped to over $3,000 million. In 1986, approvals totalled 20 new products and research expenditures rose to $4.6 billion.[27]

The implication is that the average cost of a new drug (in the USA) rose perhaps from $10 million in the late 1950s[28] to $40 million in the late 1960s, and then to $157 million by the early 1980s and as much as $230 million in 1986.[29] Estimates put forward by industry specialists are shown on Table 5.5. Three components of computed costs need to be distinguished: (i) out-of-pocket costs in current (actual) money terms; (ii) adjustment for inflation over the development period and the period of waiting for regulatory approval; and (iii) benefits foregone during the development and regulatory period – the imputed cost of capital – in

Table 5.6 Prices of selected biotechnology products

Product	Producer	Price (US$)	Comments	Source
Activase (TPA), blood clot dissolving drug	Genentech	2,000–2,200 per dose	Competitors: Eminase (Beecham), $1,700; Streptokinase, $300	Chase, 1990; Moore, 1991
Synthetic human growth hormone, against pituitary dwarfism in children	Eli Lilly, Genentch	10–30,000/year or more, depending on dose, several years		Okie, 1988, p A4; Katz Miller, 1992
Anti-endotoxin, treatment of septic shock (pervasive bacterial infection)	Centocor, Xoma	To be priced at 3,750 per dose		Fisher, 1993a, p. D3
Inunomax, recombinant gamma interferon, for treatment of kidney cancer	Biogen through Japanese licenser Shionogira Co.	¥25,770 ($170) per dose; 10–15,000 for typical adult course of treatment	To be sold in Japan	Biogen press release, 18 December 1989
Erythropoiten (EPO), hormone stimulating bone marrow to produce red blood cells	Amgen	6,240 for a one-year supply	For treatment of kidney dialysis patients with anemia	Freudenheim, 1989, p. D6
Factor VIII, blood-clotting drug for hemophiliacs	Armour Pharmaceuticals	25,000 per year	Costs 5–8 times as much as older versions	Pollack, 1988
Alpha interferon, for treatment of Kaposi's sarcoma, cancer affecting 10% of AIDS patients	Schering Plough and Hoffman-La Roche	9,800 limit on annual cost of treatment		*Genetic Engineering News*, January 1989, p. 32
Vaccine against hepatitis B	Merck	120 a treatment		Pollack, 1988
Monoclonal antibody imaging agent for detecting tumors, heart damage	Centocor, NeoRx	Likely cost 200–400	Cost of isotope to be added, resulting in 600 total cost to patient	Pollack, 1989

real terms. These three components can be clearly distinguished in Professor Wiggins's study. The out-of-pocket costs incurred during 1970–85 were adjusted for inflation, and this yielded a total of $65 million in 1986 dollars (see Wiggins, Table 5.5). Wiggins then applied an interest rate of 8 per cent as representing the cost of capital (benefits foregone), which raises the cost by $60 million, giving a grand total of $125 million. Wiggins also provided a range of capital costs: with a 5 per cent interest rate for benefits foregone, the grand total development cost works out at $103 million; and at a 10 per cent rate, the grand total is $142 million – the higher point of his range.

These are very high interest rates. Historically, the real rate – the money rate adjusted for the rate of inflation – in developed countries has been 1–2 per cent. The decade of the 1980s was an exception, with an average real rate of 4–5 per cent in these countries.[30] Using the 8–10 per cent interest rate possibly reflects the expectation that the biotechnology industry should aim at earning the kind of profit rates achieved by the pharmaceutical industry – rates that were much higher than in manufacturing in general or in the economy as a whole.[31]

While there is no doubt that real factors make biotechnology an expensive proposition during the gestation period, the situation is aggravated further by high financial costs and expectations of high profitability, which in turn have served to push upwards factor incomes and selling prices.

Product prices

Prices of biotechnology products have, as a rule been set quite high thus far, (see Table 5.6). Some of the known protests by biotechnology drug consumers against high prices include the following: (1) Anti-endotoxin (treatment of septic shock) pricing has prompted "an outcry of protests from infectious disease specialists, but renewed excitement amongst investment analysts."[32] (2) The cost of the EPO drug (kidney dialysis patients) has placed it "beyond means of many patients".[33] Amgen, the drug's producer, has offered to give free supplies to several thousand patients who do not have medical insurance.[34] (3) Vaccine against hepatitis B: "developed at great expense, it is already apparent that few people in the poorer Asiatic countries, where hepatitis B is endemic, can afford US$100 for a course of treatment. So the company's scientists are working towards a version made in a chemical factory. In this instance, the much-heralded biotechnology revolution may be over before it is begun."[35]

> Hepatitis B vaccine, the first vaccine made by genetic engineering, sells for US$120 a treatment, higher than most vaccines and out of reach of developing nations where the disease is prevalent.[36]

> One of the biggest killers in the Third World is hepatitis-B. Simple diagnostic and preventive treatments have been devised, but are currently too expensive to be widely deployed.[37]

It is not clear on what principles the pricing is based. "Genentech officials decline to say how they determined TPA's price, except to stress that $2,200 is not out of line for a potentially life-saving drug."[38] The price of anti-endotoxin "is based on a recent sale of the experimental drug."[39] "Britain's Celltech is a leading supplier of bulk monoclonal antibodies. This can be a highly lucrative activity. Celltech charges an average of US$400/gram for antibodies." It would seem that the guiding rule in pricing is what the traffic will bear, influenced by market pressure to show profits as soon as possible, after years of sustained deficits.

The overall conclusion that emerges is that biotechnology thus far has been a very expensive industry: very high R&D costs; a long gestation period, particularly influenced by long periods of testing and trials; high skill requirements in all phases of production and distribution; and high profit expectations. The major exception is the diagnostic products industry, where costs are much lower and entry into the industry much easier (see Chapter 9).

Notes

1. Estimate by US Department of Commerce (DOC), 1991, p. 18-3, refers to products developed through recombinant DNA and monoclonal antibody technologies, mostly pharmaceuticals and diagnostics. Revenue of firms refers to sales of products and services, the latter mostly for research contracts. Despite this deficiency in comparability, there is no doubt that the thirty-one companies produce the bulk of US aggregate biotechnology output and a substantial proportion of world output.

2. ICC Information Group, 1988, p. 1.

3. US DOC, 1991, p. 18-4.

4. Spalding, 1988. In 1995, overall, R&D expenses were 85 per cent of sales (Burrill and Lee, 1996, p. 70).

5. *Ibid.* The 14 per cent held steady to 1995.

6. The fourteen firms are listed on p. 60 above.

7. US DOC, 1991, p. 18-3.

8. Coy, 1994, p. 44.
9. Stewart, 1988, p. 59.
10. Green, 1994.
11. Graff and Winton, 1987, pp. 21–2.
12. Burrill, 1988, p. 1191.
13. Dibner, 1986, p. 1370.
14. Shmergel, 1986, pp. 233–4.
15. Yuan, 1987, pp. I-15, 16.
16. Newmark, 1988.
17. Shmergel, 1986, p. 234.
18. Spalding, 1988, p. 37.
19. Furguson, 1988, p. 60.
20. *Wall Street Journal Europe*, 1991b.
21. Yanchinski, 1987, pp. 45–6.
22. *Ibid.*, p. 46.
23. Stewart, 1988, p. 61; Gannes, 1987.
24. US Congress, 1991, p. 89.
25. Stewart, 1988, p. 58.
26. Chemical entities not previously marketed. These single chemical entities are the primary building blocks of drug therapy and represent the most important source of therapeutic change (source: Steven Wiggins of the Department of Economics, Texas A&M University, 1987, p. 1).
27. *Ibid.*, 1987, p. 1.
28. US$4 million financed by the industry (176/47) plus perhaps as much by the government.
29. *The Economist*, 1991b, p. 15 refers to the pharmaceutical industry stating that it costs roughly $230 million to offer a new medicine to the public; however, US DOC, 1988 implies that the average cost was $192 million as it states that twenty-four new products were developed at a total cost of $4.6 billion.
30. Derived from The World Bank, 1991b. The historical data refer to 1890–1913 and 1955–79, and those of the 1980s to 1980–89. The countries covered the USA, UK, Japan, Italy, Federal Republic of Germany and France. Real interest rates are computed by dividing long-term bond yields by the GDP deflator.
31. In 1986–89, profits as a percentage of stockholders' equity amounted to 11.5 per cent in all US manufacturing corporations. In the drugs industry, they were 19.6 per cent (US Bureau of the Census 1988, p. 516). These rates are in current money terms; adjusted for inflation, they were about five percentage points lower.
32. Fox, 1990, p. 1241.
33. Kehoe, 1989.
34. *New York Times*, 10 November 1989.
35. Yanchinski, 1987, p. 47.
36. Pollack, 1988, p. 13.
37. Wald, 1989, p. 18.
38. Fox, 1990, p. 1241.
39. Gladwell, 1988a, p. H6.

Chapter 6

Sources of Business Finance

Given that the DBFs have suffered substantial losses over a long period of time due to the long gestation periods involved in product development (with the exception of monoclonal antibody-based *in vitro* diagnostic tests), obtaining outside finance becomes critical to the firms' survival. The prolonged losses have made it difficult to contract large amounts of loans with which to finance operations and expansion. It was necessary to search for risk (equity, non-debt) finance from rich individuals, venture capital companies, and the public share (stock) market.

The low proportion of debt (loan) finance

Out of thirty-one major US biotechnology companies, nine did not show any long-term debts in their balance sheets at the end of the 1980s. In another five companies long-term debt outstanding was equivalent to under 5 per cent of total assets. For all thirty-one companies, the median proportion of debt financing (long-term debt outstanding as a percentage of total assets) was only 13.2 per cent.[1]

Case studies of individual companies would be needed to determine whether loan finance was sought but could not be obtained, or was not sought at all because the terms were considered unsustainable by the debtor companies themselves. Cutting across both classes of case study, however, the conclusion is inescapable that for the large majority of biotechnology companies debt capital was a marginal source of finance. Only in two cases did the long-term debt provide finance for more than half of total assets, and only in four cases did debt exceed equity.

Suppliers of equity finance: wealthy individuals

Equity finance – also referred to as risk or proprietary capital – is the main flow of biotechnology finance external to the firm. It essentially comes from three sources: wealthy individuals, venture capital organizations, and the public market for shares (stocks). The greatest amount of knowledge exists with respect to the share market, and a fair amount is available on venture capital; less is known about wealthy individuals and the scope of their operations. According to one observer,

> an increasing number of small businesses are doing without the services of the professional providers of finance altogether and are turning to private individuals for funds. "Business angels", as private investors are known in the US, have twice as much money available for investment as the professional US venture capital industry, according to some estimates. Private investors, many of whom have business experience with larger businesses, often seek both a part-time involvement in the management of the companies in which they invest, as well as providing equity and loan capital. Business angels are usually willing to take a far more long-term view of their investments than are banks or venture capital funds.[2]

The tendency for young startup companies to turn to private individuals was stimulated as venture capitalists began increasingly to invest in management buy-outs and buy-ins, which were more profitable than the riskier early-stage investments, and usually required far less work;[3] and as "angels" tried to fill the gap left by prominent venture firms that had lost their appetite for startups in favor of ongoing enterprises in which they could invest $5 million or more at a time. As more money became available – a record amount of nearly $5 billion was raised by US venture capital firms in 1994 – less of it went to start-ups. "That's because new companies tend to need small amounts of capital but lots of handholding."[4]

In another assessment, by Hacking, a UK industrial research scientist, "in the United States in particular, wealthy individuals paying a high marginal rate of tax are prepared to make high risk investments, particularly if there are tax advantages in doing so. Doctors have been a source of funds to small medical and biological companies."[5] There is a view that for "every active angel trying to nurture a start-up, there are 10 'virgin angels' who could be, but for a variety of reasons that have nothing to do with money, are not" and that "this investment subculture will become even more significant."[6] But Hacking adds that "there are disadvantages to this method of financing, however, often arising from personal friction between the entrepreneur and investor."[7]

Further, to the extent that venture capital companies had shifted their attention and resources from financing real investment to financing transfer of assets by the late 1980s, this was expected to change as some important financial transfers had been followed by debt-servicing difficulties; but this change had not occurred by 1995, according to US and UK data.[8] The need for capital in biotechnology companies is likely to increase as investment in processing and marketing networks is added to continuing R&D laboratory work: the survey of 1989 biotechnology industry intentions showed a yearly average capital requirement of $3 million for a small company (one to fifty employees), but $9 million for a large company, in the period 1989–93.[9] The net effect of these factors – with likely preference for real investments and rising capital requirements as firms expand – should be an increase in the role of organized rather than individual finance in meeting biotechnology needs, as the industry matures.

Suppliers of equity finance: venture capital

Venture capital is a type of direct investment in the securities of new speculative firms or expanding technologically oriented firms. It is usually characterized as a high-risk investment carrying an expectation of large returns in dividends and capital gains. It has played a highly significant role in funding new biotechnology companies. Investors in ventures cover the whole range: commercial and merchant banks, insurance companies, large manufacturing corporations, investment companies, and private individuals.

> Venture capital groups act as intermediaries between investors and entrepreneurs, but they are not only suppliers of funds; they analyze the business and its prospects and actually function to assist the company. They will work with the company on its internal problems such as marketing and financial structure without taking direct control. Initially an entrepreneur or firm seeking capital is subject to rigorous evaluation.[10]

The funds mobilized by venture-capital companies for biotechnology have been impressive, particularly in the early 1980s, and picking up again from 1993 onward (see Table 6.1). The rate of return in biotechnology projects aimed at by venture-capital companies is not known. Batchelor states that "venture capitalists normally want a big slice of the equity of

Table 6.1 Biotechnology venture-capital investment in the USA, 1976–90

Year	US$ million
1976–81	870.00
1982	332.60
1983	849.50
1984	327.85
1985	200.00
1986	115.00
1987	220.00
1988	331.00
1989	251.00
1990	152.00
1991	112.00
1992	217.00
1993	459.00
1994	639.00
1995	562.70
Total	5638.65

Sources: 1976–85: Fujimura, 1988, p. 144. 1985–95 figures are for the fiscal year 1 July of the year preceding through 30 June of the year stated. 1986–90: Burrill and Lee, 1991, p. 23. Burrill and Lee note that in the period 1989–90 total venture capital declined by about the same 39 per cent that biotechnology venture capital did. 1991: Burrill and Lee, 1992, p. 35. 1992: Burrill and Lee, 1993, p. 63. 1993 and 1994: Burrill and Lee, 1994, p. 28. 1995: Burrill and Lee, 1995, p. 74.

companies in which they invest and are also only interested in companies which can provide a high rate of return – target rates for start-ups of between 50 per cent and 60 per cent compounded annually are not unknown – to compensate them for the inevitable failures."[11] (This statement refers to all industries, not only to biotechnology; and it focuses on start-ups, the riskiest stage, not on expansions which are the preferred investment by venture capitalists.) The rates of return actually achieved across industry in the USA "for those funds started in the late 1970s and early 1980s, according to Mrs Vincent, a vice president at Venture Economics, ranged from 5 per cent to more than 50 per cent However, rates of return had by the end of 1989 fallen back to more normal levels of between minus 10 per cent and over 20 per cent compounded per annum. As returns dropped, the perception of venture capital as an easy

Table 6.2 UK venture capitalists' preferred industries[a]

	January 1991	June 1990
Engineering	1	1
Communications	2	2
Health care	3	3
Chemical	4	5
Leisure	5	6
Electronics	6	4
Publishing and education	7	8
Other services	8	7
Computer services	9	9
Computer software	10	10
High-tech	11	11
Biotechnology	**12**	**14**
Financial services	13	13
Computer hardware	14	12
Advertising and marketing	15	15
Entertainment	16	19
Hotels and restaurants	17	17
Construction	18	16
Film industry	19	18

Note: [a] Views of 163 venture capitalists in January 1991 and 158 in June 1990.
Source: Batchelor, 1991.

way to make a quick buck was dispelled and investors became wary of pumping more money into the sector."[12] In West Germany, a venture capitalist could ask for a 20 per cent return, compared to a rate of interest on borrowing from a bank of 10 per cent.[13] In what appears to be a summary of experience, two Swiss analysts state that "while it is expected that not all ventures financed will survive, for those that do the expected annual return on capital is between 25 to 35 percent."[14]

The usual maturity cycle – or the time when the target company becomes ripe for disinvestment – is between five and seven years, according to Helmut Kirchner, a partner in Matushka Group, an international investment and venture capital concern headquartered in Western Germany.[15] In a survey of British venture capitalists, asked how many years they would consider it reasonable to wait for first profits from a biotechnology investment, all said they would be satisfied with profits inside four years. Only four (out of fourteen venture-capital funds interviewed) said they were willing to wait more than seven years to realize their investment.[16] According to the Swiss analysts' summary, "normally after a four to seven year period, the venture capital company will sell its share in the new company at a large profit, and reinvest the proceeds in another start-up situation... The normal exit route for divestiture is the over-the-counter market or second board stock exchange."[17]

Venture-capital funds which have managed to sell their holdings of biotechnology stocks at public share markets or otherwise at satisfactory prices have made profits, which in some cases have been handsome. But in the USA, for example, publicly owned biotechnology companies at the outset of the 1990s numbered 186, and there were at least twice as many privately held.[18] It is unlikely that much profit from sale could have been made on many of these privately held companies (due to the long gestation period required by most biotechnology products), and venture capitalists that continued to hold them did so at the cost of interest foregone and at the risk of loss in asset value when sold, or assets declared of very low value, in case the company goes into default due to continued deficits which cannot be financed. According to one biotech-industry leading venture capitalist,

> There was this theology round here that if you worked as a team and had a company cheer like Genentech, you'd go further than the regular drug companies. They were very naive and so were investors who thought this was another electronics industry. This is not Silicon Valley: there are major technical, regulatory, patent and marketing risks. There is not a venture capitalist who has not lost money in biotech.[19]

This seems an exaggeration: there have probably been losses on individual investments, but not on the industry as a whole. A British analyst noted that, "surprisingly, most of the boutiques launched in the late 1970s and early 1980s survive."[20] But there was a down-side. The inflow of venture capital into US biotechnology slowed up in the mid-1980s.

> Venture capital is harder to come by today [1988], but some money remains out there. According to Venture Economics (Wellesley, MA), the invested venture capital funds for all industries grew at a 17.5 percent compound annual growth rate from 1982–86. While funds for medical (health-related) companies exceeded this rate, growing at 22.7 percent during this period, those for genetic engineering investments posted only a 5.3 percent gain.[21]

Another effect is that in 1990–91 biotechnology ranked twelfth in a group of nineteen activities preferred by British venture capitalists, i.e.

two-thirds down the list (see Table 6.2). Data provided by the European Venture Capital Asociation (Brussels) show that venture capital investment in European DFBs as a whole fell gradually, from a peak of about $123 million in 1989 to about $47 million in 1993.[22] It should be noted, however, that investor preferences have proven extremely volatile in the biotechnology industry's short history. They have been excessively influenced by even single company discoveries and failures.

Suppliers of equity finance: the stock market

Leaders of biotechnology companies and owners of venture-capital firms have managed to sell a substantial quantity of biotechnology shares to the investing public – institutions and individuals, mainly in the USA. This has been done in the face of continuing deficits in most of the industry and the associated lack of any dividend payouts for over ten years. The reason for the success in selling biotechnology stocks against these odds has been the expectation that ultimately biotechnology is going to earn enormous profits, which, even after heavy discounting for lack of any cash dividends in the near future, would justify buying and holding biotechnology stock today.

There is a basis for this reasoning, although uncertainty remains. Predicting in 1987 the future of Amgen – one of the best known US biotechnology companies, second largest after Genentech – Peter Drake, a biotechnology analyst at the brokerage firm Kidder Peabody, estimated that the company, then the potential producer of erythropoietin (EPO), could earn $3.60 per share in 1991 (from as little as 8 cents in 1987); these earnings would justify a price per share by mid-1988 of close to $60, or nearly 50 per cent above the 1987 actual price, in Drake's calculation. The price:earnings ratio (the inverse of the rate of capitalization of income divided by the value of the asset) used by Drake was reportedly 25, which would give a share price of $90 in 1991 ($3.60 × 25); this price was then scaled down to around $60 for mid-1988 to take into account the risks of biotechnology and, presumably, the benefits (interest) forgone.[22]

Amgen did develop and market the anti-anemia drug EPO, and it is now successfully selling: sales in the fiscal year 1 April 1990 to 31 March 1991 were estimated by Merrill Lynch at $285 million,[23] which represents a doubling of Amgen's total revenue in one year. Amgen's scientists began presenting data on its new number two product,

Neupogen, to blood disease and cancer specialists. Amgen's earnings per share, which amounted to 56 cents in 1989 and 82 cents in 1990, were estimated by Merrill Lynch at $2.25 in 1991. This is 37 per cent below Drake's $3.60 projection for the year; but anybody who has made this kind of projection four years into the future, starting from a level of virtually zero, will be impressed by this analyst's work. The expected increase in earnings gave rise to a boom in the price of the stock. On 20 February 1991, it reached $88, almost exactly the $90 level calculated by Drake for 1991. The $88 price implies a price:earnings ratio of 39 (88/2.25), compared to Drake's assumption of 25. His overestimate of 1991 earnings has been compensated, in its effect on the stock price, by his underestimate of investors' faith in the long-run future of biotechnology and their associated willingness to accept lower earnings today in the expectation of higher earnings and correspondingly higher asset values the day after tomorrow.

The average price:earnings ratio in US industry was 15 in February 1991, implying a capitalization rate of 6.6 per cent (100/15), the investors being willing to hold average stocks if they yield this rate.[25] But in the pharmaceutical industry, price:earnings ratios are normally higher than the average, in response to a traditionally higher growth rate of earnings, higher expected rate of profit, and greater faith in the industry's future, compared to other industries. Drake has used the price:earnings ratio of 25 for biotechnology, following the example of pharmaceuticals: at this ratio, investors are willing to hold stocks even if they earn 4 per cent a year (100/25). In fact, in the case of Amgen and of many other biotechnology stocks quoted on stock exchanges, the willingness to hold them has gone beyond the pharmaceutical stocks. Amgen's price:earnings ratio of 39 implies a capitalization rate of 2.5 per cent (100/39). Acceptance of this low level cannot be interpreted simply as a reflection of ignorance and lack of experience and of the caution of average investors, although all these elements are present. The fact that a very sophisticated investor, Hoffmann-La Roche, was prepared to accept a price:earnings ratio of 79 in the case of its 1990 Genentech purchase by paying $2.1 billion for a yearly earnings stream that, based on 1989 data, amounted to $26.4 million,[26] indicates a great deal of faith in rapid future earnings growth of the US largest biotechnology enterprise (at the time) and by implication in much of biotechnology generally. A US official study noted in 1988 that "biotechnology continues to boast the highest price to earnings ratio of any industry."[27]

Three major waves of placement of biotechnology stocks on the US market occurred in 1983, 1986–87 and 1991. In the first, some $500 million was mobilized;[28] in the second, lasting until mid-1987, some $1,200 million;[29] and in 1991, $3,700 million.[30] How much of these resources, and of those raised in other years, actually went toward productive investment in the industry is not clear, as part was used to reimburse venture capitalists who withdrew from the industry entirely.

Successful sales of biotechnology stocks would not have been possible without comprehensive information on company operations, plans and prospects, and without an extensive analytical apparatus in brokerage firms, banks and the government advising institutional and individual investors and disseminating knowledge. The need for information, analysis and knowledge was particularly important in view of the novelty of the industry.

The total market valuation for US biotechnology was $9–10 billion prior to the 1987 stock-market crash, excluding any participation by large established companies with diverse businesses, such as large drug and chemical companies. The stock-market crash of 1987 devalued biotechnology companies 40 to 60 per cent on average, reducing total industry market capitalization to about $4.5 billion.[31] The negative impact of market volatility is particularly severe in the case of stocks like those of biotechnology which do not yield any dividends, as there is no cushion for investors to fall on: their only reason for holding such stocks is price appreciation, and this reason disappears when prices fall. After a prolonged slump in 1988 and 1989, stocks recovered during 1990 and early 1991 as new expectations concerning product developments and use were generated.

During the 1989 slump, one financial writer, commenting on biotechnology stocks, noted that "rarely has Wall Street paid so much attention to so many companies that have lost so much money for so long."[32] The mood in 1991 changed and some important investors bought biotechnology stocks.[33] It is inevitable, however, that much uncertainty and associated volatility will remain until the industry as a whole becomes clearly profitable.

The 1991 US public financing window lasted until the end of the second quarter of 1992, with 132 DBFs raising $5.2 billion in that eighteen-month period.[34] Since mid-1992 and ongoing into the second quarter of 1995, however, the US stock market has experienced a protracted decline. This has resulted, in substantial part, from a string of clinical trial failures of promising products, and a ballooning in the number of companies – since 1990, the number of public companies has grown from 150 to 265 in 1994,[35] with the total number of DBFs (public and private) increasing dramatically in the decade 1984–94, from some 330 to 1,300,[36] all of which are competing for investors' capital.

Investors also revised their thresholds for risk and reward sharing when, in 1993 and, particularly, in 1994, products being developed by various DBFs suffered a series of clinical trial failures: leading drug candidates worked no better than placebos, or they caused unacceptable side-effects, or trials were poorly designed. These included, amongst other DBFs and their lead products, in development: Centocor's, Cortech's and Synergen's drug candidates to counter septic shock; Glycomed's heart drug; Magainin's impetigo (skin disease) therapeutic; Medimmune's drug for respiratory infection; and Regeneron's drug against Lou Gerhig's (nerve) disease. These companies saw their share prices lose between 76 per cent and 93 per cent of their (all-time high) value by 13 September 1994.[37]

In 1992, US public share companies raised $2 billion.[38] For fiscal years 1993 and 1994 (1 July–30 June), the sums raised were $1.1 billion and $1.8 billion, respectively.[39] Biotech stock prices plunged an average of 32 per cent in 1993, and a further 29 per cent in 1994 – well over 50 per cent from their zenith in mid-1992, according to the American Stock Exchange Biotechnology Index.[40]

Since the early 1990s, the UK has been considered second in strength to the USA in biotechnology. In June 1992 the UK DBF British Bio-technology persuaded the London stock exchange to become the first European exchange to relax its listing rules (the rules a company must abide by in order for its securities – for example, stocks and bonds – to be permitted to trade on a particular official stock exchange), thereby allowing the company to be the first DBF to be listed, whereupon it raised £30 million ($53 million).[41] In December 1993 the London stock exchange officially relaxed its listing rules for research-based companies; these included a three-year profit record as a qualification for listing.[42] Since British Bio-technology's flotation, fifteen additional UK DBFs have gone public on the London stock exchange through March 1995,[43] creating a quoted (that is, listed on the official stock exchange) biotech sector in the UK with a market capitalization worth around $1.5 billion (£1 billion) by September 1994 – the largest such sector in Europe[44] – and a doubling of its value from June 1992.[45] For the purposes of comparison, in June 1993 there were 225 quoted DBFs in the USA, with a combined market capitalization of some $35 billion (£23 billion).[46]

The UK's public biotech sector has also experienced volatility during its short quoted history. The Andersen BioIndex (Arthur Andersen is a UK accounting firm) has tracked the performance of this emerging sector since 1992. Up to the end of 1993 these companies outperformed both the health-care and pharmaceutical sectors, as well as the Financial Times Stock Exchange (FTSE)-100 index of leading UK quoted companies. But, for 1994 the Andersen BioIndex had fallen nearly 20 per cent by October.[47] Several factors helped to account for this fall, including the general downturn in the UK stock market, with the FTSE-100 index itself falling 10 per cent in the six months following its all-time high at the beginning of 1994. More importantly, the new issues market, which had been running at record levels since 1993, lost its momentum in the first half of 1994, as initial public offerings (IPOs) were postponed or their asking prices were revised downwards to help ensure the success of their flotations.[48] This, in turn, had an adverse effect on the sector, as without a number of headline-making IPOs it was difficult for this relatively young sector to maintain investor enthusiasm when news reports were typically those detailing R&D expenditures and concomitant company losses, with occasional patent approvals or collaboration announcements. The situation is not helped by the fact that (unlike in the USA) the sector is not quite active or large enough to warrant the full-time attention of stockbroker analysts, whose research and recommendations can stimulate institutional and smaller investor buying and selling. However, according to Arthur Andersen's Biotechnology Group, there are signs that by the end of 1994 one or two brokers were starting to build teams with biotech expertise in anticipation of the future growth of the UK DBF public sector.[49]

The UK DBF public sector was dealt further blows in early 1995, for a similar reason to those sustained by its US counterpart: poor results in clinical trials. In mid-February, British Bio-technology announced that it was suspending phase III clinical trials (the last phase) of its drug for treatment of abdominal cancer, due to glitches in its effort to scale up manufacturing of the product. The drug was the company's – and the UK biotech sector's – first product to have progressed successfully through earlier phase trials. By mid-March the company's value had fallen 30 per cent to £230 million.[50] Shortly after British Bio-technology's announcement, at the end of February, another prominent public UK DBF, Cantab, announced that it was abandoning phase III trials of its organ-transplant drug, following disappointing phase II trial results. Cantab's share price plummeted 40 per cent in response to the news, and its market value more than halved to £16 million by mid-March. In fact, by mid-March *The Economist* was reporting, "most [UK] biotech firms now trade at barely half their level at listing."[51]

In Europe generally, biotech IPOs (flotations) were still a relatively infrequent occurrence through 1994 and the first half of 1995. Money raised through IPOs by European DBFs was about $167 million in each of the years 1993 and 1994.[52]

Gaps in business finance

Despite the major involvement of venture-capital firms and share markets, three important gaps remain in the availability of business finance. The first gap refers to companies requiring large amounts of capital, but not belonging to the top-tier group of companies (larger companies which cannot obtain sufficient finance from the public share market). The second gap refers to small biotechnology companies which cannot get start-up or development capital. The third gap concerns the situation of biotechnology companies, usually small, which face a cash squeeze when usual sources of funding dry up.

With respect to the first gap, "the single most important problem facing the biotechnology industry during the 1990s continues to be its ability to raise vast amounts of capital ... Last year [1990], perhaps as a sign of hard times ahead, some biotech companies were being pressed to sell their stocks at discounts below prevailing market prices (Immunex and Epitope) or forced to reduce the size of their equity offerings (Neozyme)..."[53] As indicated in Chapter 3, only 10 per cent of the industry received over 70 per cent of all financing during 1989.[54]

On the second gap – the difficulties of small companies in obtaining financing – two British studies have provided relevant evidence:

> Finance is a problem for many of Britain's small biotechnology companies, with venture capital sources unversed in the technology and companies believing the returns required of them to be unrealistic... Government grants, an important source of support in launching nearly half the biotechnology companies surveyed, are expected to disappear with changes in rules for research support.[55]

Few small British businesses in biotechnology will expand to provide significant sources of wealth and employment ... many small companies face long lead times in developing products. They also find it difficult to discover small market areas for products that are free from large established groups in fields like chemicals and pharmaceuticals... Many of the companies face funding problems.[56]

US small firms face similar difficulties in getting finance, and these difficulties may affect even the most prominent scientists/potential entrepreneurs. Dr Jonas Salk, the developer of a vaccine for polio, had to postpone the initial public offering of $36 million for a firm of which he is a co-founder, Immune Response Inc., which is developing an AIDS vaccine. "The move by a company that has been viewed as a bellwether for biotech stock offerings is an illustration of the difficulty small, cutting-edge biomedical companies are having raising funds in public equity markets, analysts and venture capitalists said."[57]

In the third gap – emergency cash-squeeze situations – company founders and small businesses are being forced to give up large chunks of their ownership shares in exchange for money to stay in business. "There is a terrible conflict of interest among investors when a scarcity of new capital gives the wealthiest partners power to dictate financing terms. Unless founders and early investors come up with money to protect positions, their equity can be squeezed. This is especially unfair to scientists and founders whose 'intellectual property' is the company's main asset", according to Howard E. Greene, Jr., chairman of a now-dissolved venture-capital concern, Biovest Partners, which tried and failed to protect founders in turning off "hardball financing tactics of bigger venture capital firms" and "predatory venture capitalists".[58] Employees of one of the companies that Green and Wallaeger, his partner, tried to help, "saw their collective stake cut by 50 per cent as the price for raising $1.5 million."[59]

The sociology of biotech finance: two notes

Employee stock-ownership plans

Thirty of thirty-one biotechnology companies surveyed operate stock-option plans which give their key personnel and management, and in some cases other employees as well, the option to buy specified quantities of the company stock at the price ruling at the time the option was granted, thus enabling them to benefit from the difference between this price and the market price, if higher, when the option is exercised. Stock-option plans can serve as a powerful device to raise salaries of all beneficiaries. They also provide incentives to management to drive the company harder or more efficiently in order to improve its performance.

Eleven of the same thirty companies also operate employee stock-ownership plans, which distribute predetermined quantities of stocks to all employees at a preferred (lower then the market) price, and some operate profit-sharing plans. The effect is to increase wages marginally across the board and to provide a sense of participation to all employees. The quantity of shares included in stock-option plans (selective) has been much larger than the quantity included in employee stock-ownership plans (general).

Biotechnology companies have found share distribution to employees a particularly suitable practice: "it promotes the recruitment of key talent ... share ownership is also viewed as a strong incentive to loyalty and dedication";[60] and it saves company cash in the initial stages of company life, when it is likely to be particularly scarce. According to a survey of twenty-six leading biotechnology firms conducted in 1991 by the human-resource-management consulting firm William M. Mercer, biotechnology firms use stock as a form of compensation more extensively than any other industry. "In biotech, long-term incentives are needed to retain senior executives while a product goes through the lengthy development and approval process in getting to the market ... Biotech executives expect these incentives as part of the overall compensation package", explained R. Rich, a principal at Mercer. The survey found that more than 75 per cent of the executives had received an equity incentive award.[61]

The experience of Genentech, which has a very broad employee ownership (in 1989, 1,678 out of 1,790 employees held stock options, and 1,402 participated in the employee stock plan), has been very good.

> Because of this, managers pass on confidential information to employees. Last August [1987], all the employees were brought together and told of a crucial forthcoming visit by the Food and Drug Administration just before the approval of Genentech's drug TPA, used to combat heart attacks. None of the employees leaked the price-sensitive information to Wall Street. Such openness would be unimaginable in a big pharmaceutical firm.[62]

"Molecular millionaires"

The specific pattern of biotechnology financing – through venture-capital funds and stock-option plans – and the general practices of share pricing in a capitalist economy combined to produce great personal wealth for a limited number of people even before the biotechnology industry had started generating any significant profits. When initial stock (share) offerings to the market are made, stocks are priced on the basis of expected profits from future product sales, capitalized into assets by using a capitalization rate (price:earnings ratio) and discounted to present value (see the Amgen example above). This share price can be, and frequently is, much higher than the price which would result from actual development costs. The beneficiaries of the difference in pricing are the initial owners of the stocks: the people who hold stock options if their exercise time has arrived, and the venture capitalists who have financed the founding of the company and its initial production. The buyers of the stocks may finance a large part of the purchases by borrowing from banks – that is, by drawing on the savings of the general public. They expect to be reimbursed, at a profit, when, in turn, they sell the stocks in a subsequent round as production and earnings expand, or as expectations (price and profit) go even higher. The system is based entirely on expectations of future earnings; but the profits made on initial stock offerings have to be paid for today, out of collective current savings rather than out of profits which do not yet exist.

The scientists and physicians who provided the initiative for the founding of biotechnology companies were one class of beneficiaries, through stock options.

> When *Genetic Engineering News* published the first list of biotech's "molecular millionaires" in February 1987, almost half of those listed were Ph.D.s... Genentech's Herbert Boyer tops the list of former university professors turned millionaires – with an estimated personal fortune of $88 million. William C. Rutter, formerly of University of California Medical Center and now Chairman of Chiron Corporation, is worth an estimated $21 million. Steven Gillis and Christopher Henney, formerly microbiologists at the University of Washington made their fortunes (worth an estimated $6.3 million each) at Immunex.[62]

The other class of beneficiaries, most likely more significant, were venture capitalists.

Perkins helped start Genentech in 1976 with $100,000 in Kleiner Perkins' [venture-capital firm] money; the following year the firm put another $100,000... At the stock's price high of $64.75 on 24 March 1987, Kleiner Perkins $200,000 investment would have been worth $360 million.[63]

Great volatility in the overall flow of biotechnology business finance, with small and large firms not having equal access to this finance, and occasional financial cash squeezes to which the weaker biotechnology firms are especially vulnerable, make the issue of finance central in biotechnology in developed countries. It can be expected that this issue will be even more decisive in developing countries in view of their overall financial situation and problems. Chapters 7 and 8 review the position in developing countries, focusing on domestic financial constraints (Chapter 7) and access to foreign finance (Chapter 8), respectively.

Notes

1. Balance sheets of thirty-one companies. The list of companies is given in Chapter 5.
2. Batchelor, 1989.
3. *Ibid.*; Carty, 1995.
4. Bylinski, 1995, pp. 78–9.
5. Hacking, 1986, p. 250.
6. Schrage, 1990.
7. Hacking, 1986, p. 250.
8. Carty, 1995.
9. Burrill, 1988.
10. Hacking, 1986, pp. 47–8.
11. Batchelor, 1990.
12. Zagor, 1989. Venture Economics is the US venture capital industry's research group and think-tank.
13. Relchlin, 1989.
14. Husbands and Dichter, 1989, p. 16.
15. Relchlin, 1989.
16. Peter Marsh, 1988, as quoted in Fishlock, 1988c, p. II. Managers from fourteen British venture capital funds were interviewed.
17. Husbands and Dichter, 1989, p. 16. The over-the-counter market and second board stock exhange are junior public share markets, with less stringent registration requirements than the main stock exchange.
18. Bock, 1991.
19. Marsh and Buchan, 1989. Statement of Mr Robert Kunze, who is also a banker at Hambrecht & Quist in San Francisco, a fund-management venture between British and American banks.

20. Fishlock, 1988b, p. I.
21. Ernst and Mackie, 1988, pp. 495–6.
22. Lucas et al., 1995.
23. Curran, 1987, p. 76.
24. Merrill Lynch, 1990.
25. The dividend rate will be lower than (perhaps half) the earnings rate, as a part of earnings will be reinvested by the company rather than distributed as dividends.
26. Aggregate Genentech earnings in 1989 amounted to $44 million. Hoffmann-La Roche bought a 60 per cent interest of Genentech – i.e. 60 per cent of the $44 million income stream, or $26.4 million – for $2.1 billion.
27. US Congress, 1988b, p. 86.
28. Hacking, 1986, p. 253.
29. US Congress, 1988b, p. 86.
30. Spalding, 1992a, p. 481.
31. US Congress, 1988b, p. 86.
32. Gupta, 1989.
33. One of these was the $2.2 billion Quantum Fund, directed by George Soros, a well-known financier, international figure and economics writer from New York and London (and originally from Hungary) (*Wall Street Journal*, 30 September 1990).
34. Spalding, 1992c, p. 951.
35. Burrill and Lee, 1993, p. 55; and Burrill and Lee, 1994, p. 50.
36. *The Economist*, 1994b, p. 57.
37. Hamilton, 1993, p. 67.
38. Spalding, 1993, p. 149.
39. Burrill and Lee, 1994, p. 28.
40. Rundle, 1995, p. 9.
41. Gourlay, 1993; Schropp, 1995, p. 31.
42. *New Scientist*, 1994, p. 3.
43. *The Economist*, 1995b, p. 74.
44. Spencer and Kirk, 1994, pp. 958–9.
45. *The Economist*, 1994a, p. 78.
46. Lynn, 1993; Gourlay, 1993.
47. Spencer and Kirk, 1994, p. 958.
48. *Ibid.*, p. 959.
49. *Ibid.*
50. *The Economist*, 1995b, p. 74.
51. *Ibid.*
52. Lucas et al., 1995, p. 27.
53. Bock, 1991.
54. Presumably "the industry" here refers to companies traded on the stock exchange.
55. Fishlock, 1988a. Seventy-eight biotechnology firms were surveyed.
56. *Financial Times*, 1 May 1990. Based on a survey of forty-eight UK dedicated biotechnology firms.

57. Barnum, 1989.
58. Rundle, 1989.
59. *Ibid.*
60. Lowell and Witrock, 1989.
61. *Genetic Engineering News*, 1991b.
62. *The Economist*, 1988b.
63. Fowler et al., 1988b, pp. 181–2.
64. Gannes, 1987, p. 47.

Part III

Implications for Developing Countries

Chapter 7

Domestic Financial Constraints in Developing Countries

Financial constraints for biotechnology development operate at three levels in most developing countries. First, in the case of biotechnology entrepreneurs, new entrants face the institutional gap: private venture-capital companies which could help supply equity capital do not exist in most cases. Also, share markets are frequently insufficiently developed or are limited to traditional well-established firms, rendering access to equity for new firms in developing countries difficult. Second, the public finance situation in developing countries, rarely strong, has become extremely strained in many during the last decade as a result of economic stagnation and decline, debt and falling commodity prices, forcing most of them to curtail public expenditure and eliminate most new starts in long-gestation projects. To a degree, this is partly a matter of policy priority within individual countries – some countries, for example Cuba, had resisted the cuts – but the room for policy choices has been very narrow. Third, and partly overlapping with the second, interest rates in developing countries have been extremely high in real terms during the 1980s, under the impact of shortage of savings, private-capital flight, and rising demand for borrowed funds, partly to finance swollen debt-service payments, making it extremely expensive to borrow for long-gestation projects. Even though US interest rates have fallen in the recent recession, this has had only a limited effect on the internal financial market within most developing countries. Also, there is no indication that international investment in biotechnology in developing countries is reviving on a significant scale.

Table 7.1   Public-sector finances in developing countries

	Central government deficit as a share of GNP, developing countries (%)		Public sector borrowing requirements as a share of GDP,[b] developing countries (%)
	World Bank series, 90 countries	*UNCTAD series, 21 countries*[a]	*UNCTAD series, 14 countries*[a]
1972	3.5		
1985	6.3		
1988	4.7		
1978–79		2.8	7.0
1981–82		7.2	11.5
1986–87		4.0	3.8

Notes: [a] Percentage share of GDP, median value;   [b] Includes central, regional and local governments.

Sources: World Bank, 1988, p. 46, for 1972 and 1985; World Bank, 1990a, p. 199, for 1988; UNCTAD, 1989, pp. 87–8.

Public-sector financial deficits

A comprehensive picture of public finances in developing countries is not yet available, although efforts are underway by several international agencies. Partial data indicate a sharp deterioration of the situation in a very large number of cases during much of the 1980s (see Table 7.1).

Industrial countries have also run deficits in their fiscal accounts, but of a substantially smaller size. Seven major industrial countries – the USA, Japan, Germany, France, Italy, the UK and Canada – showed central-government deficits as a percentage of GDP of 4.6 per cent in 1985 and 2.6 per cent in 1988.[1] The comparable figures for developing countries, also referring to central government expenditures, are 6.75 per cent in 1985 and 4.3 per cent in 1988 (see Table 7.1 above: [6.3 + 7.2]/2 = 6.75, average for 1985; and [4.7 + 4.0]/2 = 4.3, average for 1988).

Following the enormous increase in the deficit in the early 1980s, under the combined impact of a sharp increase in debt service payments as interest rates rose, and a fall of income from commodity sales

Table 7.2 Public and total investment in a group of twenty-nine developing countries, 1970–88 (% of GDP, World Bank series)

Group	1970–80	1981–82	1983–84	1985–88
29 countries				
Public investment	8.2	10.5	9.0	8.0
Total investment	20.3	22.2	18.8	17.6
Of which 13 highly indebted countries				
Public investment	7.8	9.2	7.0	6.5
Total investment	20.1	20.2	15.1	15.2

Source: World Bank, 1990b, p. 88.

as export prices collapsed, the developing countries carried out a sharp retrenchment of both capital and current expenditures in the mid- and late 1980s.

Public investment as a proportion of GDP fell by about one-quarter from 1981–82 to 1985–88 (see Table 7.2). Aggregate current expenditures of a group of fourteen countries fell almost as much as capital expenditures (see Table 7.3).[2] In forty-two low-income countries, education expenditures – a key component of current central government expenditures – amounted to 9 per cent of GNP in 1988, compared to 20.5 per cent in 1972; health expenditures, another key component, fell from 5.5 per cent to 2.8 per cent of GNP.[3]

It is possible that substantial social pressure will compel governments to restore many of the cuts in public capital expenditures and in expenditures on education, health and social welfare before starts in new fields of public spending such as biotechnology research and support to biotechnology industry are approved. This does not mean that no starts in new fields are possible – room can always be made for new projects. But such new spending claims will have to compete against the severe competition for public funds likely to prevail through the 1990s. While the pressure of the debt problem has been alleviated in some countries of Latin America, it has remained severe elsewhere; and almost all developing countries experienced a renewed fall in their export commodity prices in the early 1990s, and resulting pressure on their budgetary revenues. Public funds will probably remain scarce for some time.

Table 7.3 Reduction of capital expenditures, in fourteen developing countries, 1981/2–1986/7 (change as % of GDP, median values, UNCTAD series)

	Decline as % of GDP
Public-sector capital expenditures, 14 countries	2.8
Public-sector current expenditures, 14 countries	2.6
Central-government capital expenditures, 7 countries	3.5
Central-government current expenditures, 7 countries	1.5

Source: UNCTAD, 1989, p. 91.

The paucity of venture-capital facilities

Country review

A highly placed official of the International Finance Corporation (IFC), affiliate of the World Bank and main international agency promoting private investment, described the supply situation of equity capital in developing countries in the early 1980s as follows:

> Having made equity investments as part of total financing packages in over 75 developing countries and in over 400 separate private enterprises, and having conducted an extensive survey on venture capital in 23 countries, we have considerable first hand knowledge of the two key issues concerning the growth of private businesses. First, there is a general shortage of venture capital, particularly equity, available either domestically or from international sources of finance. Second, small and even medium-size companies suffer from this shortage to a far greater degree than do large companies.[4]

> Institutional equity financing, relevant management expertise and professional support, which are typically funnelled through venture capital companies in the larger more sophisticated economies, have been conspicuous by their absence in developing countries.[5]

A 1980 country-by-country review shows that only in India and South Korea was the institutional structure for the supply of equity capital largely satisfactory. This was mainly due to the existence of a substantial network of government and government-sponsored institutions endowed with considerable resources for this purpose.[6] (No review could be obtained for a later date.) It is unlikely that the situation in the domestic supply of venture capital improved to a significant extent during the 1980s in view of the financial crisis that affected most developing countries. Exceptions are several Southeast Asian countries, including Malaysia, Thailand, Singapore and Indonesia; and in Latin America, countries such as Chile, Argentina, Mexico and Brazil.

Individual developed countries have provided assistance for the establishment of institutions to support capital markets development in developing countries and this may have included promotion of venture capital, but data are not available. Such assistance is known in the case of the IFC, which has considered it an important element in its lending and investment in developing countries during the 1980s (see Table 7.4). These activities should have contributed somewhat to the development of domestic capital markets in the beneficiary countries. But the amounts are too small to enable the development of biotechnology. Effective assistance on the part of the IFC to biotechnology development would call either for larger venture-capital financial injections with priority attached to biotechnology, or, more directly, for outright investment in the establishment and expansion of biotechnology companies, provided they could be expected to be profitable.

Target rate of return and timing and possibility of divestment

In IFC's recommendation,

> the venture capital company should provide a rate of return from dividends and capital gains after taxes of at least three times the prevailing level of interest rates on long-term financial assets such as bonds or time deposits. In stable price environments, this would call for rates of return after taxes of 30% per investment.[7]

With respect to sales of shares from its portfolio, the IFC suggests that the venture-capital company "should strive for a turnover of its portfolio within five to seven years".[8] It will be recalled that a similar timing of divestment and a target rate of return were indicated by two Swiss analysts of venture-capital activities.[9]

A target return in real terms of 30 per cent after tax is a formidable requirement for any enterprise. But it is in particular a target timing of divestment of five to seven years that makes it very difficult for biotechnology companies to be financed by venture-capital companies,

Table 7.4 IFC investments in venture-capital companies, 1981–90 (US$ million)

Year	Country and company	Activities	Total project cost	IFC investment
1981	Brazilpar	Agro-industry, energy, corporate financial services	15.00	1.50
1982	–	–	–	–
1983	–	–	–	–
1984	Malaysia Ventures Berhad	Investments, general	5.00	1.00
1984	Southeast Asia Venture Capital, N.V.	Regional investments, general	25.00	1.06
1985	–	–	–	–
1986	–	–	–	–
1987	–	–	–	–
1988	Industrial Promotion Services (IPS) Côte d'Ivoire	Investments, general	4.6	1.17
1989	Ventures in Industry and Business Enterprises (VIBES), Philippines	Equity, quasi equity, business consultancy services; applications of existing technology as opposed to innovative technology	15.00	2.42
1990	Capital Venture Company, India	Promotion of commercial development of locally based technology	60.00	2.87

Source: International Finance Corporation, Annual Reports.

unless there is a well-developed share market in the country concerned, where venture capitalists can sell the shares of a biotechnology company even before the latter has shown any profit (see Chapter 6). It will be recalled that it takes ten to twelve years for a biotechnology company to start marketing a new product (see Chapter 5); the exception is diagnostic products.

The importance of a well-functioning share market to back up venture-capital investments has been stressed by the IFC:

> It is not absolutely necessary to have a strong securities market in order to have successful venture capital operations. Nevertheless, a strong securities market can do two things which would certainly do a lot to help. The first is to make it possible for the venture capital company to revolve its portfolio profitably as its successful investments become acceptable to the market at an earnings multiple which could provide a true reward for entrepreneurship... The second is the role of a securities market as one of the financial mechanisms involved in subsequent stages of development of a new venture. That is, while very few securities markets provide seed capital for small and medium-sized enterprises via equity underwriting, most can arrange, through private placement or public issues, debt financing or even equity financing to supplement the original venture capital investment once an initial degree of success has been demonstrated.
>
> The country studies reveal that, in the absence of existing securities markets ... portfolio divestment limited to private placements tends to exhaust the absorption capacity of the system more rapidly and might lead to a declining level of risk exposure by discouraging involvements in start-ups and new acquisitions in general.[10]

Restricted access to the stock markets

Limitations of the markets

In its *Emerging Stock Markets Factbook 1990*, the IFC lists twenty-nine developing countries whose selected companies, listed on national stock exchanges, make up the IFC composite index. Total numbers of listed companies in each of the twenty-nine countries range from twenty-four in the Ivory Coast to an estimated six thousand in India (only some of these enter the IFC Composite Index, which consists of shares of under 800 companies). The aggregate of companies listed in the twenty-nine countries (9,767) accounted for 92 per cent of aggregate listing in all "emerging" markets. The implication is that in the remaining 120 developing countries the numbers of companies whose shares are listed

Table 7.5 Number of listed domestic companies in twenty-nine developing countries, 1989[a]

Côte d'Ivoire	24	Costa Rica	78	Mexico	203
Trinidad and Tobago	31	Colombia	82	Chile	213
Uruguay	39	Jordan	106	Malaysia	251
Jamaica	45	Nigeria	111	Peru	265
Turkey	50	Bangladesh	116	Pakistan	440
Zimbabwe	54	Philippines	144	Egypt[b]	483
Kenya	57	Thailand	175	Brazil	592
Venezuela	60	Sri Lanka[b]	176	South Korea	626
Indonesia	61	Argentina	178	India	6,000[c]
Morocco	71	Taiwan	181		

IFC composite markets: 9,767 listed companies
All emerging markets: 10,582 listed companies

Notes: [a] Emerging markets included in IFC Composite Index; [b] 1988; [c] Estimate.
Source: IFC, 1990b.

in national stock exchanges are very small, on average fewer than ten each (see Table 7.5).

The median number of listings in the twenty-nine developing countries is 116. A comparable median for twenty-three developed countries is 284 companies, ranging from 78 in Finland's stock exchange to 6,727 in the United States. A smaller number of listings, all else being equal, indicates less of a readiness to accept new companies and provide them with equity funds through the purchasing of their share issues.

> The securities market in Mexico has undergone extraordinarily rapid expansion. This is especially true of the equity market, where prices have risen dramatically, secondary market turnover has expanded rapidly, and the volume of new share issues has reached significant proportion. However, the bulk of the new issues in this market have been issues of large mature companies owned either by the principal private groups in Mexico or by the public sector. There are few new "venture capital" issues of new or rapidly growing smaller firms, and trading in the smaller firms which are listed on the Mexican Stock Exchange is infrequent.[11]

On the Colombian stock exchanges, new ventures have no access to the market. Moreover, the stock exchanges have played a minimum role in providing new equity capital for existing enterprises other than in the financial sector.[12]

Further work is needed to establish whether the Mexican and Colombian experiences have also been encountered in the securities markets in other developing countries and whether the situation has changed since 1980. This might well have been the case, particularly in the rapidly growing financial markets of some countries in Southeast Asia.

Volatility and high returns

The share markets in developing countries are more volatile than those in developed countries.[13] "Excessive market volatility ... is unlikely to inspire confidence in firms and investors."[14] It will attract speculators/traders counting on short-term gains, but it may discourage long-term investors.

Cutting across short-term variability, it appears that the share markets of developing countries have offered higher realized returns than those of most developed countries. In Dailami and Atkin's computation, which includes both dividends and capital gains (stock appreciation), total pre-tax median return on shares in real terms for twenty-three developing countries was as high as 25.5 per cent during the 1980s (1980–89 or selected years in this period), on average.[15] A general impression of high returns on stocks in developing countries has been the major factor in the attractiveness of these markets to foreign investors in recent years, as evidenced by the establishment of a number of "country stock funds" whose shares were offered in developed countries worldwide. An additional attraction is the opportunity for diversification, as these markets are not highly covariant with markets in OECD countries.[16] In 1990, there existed a worldwide developing-country fund, six regional funds (developing countries), two Brazil funds, two India funds, three Indonesia funds, six Korea funds and three Malaysia funds, amongst others.[17]

Firm figures on aggregate flows of foreign investment in the share markets in developing countries are not available. In 1990, Latin America funds attracted US$475 million, Korea funds about $430 million and Indonesia funds around $325 million. In IFC's estimate, aggregate flows have been running at $1–2 billion per year in recent years.[18]

Table 7.6   Gross domestic and national savings ratios in selected developing countries

Indicator/region	1970–80	1981–84	1985–88
Gross domestic savings/GDP			
Total	0.15	0.12	0.13
Africa	0.11	0.06	0.08
Asia	0.19	0.19	0.21
Europe/Middle East/North Africa	0.15	0.16	0.15
Latin America and Caribbean	0.20	0.17	0.17
Gross national savings/GNP			
Total	0.14	0.10	0.10
Africa	0.11	0.06	0.06
Asia	0.18	0.18	0.19
Europe/Middle East/North Africa	0.15	0.14	0.12
Latin America and Caribbean	0.17	0.12	0.11

Source: World Bank, 1990b, p. 95.

The impression of high returns on stocks in developing countries was shaken somewhat by the sharp fall in their prices in 1990: 32 per cent in dollar terms in a single year, according to the IFC Composite Index.[19] Nonetheless, the Index shows an annual rate of return in US dollars of 20 per cent in the period December 1985 to March 1991. This is considerably higher than the return on stocks in the USA and Europe.[20] The upswing in the stock markets of a number of developing countries resumed during 1991, with Argentina, Colombia, Brazil, Mexico, Chile and Pakistan in the lead.[21]

An opportunity for biotechnology?

Out of 762 stocks in the IFC's composite index of twenty-nine developing countries at the end of September 1990, only forty-one were in the group of "chemicals and allied products". This group most likely includes pharmaceuticals (drugs) and probably biotechnology products, if any exist. These forty-one stocks accounted for only 4 per cent of the total market value of 762 stocks at the end of September 1990.[22]

The Templeton Emerging Markets Fund, managed by a well-known US financier, included stocks of eighty companies from thirty-eight developing countries at the end of August 1988. Only two companies producing chemical products were included, both in petro-chemicals, rather than drugs and biotechnology products.[23]

Considerations of diversification would require the inclusion of pharmaceutical and biotechnology products in worldwide, regional and country funds in developing countries: pharmaceuticals in view of their proven growth record, and biotechnology products in view of the promise they hold – not only judging by Amgen's and Genentech's successes, but also in light of the possibilities of diagnostics production in developing countries (see Chapters 9 and 10). What needs to be proven, however, is that developing countries have the technological capacity to make these products and can do so profitably.

The lag in aggregate savings and high interest rates

The crisis of the 1980s adversely affected the savings flow in developing countries in two ways. First, it led to a reduction in the proportion of domestically generated income that was saved, as marginal domestic savings rates fell below the average, in reaction to stagnation or fall in income. Second, from such adversely affected domestic savings an increased portion was transferred abroad as debt service rose due to rising international interest rates; hence the national savings rate – the rate of savings remaining for use by national factors of production – fell even more than the rate of domestically generated savings (see Table 7.6).

Falling savings rates have not been accompanied by an equivalent fall in borrowing needs. Governments experiencing high budgetary deficits have remained heavy borrowers; and companies, while reducing their new fixed investments and associated financial needs, have experienced rising debt-servicing obligations as a result of rising interest rates. The net effect has been rising interest rates in both nominal and real terms in many developing countries. Average real rates of interest in a sample of developing countries amounted to a formidable 11 per cent per annum on average in 1980–86 (see Table 7.7).

At an 11 per cent interest rate, debt doubles in seven years if interest is capitalized. A gestation period of ten years or so, at this interest rate, leads to very high capital requirements; and they are increased further

Table 7.7 Real loan interest rates in selected developing countries, 1980–86

	1980	1981	1982	1983	1984	1985	1986	Av'ge
Argentina	5.1	31.2	−18.7	−22.9	−29.7	−6.3	3.9	−5.3
Brazil	−2.5	4.9	26.2	0.2	7.5	−0.1	−0.1	5.1
Chile	12.1	38.8	35.7	15.9	11.5	11.1	7.5	18.9
Colombia	n.a.	n.a.	n.a.	n.a.	n.a.	14.1	11.8	12.9
Indonesia	n.a.	n.a.	10.9	9.9	16.4	17.4	13.1	13.5
Rep. of Korea	−12.3	5.1	6.6	7.9	7.4	6.6	8.6	2.8
Philippines	n.a.	4.2	8.9	−5.4	−15.0	21.7	17.9	5.4
Thailand	1.4	5.9	16.0	13.3	19.2	15.2	15.1	12.3
Turkey	−0.6	50.2	37.7	28.0	28.7	42.0	51.0	33.9
Average	0.5	20.0	15.4	5.9	5.9	13.5	14.3	11.0

Source: World Bank, 1989a, p. 66.

if additional expenditure is incurred to support the existing manpower and plant – that is, if current operating losses are experienced. It follows that, for biotechnology development to be able to compete for resources with other activities, ways need to be found, first, to finance operating expenditures out of current revenue; second, to cut the gestation period to a minimum; and third, to obtain abroad as large a proportion of resources as possible to finance the initial capital outlay.

The severity of the financial problem would be reduced if real interest rates were to fall. But there is a limit to the extent that the interest rates in developing countries can fall; not only do doubts arise regarding their ability to increase national savings, but the demand for these savings is also likely to remain strong.

Notes

1. IMF, 1992, p. 106. Percentages given are an average for the seven countries.
2. UNCTAD, 1989, p. 91.
3. World Bank, 1990a, p. 198. The figures exclude China and India, for which data are not shown.
4. Gill, 1981, p. 2.
5. Gill, 1984, p. 5.

6. IFC, 1980.
7. IFC, 1986, p. 16.
8. *Ibid.*
9. Husbands and Dichter, 1989, p. 16.
10. IFC, 1980, pp. 26–7. A major factor accounting for the relatively small amount of venture capital invested in European DBFs (compared to the USA) is the stringent listing rules on the European stock exchanges – with the exception of the UK (see Chapter 6, p. 85); venture capitalists thus do not have an easy exit available for divestment. In 1992, the UK was only slightly ahead of the other two leading European countries – Germany and France – in attracting venture capital for DBFs. In 1993, when the UK relaxed its listing rules, UK venture capital investment for DBFs was double the level of France and Germany (Lucas et al., 1995, p. 35).
11. *Ibid.*, pp. 101–2.
12. *Ibid.*, p. 32.
13. Statement by Peter Topper, the editor of *IFC Quarterly Review of Emerging Stock Markets*, of 11 December 1990, IMF Visiting Center, Washington. See also Dailami and Atkin, 1990, pp. 30, 32.
14. *Ibid.*, p. 30.
15. *Ibid.*, p. 18.
16. *Ibid.,* p. 34.
17. IFC, 1990b, p. 13.
18. IFC, 1991, p. 10. According to ING Barings estimates, the global flow of funds into emerging stock markets surged in the early 1990s, peaking at $62 billion in 1993, dropped to $40 billion in 1994, and plummeted to $15 billion in 1995 in the wake of the Mexican crisis, although inflow is expected to recover in 1996 (*Financial Times*, 1996).
19. *World Bank News*, 1991, p. 1.
20. IFC, 1991, p. 11.
21. *Washington Post*, 21 April 1992.
22. IFC, 1990a, p. 10.
23. Templeton, 1988.

Chapter 8

Access to Foreign Finance

Contract research

In the experience of developed countries, especially the USA, many of the funds needed in the initial years for operational expenses, before the products could be developed and marketed, were generated by selling research services to larger, already established multiproduct, multinational companies (see Chapter 3). In a sample of seventeen US biotechnology companies for which fairly consistent data are available for a part of the 1980s, this contract research provided as much as 64 per cent of total current revenue, on average. It ranged in individual companies from 27 per cent to 90 per cent (see Table 8.1).

The need of companies and research institutes in developing countries for revenue from contract research is even greater than that of companies in developed countries, as other sources of financial support are more scarce. And since the number of domestically registered large companies is limited, they will have to sell their specialized research services to companies abroad.

The benefits to both parties of international contract research would be substantial. Companies and institutes in developing countries would obtain a cash flow without which their own research projects might be jeopardized; in some cases this would make all the difference to their survival. In addition, by being paid by institutions located in rich countries abroad, their scientists are likely to receive salaries higher than the domestic average. In turn, companies and governments in the developed countries would acquire research data at a much lower cost than if they bought them within their own countries, as salaries in developing countries, even if above their own domestic average, are

Table 8.1 Share of contract research revenue in total revenue of seventeen US biotechnology companies

Company	% share of contract research revenue in total revenue	Period covered
Chiron	90.3	1983–87
Cetus	81.7	1986–89
Integrated Genetics	80.8	1983–88
Nova Pharmaceuticals	78.8	1984–87
Immunomedics	76.8	1982–88
T-Cell Sciences	71.1	1986–89
Genex	70.8	1981–88
Repligen	70.3	1984–90
Biogen	67.4	1983–87
Immunex	67.1	1985–89
Centocor	64.5	1981–89
Praxis Biologics	57.0	1984–88
Enzo Biochem	50.1	1983–85
Molecular Genetics	43.6	1981–89
Biotech Research	30.6	1984–90
Techniclone International Corp.	28.1	1985–89
Collaborative Research Inc.	27.3	1984–90
Weighted average	64.4	
Median	67.4	
Arithmetic average	62.1	

Source: Annual Reports of the seventeen companies.

much lower than in developed countries. For instance, the salary of a scientist with a Ph.D. in the Genetic Engineering Center in Belgrade, Yugoslavia, which has a research contract with a US institution, was US$1,200 per month in June 1991,[1] far below the salary in the USA for this type of work. In early 1994, the Indian founder of a Bangalore-based enzyme-producing company boasted: "India is the most cost-effective place in the world for high technology research. The salary of a good PhD-qualified researcher is only Rs 10,000 [US$319] a month – a fraction of rates in the US."[2]

The disadvantage of contract research is the likelihood of biotechnology work being diverted from domestic needs in developing countries to predominantly and perhaps exclusively foreign needs. This can be circumvented if there is sufficient domestic support for biotechnology so that foreign and domestic demand can be appropriately balanced.

Evidence from developing countries and future prospects

The Genetic Engineering Center in Belgrade was established in 1984 at a cost of US$2 million, obtained from the Serbian Science Foundation. Approximately forty scientists work at the laboratory, some of them partly trained in Western universities, working on six different projects. Most of the operating expenses are financed from abroad. The USA has been funding the Center's project of sequencing by hybridization of megabase plus DNA, theory and methodology. The research results are supplied to several US laboratories. The other five projects are being worked on in collaboration with the United Nations Industrial Development Organization's (UNIDO) International Center for Genetic Engineering and Biotechnology (ICGEB), which is providing the Center with $150,000 a year. In addition, the Center received a three-year grant of US$1.4 million from the Italian government.[3]

In India, in addition to a significant independent domestic biotechnology development, some companies and public institutions have been entering the biotechnology field with foreign collaboration. To tap the availability of cheap and competent skilled scientific and technical personnel in India, some multinational companies like Astra AB of Sweden are setting up biotechnology research and development centers in India.[4] The US Agency for International Development (USAID) has granted funds for equipment and supplies and to support collaborative research with India's National Institute of Immunology (NII), a New Delhi public-sector institution, on a new range of birth-control vaccines. The Pasteur Institute in Paris has collaborated with researchers at NII on immunological control of tuberculosis, leprosy and gastro-intestinal tract infections. NII also had a joint programme with the Population Council of the Rockefeller Foundation in New York to develop a male antifertility vaccine.[5]

In Mexico, a group of scientists located in Irapuato has been chosen by the US company Monsanto to study plant cell transformation and regeneration. According to the director of Monsanto's biological science department, the collaborative work is focusing the molecular and cellular aspects of crop transformation, for which Monsanto is supplying genes and some funding.[6]

The future of contract research in North–South biotechnology relations will depend mainly on two factors: continuing scientific education and the advance of high quality science in the South, and the price competitiveness of its research in the North's markets. In both respects, the developing countries will meet competition not only from domestic companies in the North, but also from Eastern Europe. In considering the effects of economic reforms in Eastern Europe and the region's efforts to expand its trade and financial ties with Western countries, Nimgade made the following comment on contract research:

> With over one million scientists in the USSR, the world's largest research pool, and over a quarter million scientists and technologists in the rest of Eastern Europe, it is no wonder that most East–West biotech ventures involve contract research. Numerous multinational firms have leveraged modest sums into sizeable projects. In 1989, Monsanto (for US$500,000) contracted the services of 10 researchers from Moscow's prestigious Shemyakin Institute for Bio Organic Chemistry. For about half that sum, Millipore opened a joint R&D center with Moscow's Institute of Genetics.[7]

It is probably too early to project the possible outcome of South–East competition in this field. Scientists and managers in developing countries have the advantage of a long and close association with Western scientists and Western markets and institutions. The East currently has the advantage of being very cheap because of the extremely low exchange value of its currencies, particularly that of Russia. Neither of these two factors will last forever. Ultimately, it will be the difference in scientific advance that will prove decisive.

Financial and marketing interaction between the private and public sectors

Recent policy shifts

The recent emphasis on private-sector involvement in international trade, marketing and financial policies has not bypassed international biotechnology policy and related biotechnology studies. The World Bank, in a major 1991 study prepared under its auspices, has referred to this shift:

A new feature in the evolution of biotechnology has been the increasing collaboration between the public and private sector. Private companies often contract specific research projects at public sector institutions and in return obtain some proprietary rights to the technology generated.

Continued public sector investments in biotechnology and creative partnerships between public and private sector interests are an essential prerequisite for establishing a competitive national strategy in biotechnology... A new pattern of ... research funding has also emerged from the linkages between biotechnology and academia and commerce ... the result has been that the traditional systems of open interaction and communication in research are being rapidly altered...[8]

USA–Thailand biotechnology commercialization agreement, 1991

A practical application of this policy shift, at least in part, is the US Thailand Commercialization of Science and Technology Program (UST/COST). The goal is to match US and Thai companies in selected areas of technology: biotechnology, electronics, and advanced materials. The first, already identified, part of the Program refers to biotechnology. The principal partners are: USAID, the Thai Science and Technology Development Board (STDB), the State of Maryland International Division (MID), the US National Research Council through its Board of Science and Technology for International Development (BOSTID), and BioTechnology International (BTI), a program at the University of Maryland. USAID, STDB and MID provided the funding. BTI assessed the needs of Thai industry, agriculture and infrastructure in the biological sciences; and MID identified and recruited Maryland companies that can provide the appropriate products and technologies. The state of Maryland was chosen for this experimental project because of its existing biotechnology industry, its well-developed international trade office, and the allocation of matching funds to the USAID contract.

As of January 1992, there were over twenty agreements under consideration with an estimated value of US$5 million (presumably referring to capital expenditures). Negotiations are proceeding on sixteen agreements: seven are for distribution and marketing within Thailand, presumably all of US-produced goods (diagnostic kits or devices for infections, including sexually transmitted diseases, predominate); three are for research and development; two are for manufacturing projects; three are for agricultural projects (fish growth hormone, shrimp feed and the development of new eucalyptus strains); and one is for clinical trials – these nine are presumably all to be based in Thailand.[9] The arrangement seems in considerable part to promote export sales of US biotechnology products; but the full balance of benefits and costs, including those from transfer of technology to Thailand, will only become apparent when all agreements are concluded and implemented.

Worthy of note is the scope of public-sector-agency involvement in the program. This is not only the case on the Thai side, where a number of government and para-statal agencies, including the Armed Forces and Naval Medical Research Institutes, are involved (this appears to confirm the generalization made by James and Persley in a companion research volume to the World Bank study: "Currently in the developing countries, the public sector is the main supporter of biotechnology, and therefore in the short term it will be the public sector that will normally have to pursue joint venture with industry"[10]). On the US side, too, there is broad involvement on the part of public bodies, covering the range of federal and state government, high-level science management, and a university department, in the planning of the Thai program. The shift in policy concerning the roles of the public and private sectors does not seem to involve a diminution of public-sector activity, at least in this case; rather, it appears to aim at making sure that private industry is guaranteed a market and sufficient profit opportunities.

Joint ventures and equity investments

Emerging patterns in developing countries

Of 165 collaborative ventures between US dedicated biotechnology companies and foreign corporations, including joint ventures and equity investments, between 1981 and 1986, only three were with developing countries – two with China (probably Taiwan), and one with Malaysia.[11] As US investors accounted for an estimated 90 per cent (or $3.7 billion)[12] of all international biotechnology investment (through 1985), it follows that total foreign investment in biotechnology in developing countries could not have been significant prior to the mid-1980s.

Developments since 1986 may have been more favourable. One case is Diagnostic Biotechnology Limited in Singapore, which produces diagnostic kits, with a US company providing the technology.[13] In São Paulo, Brazil, a biotechnology company called Imovall was launched in

1988 – 48 per cent owned by Rhone Poulenc subsidiary Institut Merrieux, a world leader in vaccine production, and 52 per cent by Vallee of São Paulo, which is primarily involved in veterinary vaccines. Imovall will produce human vaccines, blood derivatives and immuno-modulators. The joint venture gives Vallee access to world-class technology and the ability to commercialize Merieux products in Brazil. Institut Merieux gains a national administrative, commercial and technical service infrastructure in the largest country of Latin America.[14]

There have been instances of joint ventures among developing countries, or with their involvement. A leading Indian industrial company, Tata, has set up a joint venture, Plantech, in Singapore with Native Plants International of the USA to develop new strains of plantation crops such as tea and palm oil through tissue culture.[15] In Argentina, a Buenos Aires venture-capital firm, Desatek, with a partner, Embrabio from São Paulo, Brazil, financed scale-up and is now marketing a non-recombinant rotavirus vaccine for cattle, developed by the Argentinian government-funded Center for Advanced Veterinary Research (CIVAN) under the leadership of Dr Jose la Torre, an Argentinian scientist. The vaccine, based on tissue-culture techniques and the use of micro-carriers, sharply reduces the disease incidence and mortality of new-born calves.[16] While not a part of the "new" biotechnology, the vaccine appears to represent a major advance: it is considerably cheaper than similar European vaccines. A similar porcine vaccine is also being developed.[17] In China, contacts with the neighboring newly industrializing countries (NICs) are taking place. Hong Kong plans to staff its newest biotechnology research institutes with a number of researchers from China; in addition, there are many joint ventures between China and Hong Kong.[18]

> Singapore, Taiwan and Thailand have placed a high priority on biotechnology and have good access to foreign capital and technology. Their experience with manufacturing is more adaptable to China than the experience of many European and US investors is. For many NICs China is considered an attractive location for future investments. It is expected that Western companies will take advantage of the NICs experience in exploring the Chinese market.[19]

Need for a new company survey of attitudes to collaborative arrangements

A 1989 OECD study, based on interviews carried out in 1986 and 1987 with a sample of ninety-four companies in the pharmaceutical, food and feed, agricultural and chemical sectors, and biotechnology equipment supply firms in developed countries, concluded that the prevailing attitude was one of caution concerning biotechnology development in developing countries. The sample comprised 14 US, 58 European, 15 Japanese and 7 Canadian companies. Among the main findings of the 1986–87 survey are:

1. Indifference seems to be the prevailing attitude. However, Japanese companies indicated particular interest in the Third World.

2. Strong interest in the food needs of developing countries can be found in some cases. Some companies hope that microbiologically produced proteins, or, more specifically, the relevant manufacturing technologies, will find better markets in the Third World than in OECD countries.

3. Third World needs for pharmaceuticals, including diagnostics and vaccines, are recognized by everyone, but no one seems to be sure how such developments, deemed to be desirable, could be financed. Some companies suggest the creation of new international financing instruments for this purpose.[20]

The sample of companies interviewed clearly understated the role of the US biotechnology industry. US firms accounted for only 15 per cent of the sample, even though they accounted for over one-half of the world biotechnology industry.

A new survey is needed, first, in order to update the earlier findings; second, to improve the composition of the sample by giving greater weight to companies already involved in biotechnology; and third, to focus explicitly on the prospects of investment in biotechnology in developing countries and the conditions under which it could take place, as well as the prospects for contract research and other types of collaboration.

Lessons from the experiences of developed countries

As indicated earlier in this chapter and in Chapter 3, collaborative ventures have played a pivotal role in the financing and marketing of the products of US DBFs; companies and research institutes in developing countries are even more dependent on these collaborative ventures. This holds true for all types of collaboration: joint ventures, equity purchases, marketing and licensing agreements, and contract research.

Moreover, as developing countries do not have sufficient access to venture capital in significant amounts in their domestic markets, they may consider approaching venture-capital firms in developed countries which have an established tradition and experience in providing biotechnology investment finance. The terms will probably be stiff, but the alternatives – other than borrowing from international financial agencies – are not plentiful. Additionally, financiers and companies active in biotechnology-based work in industrialized countries are reported by the World Bank to be reluctant to become involved in biotechnology ventures in developing countries unless arrangements have been made to protect intellectual property rights (see Annex 1).[21]

Much of what was said in Chapter 3 concerning the relationship between small and large companies is relevant to developing countries with respect to their bargaining position with developed countries. The major point is that, while maintaining other forms of collaboration, the developing country company should hold on to its proprietary rights as long as possible if it has prospects for making a major advance which may be of commercial value.

This point was further underscored by Mr J. Thurston, a partner in Mckenna and Company, a firm of London solicitors, during a conference held in London at the end of 1987 on legal issues concerned with biotechnology. Thurston stated that smaller companies often fail to secure a proper agreement and instead do a deal quickly because they are desperate for cash. Many companies which sponsored research at a smaller firm impressed on the latter the need to take on the commercial rights to any inventions that resulted. Thurston went on to say that the company performing the research should, however, stand its ground and ensure that it has legal ownership to the enabling technology that is behind the work, offering, if necessary, to license this to the larger company at a later stage. If this approach is not adopted, small companies could lose out commercially.[22]

Support by international institutions

Several international agencies are involved in assisting biotechnology in developing countries. The greatest financial support has been extended by the World Bank as a result of its project-lending activity in the areas of health, education and agriculture. The second major supporting agency is the International Center for Genetic Engineering and Biotechnology sponsored by UNIDO and operating from its two headquarters in New Delhi, India and Trieste, Italy. Other UN agencies, such as the United Nations Development Program (UNDP), the World Health Organization (WHO), the United Nations Environmental Program (UNEP), and the United Nations Conference on Trade and Development (UNCTAD) have also carried out studies and provided assistance for biotechnology in developing countries. It is likely that these institutions will increase their support, but the extent of the increase cannot be predicted at this time.

What is known is that the leading UN agency concerning itself with the development of biotechnology, the International Center for Genetic Engineering and Biotechnology, was able to distribute only US$1,005,000 worth of grant money for collaborative research programs in developing countries for the year 1990. Thirty proposals were submitted, of which twenty received grants[23] – an average of $50,000 per project. It is clear that no developing country could sustain a biotechnology development program by relying exclusively on UN assistance at this scale.

More generally, it is also clear that developing countries need to choose projects in biotechnology where the pay-off is quick and where scientific and technological uncertainties are likely to be manageable (see Chapter 9).

Notes

1. Dr Vladimir Glisin, Director of the Center, Belgrade, personal interview, June 1991 (the interview took place prior to the outbreak of the Yugoslav–Croatian war).

2. Wagstyl, 1994. Statement of Ms Mazumdar, founder of Biocon India (Bangalore), with annual sales of Rs 165 million and currently employing 105 people of which 25 are scientists with advanced degrees. The exchange rate Indian Rs/US$ used was 31.31, indicated in the *International Herald Tribune*, 19–20 February 1994, p 9.

3. Glisin, personal interview, 1991.

4. Kumar, 1987.

5. Jacob, 1989.

6. Kaplan, 1989.

7. Nimgade, 1990.

8. World Bank, 1991a, p. 9.

9. *Genetic Engineering News*, 1992.

10. James and Persley, 1990, p. 374.

11. US Congress, 1988b, p. 90.

12. *Ibid.*

13. Yuan, 1988, p. A-13.
14. Kaplan, 1989.
15. Kumar, 1987, p. 55.
16. Kaplan, 1989.
17. *Ibid.*
18. *Biotechnology and Development Monitor,* 1991a, p 15.
19. *Ibid.* This expectation proved to be well-founded. In the period 1991–95, China was noteworthy amongst developing countries for the string of joint-venture and research-collaboration agreements forged between Western European multinational corporations (MNCs) and US MNCs and DBFs in biomedicine and agriculture and Chinese companies and public research institutes involved in these sectors.
20. OECD, 1989, p. 41.
21. World Bank, 1991a, p. viii.
22. Marsh, 1987c.
23. International Center 1991, p. 1.

Chapter 9

Diagnostic Products: A Biotechnology Priority for Developing Countries?

It was indicated in Chapters 2 and 5 that production of diagnostic kits, based on monoclonal antibodies, was one of the fastest growing applications of biotechnology. Furthermore, it is an industrial application which has a substantially shorter gestation period than products based on recombinant DNA technology; which calls for a substantially lower capital cost; which is less demanding on research expenditures than other applications; which may become an exportable product; and which can serve as a stepping stone in developing skills and a financial basis needed for future production of novel vaccines and recombinant DNA products. One of the limitations of diagnostic products is that they do not cure or prevent diseases; but at least they help identify them (or exclude their possibility) with precision, which is essential for a timely and adequate cure. The other limitation is that the main focus of diagnostics thus far has been on human health care, although the field is being extended to agriculture – livestock and aquaculture, as well as to plants. On these grounds, diagnostic products seems to be an industry *prima facie* suitable for entry into biotechnology by those developing countries which have the required technical wo/manpower and managerial capacity.

The need for diagnostics

Diagnosis of disease – be it human, animal or plant – serves three important functions: (1) to determine the nature of a given disease for the purpose of timely and appropriate treatment. Early diagnosis of disease can be instrumental to higher survival rates, improved quality of life and reduction of overall health costs; (2) to determine the prevalence of specific disease-producing organisms or agents in populations, to allow assessment of the impact of public-health interventions (or disease control/eradication measures for animals and plants); and (3) to determine the range of diseases affecting a population, the immune stages and status of the population, for research and planning purposes.

Of particular importance to developing countries, and to diagnostics for determining the prevalence of disease, is that survey teams must be able to apply diagnostic methods under field conditions to large numbers of local people in isolated and often tropical areas where disease is endemic. Successful application in the field necessitates simple, reproducible and inexpensive diagnostic methods that can provide an unambiguous indication of the status of an infection, and a specific identification of the causative agent. This is especially the case in the ongoing work to develop safe and effective vaccines for a variety of tropical diseases. Without a means of accurately determining (or at least reliably estimating) prior exposure and the immune status of vaccinees and control groups, and their post-inoculation follow-up, valid field testing of these vaccinees will not be possible.[1]

A wide range of biochemical tests are available to supplement the observational abilities and skills of medical personnel in the physical diagnosis of health and disease. Prior to the advent of new technologies and the knowledge generated and continuing to be generated by new biotechnology, one could classify conventional diagnostic technologies in two broad groups:

1. Direct examination of urine, stool, blood, sputum, tissue biopsy or cultured isolates using unsophisticated equipment (for example, a light microscope) and reagents.
2. Serologic examination to detect antibodies to the pathogen, or to detect the pathogen or its byproducts in a sample of patient's blood.[2]

New biotechnology has led to the development of new diagnostic methods and products. These fall into two categories:

1. Diagnostics based on monoclonal antibodies (MAbs).
2. Diagnostics based on DNA hybridization probes, termed "DNA probes", "gene probes" or "probes" for short.

This chapter concentrates on diagnostics based on monoclonal antibodies. The sensitivity[3] of gene probes, and hence their utility and effectiveness, has been enhanced when used in combination with another major advance in new biotechnology – the polymerase chain re-action, which can amplify minute quantities of DNA to millions of copies within a few hours. While DNA probe-based diagnostics hold promise for the future, in mid-1992 they would probably not have been found in even 5 per cent of US diagnostic laboratories.[4] In other countries the proportion would be even smaller. Glitches encountered in the widespread use of DNA probes for clinical diagnosis during the 1980s were still being sorted out at the turn of the 1990s. The use of DNA probes in diagnosis, as well as the problems encountered and strategies adopted to surmount these problems, are discussed in Annex 2, as is the polymerase chain reaction. Given the experience to date in developed countries, this area of diagnostics does not seem suitable as a field of entry into biotechnology for developing countries, in marked contrast to MAb-based diagnostics.

Monoclonal antibodies are homogenous antibodies derived from clones – that is, genetically identical copies – of a single cell. In order better to understand MAbs and to lay the foundation for understanding their significance and uses in biomedical and agricultural research, as well as their uses in prophylaxis and treatment, it is necessary to refer to certain concepts and terms in the field of immunology; these are briefly outlined below.

The immune system[5]

The immune system's role is to protect and defend the individual against foreign materials. All vertebrates including humans consist of hundreds of distinct cell types that differ in appearance and act in unique ways. Our bodies, at the same time, also provide a particularly hospitable environment for a multitude of inventive and aggressive invading organisms and pathogens. We need, therefore, a mechanism to identify each cell in our body as our own, a way to recognize the complete range of invaders as foreign, as well as mechanisms to get rid of/kill the foreign invaders efficiently. These tasks fall to the immune system, and an often used analogy compares the immune system to an army.

Infectious diseases can have devastating effects on health and welfare, especially in previously unexposed populations. It was appreciated early on, however, that those people who survived an infectious disease would usually not contract the disease again during their lifetime. Already in the tenth century the Chinese had introduced the practice of inoculation of human smallpox material – variolation – to protect people from natural infection. What marks the beginning of immunology as a systematic subject is when the practice of variolation spread to Europe, and at the end of the eighteenth century Edward Jenner in the UK deliberately inoculated a young boy with cowpox virus. This virus was not virulent for humans, and, as Jenner had observed the pox-free skin of milkmaids, he reasoned that the cowpox virus might confer protection against the related human smallpox organism. Jenner duly observed that the boy became protected against subsequent exposure to smallpox. By injecting a harmless form of a disease organism, Jenner laid the foundations for modern vaccination (from Latin *vacca*: a cow).

Antibodies and antigens

The phenomenon of how people and animals, having once recovered from a primary attack by an infectious disease, became immune against further attacks by the same disease-inducing agent became the object of study; and one hundred years later, at the end of the nineteenth century, this work led to the discovery of a special class of protein molecules in the blood serum (the portion of blood from which red and white cells have been removed) which became known as antibodies (Abs).

These Abs were recognized to be capable of specifically combining with and initiating the eventual elimination of the specific type of virus or bacterium that had been responsible for the disease in infected experimental animals. Immunity was thus partially attributable to the presence of antibodies whose appearance is elicited by the primary infection. Soon after the discovery of the connection between Ab production and resistance to infectious disease, it was found that specific Abs are also formed in response to the injection into the bloodstream of non-living materials, such as dead bacteria, bacterial toxins and snake venoms. Subsequently, in the next few years it was shown that *any foreign protein*, or, as it is technically termed, "antigen" (from "generates antibodies"), whether noxious or innocuous, when injected into the bloodstream, will result in the appearance of Abs. In the 1950s it was shown that carbohydrates can also stimulate the production of antibodies in animals.[6] These Abs are specifically directed against, and by complementary shape (which crudely can be thought of as a lock-and-key type specific fit) bind to the surface of the antigen (Ag), forming so-called "immune complexes". This Ag–Ab immune complex results in the eventual elimination of the Ag. However, protein molecules obtained from an individual's own tissues cannot act as an Ag in that same individual. Ab formation is thus not just a defensive reaction against infectious disease, but a phenomenon of rather wide biological significance: a mechanism for the recognition of non-self.

Antigenic determinants

Antibodies are produced by a subclass of white cells called lymphocytes (which originate in the bone marrow). The subclass of lymphocytes which eventually produce the Abs that circulate in the blood are called B lymphocytes or B cells. It is estimated that the spleen of a mouse or human contains about one million specific lines or clones of B cells. Each individual B cell makes one specific Ab which complementarily binds to, and is directed against, one specific portion of the Ag. The portion of the antigen to which the antibody complementarily binds is called the antigenic "determinant" or "epitope".

Clonal selection

The process by which the B cell recognizes the antigenic determinant is complex, and need not concern us here; however, once the B cell does recognize and bind to the antigenic determinant, the binding has a dramatic effect on the B cell. Given the proper signals from certain regulatory cells, the B cell enlarges, divides rapidly and produces plasma cells. These plasma cells are rich in protein-making apparatus; they are, in effect, factories for synthesizing Abs. The process whereby an Ag, or more precisely an antigenic determinant, elicits the production of a complementarily shaped Ab is known as clonal selection – the Ab precursor plasma cells are genetically identical, that is, a clone.

Memory B cells

When an Ag does penetrate our non-specific defenses, such as the skin, and reaches the bloodstream, the body needs time to build up an effective stock of plasma cells from the B cells, and thus the body cannot produce much Ab initially. When challenged by a massive dose of toxin – for example, snake venom – the body will produce Abs, but sometimes cannot do so quickly enough to save the victim's life. With a disease such as measles, there is a period of illness before the body is able to manufacture enough Abs to defeat the virus.

Fortunately, during the initial exposure to Ag or the first bout of infection, so-called "memory" B cells develop from the same clone as that which produces Abs against the antigenic determinant, and these memory B cells survive and remain in a dormant state for many years. If the same Ag reappears at a later time, the dormant memory cells become active, proliferate and build up the level of Ab very quickly. If the Ag in question is an infective microorganism, the level of Ab usually increases at a sufficiently rapid rate that the individual suffers no noticeable symptoms. In other words, the person has become immune to the disease that the microorganism causes. The body's ability to create memory cells is one of the foundations upon which vaccines are made.[7]

Antibody production

Polyclonal antibodies

For decades (prior to the advent of MAb technology in 1975) researchers had obtained Abs to a particular Ag by inoculating animals, often rabbits or horses, with the Ag in question. The animal then generated Abs specifically targeted to the invader. After several weeks the animals were bled, the blood was allowed to clot, and the clear serum containing the Abs was collected. But this method was rather crude, because when exposed to the Ag, each determinant of the Ag is recognized by a distinct individual B cell, and this B cell and its progeny produce only one specific kind of Ab. The animal responds by producing large amounts of several different Abs, each Ab being specific to a distinct determinant of the Ag. This multiple B cell reaction thus produces a mixture of Abs, with each type of Ab represented in limited quantities, and is called a "polyclonal" response. Scientists devised various chemical precipitations and immunologic binding methods to try to fish the desired Ab out of the complex polyclonal pool. Many problems were encountered in these procedures. Another problem arising from this method of Ab production was that even animals from closely inbred lines vary in their individual ability to recognize and respond to particular Ags: the Abs are heterogeneous, varying from animal to animal or even within the same animal over time.

Monoclonal antibodies: cell fusion-hybridoma technology

Scientists' inability to obtain uniform, reproducible and, above all, specific antibodies hindered biomedical research and formed a major obstacle to the study of the structure and function of Abs. Thus, the discovery in 1975 by Cesar Milstein and George Köhler, working at the UK's Medical Research Council (MRC) Laboratory of Molecular Biology in Cambridge, of the technique to produce infinitely homogeneous Abs derived from the clones of a single B cell, or monoclonal antibodies (MAbs), was a landmark in the history of immunology as well as biotechnology; the technique "is revolutionizing basic research, medicine and commerce."[8] Milstein and Köhler won the Nobel Prize for their work.

Milstein and Köhler were responsible for the first immunological application of cell fusion, also called cell hybridization technique, which dates back to 1960. With the cell hybridization technique, it is possible, starting from two different types of cells, to "create" a new cell unit possessing all or part of the genetic material of the cells involved in the fusion. The hybrid cell thus obtained simultaneously expresses the biological properties of both parent cells.

For some time, immunologists had attempted to isolate and clone Ab-forming B lymphocytes in the laboratory in culture (liquid nutrient) growth media, but these cells normally have a limited life span and clones cannot be established. Malignant B cell tumors of the immune system called myelomas are capable of continuous proliferation in cultures, but myeloma cells produce little or no antibody. Milstein and Köhler devised a method for forcing the myeloma cells to produce specific Abs in quantity. They fused an immortal but non-Ab secreting myeloma cell line with an Ab-secreting but nonculturable B lymphocyte in order to produce hybrids having the desirable properties of both parental types, that is, able to produce one type of Ab indefinitely. The resulting fused cell is called a hybridoma (from hybrid myeloma).[9] As Milstein has written:

> A monoclonal antibody is a well-defined chemical reagent that can be reproduced at will, in contrast to conventional antiserum [serum containing antibody], which is a variable mixture of reagents and can never be reproduced once the original supply is exhausted.[10]

Versatility of use of monoclonal antibodies

MAbs have been made against a wide spectrum of antigenic components, including hormones, drugs, serum components, white and red blood cells, bacteria, viruses, fungi, single-cell and multicellular parasites, and natural toxins derived from plants and microorganisms. MAbs generated against rabies, influenza, parainfluenza, herpes, measles, reovirus and tumor viruses have made it possible to identify previously unrecognized substrains that complicated diagnosis (as well as the development of effective vaccines). Production of MAbs against surface antigens of parasites at different stages of their life cycle has proven helpful in dissecting the complex antigenic structure of composite membrane molecules and in identifying molecules for use in diagnosis (as well as for the development of vaccines, discussed in Chapter 10). Similar use in plants has revealed substrains involved in the pathogenesis of major crop diseases, such as those caused by fruit-tree viruses (prunus necrotic ring spot, apple mosaic and tobacco streak) and potato viruses (M, S, X and Y; potato leaf role.).[11]

The above are only examples intended to be illustrative of what MAbs can be produced against or detect. MAbs were used initially as an accurate method for molecular exploration of functional analysis in immunology,[12] but by the early 1980s left the confines of basic research for industrial exploitation. Researchers had come to value MAbs for dissecting molecular structure and mechanisms of genes; often MAb technology is combined with recombinant DNA techniques. But "high volume production of rodent MAbs has had a significant impact on the diagnostic industry in particular."[13] In fact, through the 1980s, MAb technology, in the form of *in vitro* diagnostic kits, commanded the lead amongst other biotechnology products in commercial use, measured by the number of products on the market.

Diagnostic products based on MAbs fall into two distinct categories: those using MAbs for *in vitro* (outside the body) applications; and those using MAbs for *in vivo* (in the body) applications. *In vitro* uses do not have to go through the same rigorous safety testing that *in vivo* do. *In vivo* MAb diagnostics are, from a regulatory standpoint, considered as a drug, requiring the same extensive testing that drugs undergo, prior to marketing approval.[14]

In vitro MAb-based diagnostics

In vitro diagnostics, also called chemicals-based diagnostics, involves taking samples of body fluids such as urine, stool or blood and adding to them reagents to detect specific substances which indicate a medical condition. With new biotechnology methods, notably MAbs (and gene probes, described in Annex 2) scientists can, with far greater precision, select the chemical characteristics of the substances in the reagent. These, in turn, can then be used to identify, with a higher degree of sensitivity and specificity,[15] chemicals in the body fluids. As a result, diagnostic methods are becoming more precise and can be used to detect a wider range of conditions. These techniques are increasingly becoming vital tools in hospitals and medical laboratories. Some *in vitro* diagnostics – for example, those for detecting pregnancy – can be used by the consumer directly, in the home.

Immunoassays

Of the total *in vitro* diagnostics industry, with sales of about $6 billion worldwide in 1986 (the sum including both chemicals and monitoring equipment), the fastest growing segment in the late 1980s were immuno-assays, based on both monoclonal and polyclonal antibodies, accounting for worldwide sales of about $1 billion of the total and reported to be growing at 10–20 per cent a year in the mid-1980s.[16]

In immunoassays, Abs and Ags are used for the detection of each other. The chemical reagent you start with is either a laboratory-prepared Ab targeted to the Ag you are trying to detect in the test sample fluid, or a laboratory-prepared Ag with which you detect Abs in the test fluid. A plethora of immunoassay techniques have been developed. One of the most common is where the final determination of Ab–Ag coupling involves a reagent conjugated with an appropriate label. When immuno-assays were first developed in the 1960s, the labeling was achieved using radioactive isotopes. Due to the difficulties and health hazards involved in handling even mildly radioactive sources, this meant that linked immunoassays were confined to laboratories; no one other than skilled scientists could carry out the techniques. There was also a problem of deterioration of reagents through radiation damage.

More recently, immunoassays have become far more ubiquitous, largely due to more user-friendly labeling methods. One of the most common is called the enzyme-linked immunoabsorbent assay (ELISA). ELISA involves a set of enzyme reactions (an enzyme is a protein which acts as a catalyst, speeding the rate at which a biochemical reaction occurs, but not altering its direction or nature and without itself being destroyed) which are set in motion by the appearance of a specific Ab–Ag complex and which produces an easy-to-spot color change.

The ELISA uses small sample volumes. Large numbers of specimens can be processed, so the procedure is useful in epidemiological studies (epidemiology is the scientific study of the distribution and occurrence of diseases and health conditions, and their determinants in a population). Of note for developing countries is that the procedure can be performed in simple laboratories, and the reagents are stable if refrigerated. Widespread field testing of ELISA procedures have been initiated for a number of tropical diseases, including African sleeping sickness (African trypanosomiasis), Chagas disease (American trypanosomiasis), leishmaniasis, amoebiasis, malaria, filariasis and schistosomiasis.[17] One great advantage of the ELISA procedure is that the result can often be judged positive or negative by the naked eye, obviating the need for instrumentation.

Thus, even prior to the introduction of MAbs, great strides had already been made in the use of Abs in diagnostic medicine. Routinely used in immunoassays, and in emerging areas such as immunohistology (where labeled Abs would be used to visualize the distribution of Ag in tissue and within cells), polyclonal Abs still suffered shortcomings that could often be addressed by the more specific and sensitive monoclonals. MAbs have been used, for example, to distinguish between organisms that cross-react[18] in conventional immunoassays.[19]

Additionally, monoclonals presented a somewhat easier manufacturing process[20] and allowed a level of standardization that was impossible with polyclonals. Conventional polyclonal Ab reagents must be constantly reproduced and standardized as supplies become exhausted; one of the outstanding advantages of the MAb as a reagent is that it provides a single standard material, which, in principle, could be used for laboratories throughout the world, in an unending supply, if the immortality and purity of the cell line is maintained.[21] A 1985 US Congress Office of Technology Assessment report sums up by stating that "The revolution [in immunodiagnosis using MAbs] is in making these diagnostic test procedures much more sensitive and specific, more reproducible, faster and more economical."[22]

MAb technology has also been rapidly expanding the breadth of tests and reagents available on the market, making tests available that would not have been possible hitherto. A recent example of this is the hepatitis C test, where, after isolation of the hepatitis virus in 1987, a test to detect the virus in the blood became available in 1990; the US Center for Disease Control and Prevention now estimates that at least 150,000 people in the USA alone are newly infected with hepatitis C each year.[23]

MAbs used in diagnostic tests are often sold commercially as a "kit", of which MAbs are the essential raw material. A kit refers to a complete packaged entity required to carry out the diagnostic test on the body's sample. In addition to the MAb the kit would include such things as positive and negative controls, and other standard reagents needed for the test reaction such as buffered salts to maintain the proper acidity, test tubes, and so forth.

One of the first MAbs developed commercially, and subsequently marketed as a kit for home use by early 1983, was for detection of pregnancy.[24] These test kits are based on the fact that, from the first day of pregnancy, the hormone human chorionic gonadotropin (hCG), which is essential for implantation and maintenance of early pregnancy, is produced by the developing embryo. These kits make use of MAbs to detect hCG in a sample of a woman's urine, often employing the ELISA technique.

Other MAb kits for home use include those to identify the time of ovulation (again, by testing a urine sample to detect a hormone-luteinizing hormone (LH), which women produce in large amounts just prior to ovulation), for detecting blood in the stool (an early warning sign of possible rectal cancer and other illnesses),[25] and for detecting bacteria that cause urinary tract infections.[26]

MAb diagnostics

Bacterial and viral infections and parasitic diseases

Prior to the availability of MAbs, there was little application of immuno-assays to the diagnosis of bacterial infections.[27] Generalized bacterial infection in infants is a leading cause of neonatal mortality in developing countries. The bacterial pathogens most commonly encountered in these infected infants are group B streptococci,[28] which are also the most common serious infections in newborn infants in the USA.[29] Previously, diagnosis of the infection would take several days; but rapid diagnosis – in as short a time as two hours – was achieved using MAbs.[30] Kits for other bacterial infections have been introduced, such as those to detect the bacteria responsible for meningitis, in which the bacterial strains can be detected in ten minutes.[31]

MAb-based diagnosis has also been developed for viral infections. MAb diagnosis of hepatitis B infection is reportedly one hundred times more sensitive than conventional diagnosis using polyclonal Abs.[32] Epidemics of influenza throughout the world are caused by serologically distinct subtypes of the virus. Once the human population develops immunity against the new virus subtype, viruses with minor changes begin to arise. These new strains exhibiting alterations in individual determinants can be readily distinguished with MAbs, hitherto not possible using conventional methods.[33] Other viral infections for which MAbs have been developed for diagnosis include those caused by cytomegalovirus and the rotaviruses – believed to cause one-third of all diarrheal disease worldwide, and up to 40 per cent of diarrheal disease in children in developed countries.[34]

Speedy and sensitive MAb kits have been developed for the common sexually transmitted diseases syphilis, gonorrhea and chlamydia. Conventional diagnosis of these diseases had been hampered by time-consuming cell-culture requirements.[35]

In the field of tropical and parasitic diseases, immunodiagnosis using MAbs to probe for parasite antigen has been applied to such diverse conditions as hyatid and other larval tapeworm diseases, Chagas disease, onchocerciasis, schistosomiasis and toxoplasmosis. MAbs have also been used to identify malarial organisms within mosquitos without the need for exhaustive dissection and microscopy.[36]

Alzheimer's disease

Scientists at SIBIA, the corporate spin-off of the Salk Institute for Biotechnology (California), are working on commercializing the first predictive diagnostic test for the debilitating Alzheimer's disease.[37] At present a firm diagnosis of Alzheimer's can only be made by autopsy, where characteristic lesions or plaques of amyloid beta-protein on the brain are revealed. The new test requires the withdrawal of cerebrospinal fluid (as the disease is confined to the central nervous system) and uses a MAb to assay levels of amyloid beta-protein precursor, a substance which gives rise to the protein plaques found in the brain of Alzheimer's victims.

Although at present there is no cure for Alzheimer's, the test can be used to distinguish Alzheimer's from other kinds of dementia, possibly helping to redefine treatment. The test could also be used to monitor the response of Alzheimer's patients to experimental drugs, as well as the progression of the disease.

Cancer

Potentially one of the most important applications of MAbs in immuno-assays is the detection and quantification of indicators related to malignant tumors. Certain types of cancer cells make abnormal proteins or enzymes called tumor markers. A great deal of research is underway in identifying these tumor markers. In some cases the markers are shed into the blood. For example, cancers of the gastrointestinal (GI) tract often shed carcino-embryonic antigens; liver cancers shed alpha-feto-protein; and prostate cancers shed prostatic acid phosphatase. MAb test kits have been developed to detect these blood-borne antigens shed by the tumor.[38] In other types of tumors, MAb reagents – for example, fluorescently labeled MAbs – are an accurate spotter of otherwise difficult-to-identify tumor cells, detected by staining tissue specimens. Examples include the identification of primary tumors and metastasis in breast cancer, melanoma and brain tumors. MAbs have also been used in the subclassification of lymphomas, leukemias and diagnosis of immunodeficiency diseases.[39]

The above examples are by no means exhaustive. For *in vitro* diagnostics involving the use of antibodies, with the exception of those few cases where specificity is not improved, the use of monoclonals as the antibodies of choice (as opposed to polyclonal antibodies) is virtually universal in the immunology/serology arena.[40] MAb-based tests and kits have undergone rapid commercial volume growth, replacing existing products and expanding the growing menu of immuno-based tests. Part of the reason for their rapid acceptance and deep market penetration has been that prior-generation technology employing polyclonal antibodies paved the way.

Agriculture and the environment

MAb-based diagnostics are not limited to problems of human health. Although developed commercially to a much lesser extent than in human health care, MAb technology has been and continues to be developed for diagnosis of diseases affecting the agricultural sector – both plant and animal, as well as for use in the environmental sector to detect pollutants, herbicides and pesticides.

In agriculture, prior to MAb technology, immunoassays to detect infectious pathogens of both plants and animals existed; MAbs used in the immunoassays exhibit the same advantages over polyclonals as in human health care.

An illustrative example of how MAb technology lends itself to diverse sectors in agriculture is the formation in 1988 of Stirling Diagnostics Ltd (Scotland), the first products of which are to be MAb kits for detecting diseases of both fish and potatoes. Stirling was formed from the merger of Talbero (Scotland), set up in 1985 to commercialize local research on fish diagnostics and vaccines, and Agricultural Diagnostics (Edinburgh), which specializes in developing and selling kits for the rapid diagnosis of plant diseases. Company heads from both firms stated that the similar technology base and business plans of the two companies demonstrated a case of ideal synergy.[41]

Among Stirling's first products are to be ELISA test kits to distinguish three fungal diseases of cereal crops, important for optimal treatment. Differential diagnosis, conventionally based on symptoms produced by the three fungi, is rendered difficult, as the symptoms are similar. The test is expected to produce a result in twenty minutes. The first of Stirling's ELISA kits for fish diseases will allow rapid diagnosis of the four bacterial and two viral pathogens that cause the biggest problems for salmon farmers and fish farmers in general.

In the environmental field there is increasing use in the USA of immunoassay MAb ELISA tests for pesticides, herbicides and toxic waste products such as polychlorobenzenes (PCBs), polychlorophenols (PCPs), polyaromatic hydrocarbons, gasoline and used motor oil. Such tests are needed and used by such diverse groups as agribusinesses, industries producing toxic waste, government regulatory agencies, farmers and environmental engineers. The advantage of these tests over conventional methods is that, not only are they cheaper, but many tests can also be conducted in a grid-type fashion, on-site in ground water and soil samples, with results available in minutes to hours; conventional testing procedures in which samples are sent to environmental testing laboratories can take up to two months to yield results.[42]

Further work is needed to assess the likely social distribution of benefits from the use of diagnostic products in agriculture (plants, livestock and fish) in developing countries. If the price of kits is low, if credit to small farmers is available for the purchase of kits, and if there is a cooperative organization to assist in the maintenance of kits as needed, the effects on distribution of income should be favourable – in view of the ease of use, which would enable the poor as well as the well-to-do farmers to benefit from diagnostic products.

In vivo MAb-based diagnostics

Diagnosis of some diseases requires identification and localization of the disease and its spread within the body. MAbs, because of their specific targeting abilities, are uniquely suited for this purpose. To accomplish this, the MAbs which have been developed to detect, for example, unique tumor markers on cancerous cells and cancer spread in the body, are linked to radioisotopes. These are injected into the body and the MAb transports the linked radioisotope to the tumor sites. The tumor sites are made visible outside the body with a special camera that can detect the radiation the radioisotopes emit. The general term used to designate this type of test is "radioimaging" or "immunoconjugate" diagnostic. The technique gives physicians a more accurate image of the tumor than traditional methods such as a physical examination or X-rays.[43] The bulk of sales accounting for *in vivo* diagnostic MAb applications are expected to be in the cancer and cardiovascular areas.[44]

In cancer patients, MAb *in vivo* imaging is used for tumor localization and quantification, as well as in assessing the degree of metastasis. The first such test to receive marketing approval – an imaging agent for colorectal cancer, produced by the DBF Cytogen of New Jersey – went on sale in Europe at the end of 1991.[45]

In 1991 clinical trials were underway in the USA for MAb imaging agents to diagnose eight different types of cancer.[46] Six of these cancer types – lung, colorectal, breast, pancreatic, stomach and ovarian – account for over 60 per cent of annual cancer deaths in the USA.[47] Most of these trials are intended to confirm and further the diagnosis of cancer so that appropriate treatment can be administered – for example, whether surgery is necessitated, or to determine the level of chemotherapy required. These distinctions were not possible with previous diagnostic methods.[48]

In the area of cardiovascular disease, *in vivo* MAb imaging is undergoing clinical trials in the USA and is already available in several European countries to detect the protein that is released (myosin) when heart muscles undergo a myocardial infarct (heart attack caused by stoppage or impairment of blood flow to the heart muscle). This is the most common type of heart attack, affecting about 1.5 million Americans each year, of which about one million survive and would benefit from continuing medical care. The imaging agent is used to determine the exact location and extent of heart damage, thus aiding doctors in determining whether a patient suffering inexplicable chest pain is in the midst of a heart attack or suffering from some other ailment, as well as helping to decide appropriate therapy. Other radio-imaging agents are being developed to locate dangerous blood clots.[49]

Overall market growth

Sales of diagnostic products based on MAbs are reported to have increased from $30 million in 1983 to $150 million in 1985 and then to $300 million in 1987.[50] No specific sales estimates are available for later years, but all industry and government comments indicate that growth continued to be spectacular. The US Department of Commerce's (DOC) *US Industrial Outlook 1988* stated that

> diagnostics utilizing monoclonal antibodies and DNA probes have been the fastest growing component of biotechnology, amounting to more than half of the current market for biotechnology-derived products. At least 220 diagnostic kits using monoclonal antibodies and 8 using DNA probes are now available.[51]

Four years later, the DOC's *US Industrial Outlook 1992* reported that "the US Food and Drug Administration has approved more than 520 diagnostic kits using MAbs and DNA probes since 1981."[52] It follows that the yearly rate of entry of diagnostics into the market more than doubled from 32 per year in 1981–87 (228/7) to 73 in 1988–91 ([520 – 228]/4). The main factor behind this rapid increase was the replacement of the less accurate and more expensive diagnostic devices that were used prior to the introduction of the methods of new biotechnology.

Diagnostic tests based on MAbs and DNA probes are expected to gain an increasing share of the medical testing market.[53] For the USA, estimated total sales of MAb-based products (for diagnostics and therapeutics) were $573.5 million in 1992, of which $364.5 million was for *in vitro* diagnosis. US total MAb-product sales are projected to increase to $3,778.1 million in 1998. Of this total, about $3 billion of sales are forecast to be for *in vivo* diagnostics and therapeutics. In these two cases, however, projections are less reliable, as experience is rather limited, and clinical-trial outcomes unsure. 1995 world sales of hCG and LH diagnostic kits (see p. 131) were estimated to reach $18.8 million and $48 million, respectively – an increase of 100 per cent and 120 per cent, respectively, from 1989 sales.[54] For diagnostics based on DNA probes, one leading US DBF in the field has estimated that the potential US market in the second half of the 1990s would amount to $500 million.[55]

The future for diagnostics in developing countries as a whole must be very good. Country-by-country, specific/individual biotechnology diagnostic estimates of emerging demand trends and potential market size need to be made; and this will probably be the first step in the next phase of research on specific product priorities in the biotechnology industry in developing countries.

Gestation period

Development and approval of diagnostic products require only a fraction of the time needed for the products of genetic engineering. The latter, it will be recalled, has been estimated at 10–12 years (Chapter 5), of which a large part is taken up by testing and clinical trials in addition to the time needed by government authorities for product approval. For *in vitro* diagnostic kits clinical trials are not required, while approval time is very short. In the USA, biotechnology companies have managed to obtain approval for their MAb diagnostic kits within ninety days.[56] More generally, "MAb applications often do not take long to develop, and are relatively easy to produce in large quantities and are low cost."[57]

An estimate by the Office of Technology Assessment (OTA) of the US Congress, based on an industry source, suggests that "achieving the limited goal of supplying MAbs successfully to manufacturers of *in vitro* diagnostic products will require a 3-year investment."[58] Allowing for, say, an additional six months to construct the facility which would produce the kits themselves, it would appear that the gestation period of investment in diagnostic-products production would be one-third that of investment in products based on genetic engineering (3.5 years compared to 10–12 years).

In a project considered in Cameroon, West Africa, for producing MAb-based pregnancy-test kits, to be followed by the production of diagnostics for early detection of parasitic diseases such as onchocerciasis and malaria, it was estimated that it would take three years before income would be generated.[59]

Capital cost

The cumulative three-year investment cost for an *in vitro* MAb production facility is estimated at between US$3.5 and 4 million.[60] The final immunodiagnostic product (diagnostic kit) may require five to ten times that amount,[61] implying a range of total investment costs from $17.5 to $40 million, with a midpoint of $29 million. Further investigation is needed into the reasons for what appears to be a fairly high investment cost in moving from production of MAbs – the essential core of the diagnostic – to production of the final product (diagnostic kit). As indicated above, in addition to the MAb core, the final product also includes test tubes, reagents, controls and so forth, whose specific costing should be examined and analyzed.[62] Taking the estimate as is, it needs to be adjusted upwards to account for the increase in the general price level since 1982, when the estimate was made: the equivalent in 1990 prices would be $38 million, using the US GNP price deflator. This $38 million cost is under 40 per cent of the investment cost of some $100 million estimated for the development of the new genetically engineered drugs. One reason for the lower capital cost of an *in vitro* diagnostic facility is that it does not involve investment in a sterile fermentation plant, which is required for an r-DNA pharmaceutical;[63] another reason is that the gestation period is much shorter (and hence fewer benefits are forgone).

Another 1982 estimate has placed the capital cost at a much lower level: $41–75,000, or, with added equipment, $180–353,000. This estimate, prepared by professors Davis, McGuire and Perryman from Washington State University,[64] refers to a laboratory which could produce MAbs, not a full-fledged plant. The actual cost of a plant, which would employ between fifteen and twenty persons when operating at full capacity, the Damon Biotech monoclonal antibody plant, was $3 million, according to a 1988 study.[65]

In the Cameroon diagnostics project (1992) – first phase, pregnancy test kits – the cost of technology acquisition and capital equipment is estimated at $450,000. The total three-year cost prior to generation of net income, which includes cumulative wages and salaries and a 20 per cent contingency allowance, is $1.71 million. It is expected that the price at which the kits would be sold would be considerably lower than the equivalent imported product, while still being able to generate profits.[66]

Skills: demand and supply

Diagnostics production, while calling for substantial research and corresponding skills, demands less in this regard than the development of a therapeutic drug through genetic engineering, the skill requirements for which are formidable. As indicated in Chapter 5, research and development expenditures per US employee in the diagnostics industry ($38,000 per year), amounted to 44 per cent of the expenditures in the therapeutic sector of biotechnology ($87,000) in 1995.

The capacity of the industrially more advanced developing countries to meet the skill and managerial requirements of the diagnostics industry should not be in serious doubt. Countries such as Argentina, Brazil, Mexico, China, Singapore, South Korea, India, Eastern Europe and other countries with a similar industrial capability have considerable pools of technical manpower and scientists who could be engaged in biotechnology techniques. Moreover, some of these countries' scientific talent is working abroad, in institutes and universities in developed countries, and some of them could be attracted back to their home countries, at least temporarily. These countries have well-developed industrial bases and experience in handling the complex issues involved in organizing new industrial processes. They have achieved major advances in expanding exports of manufactures to the world market as a result of successful industrialization and low, competitive costs; this should see them through entry into the diagnostics market as well. Whether they can become net exporters of diagnostic products is too early to judge, but the possibility cannot be excluded. The US-based diagnostics industry is an exporter, according to anecdotal evidence,[67] and so is a Russian 700-employee firm which exports to Turkey and some countries in the Middle East.[68] Concerning the scientific credentials of those developing countries, it is perhaps appropriate to recall that it was an Argentinian scientist working in England, Dr C. Milstein, a Nobel prizewinner, who, with G. Köhler, invented a method and was the first to produce monoclonal antibodies, thus creating the basis for the modern biotechnology-based diagnostics industry.

Diagnostics use in developing countries: international agency and expert assessment

In a 1984 study, remarkable for the accuracy and imagination with which it predicted the rapid development of the monoclonal antibody industry, UNIDO concluded that

> research and development pertaining to MAbs for use in diagnostic kits and as detection agents offer impressive opportunities for researchers in developing countries and at the future UNIDO-sponsored International Center for

Genetic Engineering and Biotechnology... The sizeable demand for MABs for these purposes could be built at a rapid pace.[69]

The World Bank, in a 1991 study prepared under its auspices on agricultural biotechnology and Bank policy options in support of it, stated:

> The new technologies are being applied to the detection of microbes, chemicals (particularly pesticides), and plant products. Improvements in assay technology have led to the development of sensitive, specific, easy-to-use methods for many agricultural purposes. Countries considering the potential application of new agricultural diagnostics should make certain that the technology is well developed and that immediate application is feasible. Once the specific target has been identified the technique should also be applicable to all crops and most pests and diseases. The use (as distinct from preparation) of monoclonal antibodies does not require high technology and their application should be feasible in most countries.[70]

The International Development Research Center of Canada is supporting an International Institute of Tropical Agriculture (IITA, Ibadan, Nigeria) project to help African national agricultural programs use MAbs in local laboratories for identifying endemic prevalent viral strains. "With MAb-methods available in African national programmes, rapid diagnosis of viral diseases will no longer be hampered by quarantine regulations, which prohibit shipment of infected plants or plant parts across international borders for analysis at IITA."[71]

A United Nations Conference on Trade and Development (UNCTAD) 1991 study on the trade and development aspects of agricultural biotechnology, prepared for its Committee on Transfer of Technology, stated:

> Diagnostics tests based on monoclonal or polyclonal antibodies constitute a particularly effective tool for the detection of diseases (in particular virus attacks) in plants, but also in soils or in carrying out plant selection programmes. Diagnostic kits are becoming a standardized technology whose use at the farm level requires no special knowledge, and whose potential contribution to agricultural productivity and, by extension, to exports of developing countries could be significant.[72]

Equally positive are the expert assessments of the need for diagnostic products and ease of application:

> Modern diagnostic technology is available or can readily be made available to produce accurate, sensitive, reliable test systems, for laboratory or field use,

to detect specific chemicals, gene sequences or micro-organisms in plants, foodstuffs and the environment.

In industrialized countries, such technology is being increasingly used for research, for regulatory purposes and to aid crop management decisions. There are no basic technical reasons why modern diagnostics could not be used for the same purposes in developing countries. In fact ... there are many potential advantages for their use in developing countries in comparison with traditional methods. The main advantages will be in the use of rapid, simple-to-use, accurate, reliable, robust, on-site kits by non-specialists, in comparison with the current use of sophisticated, costly, complicated, hard-to-maintain equipment by highly trained scientists in specialized laboratories.[73]

In the field of environmental monitoring,

One area with obvious potential lies in monitoring the presence and abundance of microbial or viral insecticides... Use of a monoclonal kit requires no special facilities or expertise; it gives a quick result; and the kit can be stored for regular reuse over several months in a domestic freezer.[74]

MAbs can be most useful for improving diagnostic capabilities for livestock diseases. In addition to improving livestock productivity by accurate diagnosis of diseases,

such diagnostic technologies may also be required by developing countries to certify that livestock export commodities, whether live animals, embryos or livestock products, are free of given diseases, as required by the importing countries. This is an area of increasing importance, of direct economic benefit to the exporting countries, and underlines the necessity for the acquisition of the relevant technologies by such countries.[75]

Concerning human health,

the resulting savings in time and money [using MAbs] has been recognized, and commercial enterprises [in industrialized countries] are rapidly turning to the new technology for the routine production of serological reagents... The reagents generated thus far would be equally useful in diagnosing diseases in developing countries and would greatly facilitate and improve their diagnostic ability.[76]

A diagnostics industry in developing countries?

According to UNIDO, "the technology necessary to produce MAbs can be mastered readily by bio-science researchers and technicians. Furthermore, the cost of designing and constructing MAbs is reasonable."[77] Two consultants to the World Bank, working in the industry, have expressed a contrary view:

It must be recognized that the development of diagnostic kits requires considerable investment and the use of sophisticated, costly equipment in modern laboratories by highly trained specialists. Therefore, the development of practical technology for use in developing countries requires equipment and trained personnel more readily found in industrialised countries ... Considering the experience gained and systems already produced or under production in industrialised countries, and the fact that there are likely to be many common targets, together with the need for high-technology facilities for system development, it would appear more efficient, at least in the short- to mid-term, for developing countries to seek ready made systems from industrialised-country organizations. These could be financed directly by the developing country or with an international development agency.[78]

Four points need to be made concerning this controversy. First, it does not apply to livestock diseases: diagnostics in this field must be developed domestically. The reason for this is that veterinary regulations in industrialized countries largely prohibit the entry of exotic infectious agents and livestock from developing countries whether for use in the public or private sectors. The technologies must, therefore, be developed, tested and applied within the developing country, region or continent affected by the disease concerned.[79]

Second, diagnostic systems developed in industrialized countries will frequently need adaptations in order to be usable in developing countries, and in some cases cannot be used at all. For example, some plant pathogens endemic in developing countries are not found in industrialized countries – for example, African cassava mosaic virus and maize streak virus.[80]

Third, locally developed diagnostics would assist in avoiding transportation of plant pathogens to areas where the pathogen is not found, thereby eliminating the possible spread of the disease in question.

Fourth, one argument in favour of developing a domestic diagnostics industry is that "third world scientists would be very quickly at the cutting edge of technology", in the phrase of a UNIDO study.[81] This is essentially the infant-industry argument being advanced in a very important industry.

The decision whether to establish a national diagnostics industry cannot be made on an *a priori* basis; everything depends on the country concerned. As two other World Bank consultants, – this time from university and laboratory research – noted, "given sufficient trained personnel, adequate facilities and capital resources, there is no major obstacle to transferring such techniques to developing countries."[82] The timing will depend partly on the price of the imported diagnostic product compared to the likely domestic costs, and, in the case of foreign private investment, on the extent of privileges it will seek, in the form of tariff protection and patent rights. The interest of the developing country is to obtain diagnostic products as cheaply as possible, while at the same time providing a stimulus for the establishment and growth of a domestic biotechnology industry and research capacity.

In many cases, the decision will be easy to make as it will be obvious whether or not the necessary skills are available. But there will be borderline cases. The benefit of the doubt should be given to the infant-industry argument in view of the importance of the biotechnology industry not only for human health, but also for agricultural growth, provided the required protection is within a reasonable range and the quality of domestic products meets international standards. (For observations on the prospects for applying biotechnology to agriculture in developing countries, and the problems involved, see Annex 3. Chapter 10 discusses how development of a MAb-based diagnostics industry can serve as the basis for more advanced phases of biotechnology applied to human health care.)

The issue of how many developing countries can usefully absorb biotechnology processes and develop their own research capacity is an open one. The World Bank estimates that there are about ten countries in this group, an estimate that is probably on the low side. This group would appear to include: Brazil, China, India, Indonesia, Malaysia, Mexico, the Philippines, Singapore and Thailand; at least these are the countries listed in the Bank's policy paper.[83] For Latin America alone, two officials of the Technology Generation and Transfer Programme of the Inter-American Institute for Cooperation on Agriculture (IICA), located in Costa Rica, listed eight countries – Argentina, Brazil, Chile, Colombia, Cuba, Mexico, Costa Rica and Venezuela – as having "internationally accepted research in frontline areas using sophisticated state-of-the-art biotechnologies";[84] this compares to the presence of only two Latin American countries on the World Bank list. The IICA officials' claim, largely convincing at the time, was borne out through 1995. The larger the number of developing countries with a promising absorptive capacity for biotechnology, the greater is the need for both multilateral and bilateral support from developed countries and the greater the justification for such support. At a European–Latin American meeting on prospects for cooperation in biotechnology held in 1987, it was stressed that "what Latin American and other developing countries need is the establishment of bilateral accords with developed nations, which permit training and the creation of a domestic infrastructure capable of supporting the benefits to be wrought by biotechnology."[85] In a sense, this statement anticipated the US–Thailand agreement of 1991, although the latter has gone much further in specifying actual projects (see Chapter 8). This agreement may be followed by others, suitably modified to meet individual country requirements.

The analysis in this chapter should not be interpreted as endorsement of the establishment of a diagnostic-products industry in every developing country. Rather, the claim is simply that sufficient grounds of a general nature exist to justify an examination of diagnostics production feasibility in countries contemplating biotechnology development as a national policy. The feasibility of diagnostics in each specific case will need to be determined in the light of: (i) the availability of skills: (ii) the existence of likely markets; (iii) prevailing and expected prices of particular diagnostics that will be produced – competition in this field may be quite severe; (iv) prevailing and expected costs of equipment, material and labor; and (v) the expected profit rate.

Notes

1. US Congress, 1985, p. 161.
2. *Ibid.,* p. 153.
3. Sensitivity refers to the ability of a diagnostic test to detect a disease-producing agent or disease when it is present. A very sensitive test correctly identifies all infected individuals. A test whose result is negative (that is, indicating no disease present) on individuals who, in reality, actually do have the disease, is termed a "false negative".
4. Hoffman and Rosenberg, 1992, p. 8.
5. Description of the immune system and the functioning of antibodies was derived from: US Congress, 1985, chs 5 and 8; US Congress, 1987, ch. 3; Coghlan, 1991a; Gamlin, 1988a and 1988b; Roitt, 1991; *The Economist,* 1987b; Watson, et al., 1992; WHO, 1983.
6. Sharon and Lis, 1993, p. 83.
7. It should be noted that the immune response does not only involve antibodies; T cells, macrophages and cytokines, amongst other types of cells, also form part of the immune system. T cells are a separate group of lymphocytes, responsible for the second line of defense, termed the cell-mediated immune response (as distinguished from the humoral or antibody response). These cells have a myriad of functions, including activation of B cells and macrophages – white cells with "phagocytic" activity (i.e., they engulf or gobble up foreign

matter). The T cells combat intracellular infections – cells that have already become infected with the foreign invader – while B cells concentrate on dealing with antigens in the bloodstream before they infiltrate cell tissue. It is a subset of T cells called "helper" T cells which the HIV virus that causes AIDS infects, rendering the body increasingly susceptible to viral and microbial infections.

Cytokines embrace a variety of extremely potent protein molecules, present in minute quantities in the blood, which orchestrate and regulate the amplitude and duration of the immune response. Cytokines include interferons, interleukins, tumor necrosis factor and colony stimulating factors, all of which are the focus of substantial biomedical research and pharmaceutical development.

8. US Congress, 1987, p. 38.

9. The basic method for producing monoclonal antibodies is as follows. First a rodent – mouse or rat – is inoculated against the antigen of interest and permitted some time to respond (the mouse will start producing different antibodies directed at the determinants of the Ag). The spleen of the mouse, which contains Ab-producing B lymphocytes is removed and minced to release the Ab-producing cells. These cells are dispersed and added to cultures of mouse myeloma cells (constantly dividing B tumor cells, selected for their inability to secrete Ab). The mixed cells are incubated in special media so that their cell membranes are allowed to fuse together, producing hybrid cells with two nuclei. After a period the hybrid cell nuclei stabilize, and the cultures, consisting of thousands of cells, are grown in a selective medium which kills off the unfused partners, and thus only hybrid cells survive. The hybrid cells are then distributed to microwell plates at such high dilution that, on average, each well will contain one hybridoma. These are allowed to grow for several days, after which the culture fluid is removed and tested for the presece of Ab that binds the Ag. Hybridomas that test positive are then cultured to start a clone of genetically identical cells, each derived from a single hybrid cell and secreting one specific, monoclonal Ab. Antibody-producing cell lines can be stored frozen in liquid nitrogen and thawed out and cultured as needed. Different methods for MAb production are being researched.

10. US Congress, 1985, p. 111.

11. "Monoclonal Antibodies", National Research Council, 1982, pp. 96–111, 98.

12. Capron and Grzych, 1983, p. 21.

13. US Congress, 1987, p. 38.

14. US Congress, 1984, p. 146.

15. Specificity is the ability of a test procedure to determine correctly that a disease-producing agent or disease is not present. A very specific test will correctly identify all uninfected individuals. Positive tests for individuals who do not have the disease are termed "false positives".

16. Marsh, 1987b. In 1993, the worlwide market for *in vitro* diagnostics was estimated at $9 billion (Griffiths and Hall, 1993, p. 127).

17. US Congress, 1985, p. 157.

18. Cross-reactivity is an aspect of immunodiagnostic tests related to, yet different from, specificity. A cross-reaction occurs when the test correctly identifies the appropriate chemical entity, but that chemical happens to exist in an organism

other than the one tested for, resulting in a false positive.
19. US Congress, 1985, p. 162.
20. Hoffman and Rosenberg, 1992, p. 8.
21. Roitt, 1991, p. 138.
22. US Congress, 1985, pp. 161–2.
23. Kolata, 1993, p. C3; Hoffman and Rosenberg, 1992, p. 8.
24. Schrage, 1984; US Congress, 1984, p. 146.
25. IBA, 1988, p. 3.
26. Stevens, 1992, p. 83.
27. US Congress, 1984, p. 144.
28. Gangal, 1987, p. 53.
29. US Congress, 1984, p. 144.
30. *Ibid.*, p. 145.
31. *Ibid.*
32. *Ibid.*, p. 144.
33. Gangal, 1987, p. 53; US Congress, 1984, p. 144.
34. US Congress, 1985, p. 86.
35. IBA, 1988, p. 3.
36. US Congress, 1985, p. 162.
37. Erikson, 1992.
38. Gangal, 1987, p. 55; US Congress, 1984, p. 146.
39. Gangal, 1987.
40. Hoffman and Rosenberg, 1992, p. 8.
41. Newmark, 1988.
42. Dramik, 1992, p. 11.
43. Cookson, 1992.
44. Koenig, 1989, p. 5.
45. Cookson, 1992.
46. PMA, 1992.
47. IBA, 1988, p. 4.
48. *Ibid.*
49. Bishop, 1989b, p 7; Centocor, 1991; Koenig, 1989, p. 5. In 1995, three such products were undergoing clinical trials in the USA (PhRMA, 1995).
50. Lancaster, 1984; *The Economist*, 1986a, p. 92; and *The Economist*, 1988a, p. 10, respectively.
51. US DOC, 1988, p. 22-7.
52. US DOC, 1992, p. 17-2.
53. US DOC, 1991, p. 18-5.
54. *Genetic Engineering News*, 1993; 1992 figures and 1988 projections were according to Frost & Sullivan Market Intelligence (Mountain View, California); Koning, 1994 for hCG and LH figures.
55. Enzo Biochem Inc., 1991b.
56. Mackler, 1990, p. 26.
57. Sercovich and Leopold, 1991, p. 51.
58. Treble, 1982.
59. Bialey, 1992. This project was being developed in cooperation with the

WHO/UNDP/World Bank Special Program for Research and Training in Tropical Diseases, with expected assistance from the International Finance Corporation (IFC), Washington, DC.

60. Treble, 1982. This estimate presumably includes interest during construction, i.e. an allowance for benefits forgone during the investment period.

61. *Ibid.*; Koenig, 1989, p. 5.

62. See p. 131 above, which describes some of the other inputs needed to complement the MAb in order to produce the final test kit product.

63. Sercovich and Leopold, 1991, p. 51.

64. Davis et al., 1982, pp. 204–5.

65. Bifani, 1988, p. 231.

66. Bialey, 1992, pp. 8, 13.

67. US DOC, 1989, p. 19-3.

68. Statement of Dr Nikolai Durmanov, Co-Chairman of the Council of "D. Mazai" Joint Stock Company, Moscow, February 1992.

69. UNIDO, 1984, p. 27.

70. World Bank, 1991a, pp. 15–16.

71. *Biotechnology and Development Monitor* 1990a, p. 19.

72. UNCTAD, 1991, p. 21.

73. Miller and Williams, 1990, p. 103.

74. Whitten and Oakeshott, 1990, p. 128.

75. Doyle and Spradbrow, 1990, p. 179.

76. "Monoclonal Antibodies", National Research Council, 1982, pp. 96–111, 98.

77. UNIDO, 1984, p. 27.

78. Miller and Williams, 1990, pp. 103, 105. Dr Miller is from Agri-Diagnostic Associates, Cinnaminson, New Jersey, USA; and Dr Williams is from Ciba Geigy, Basle, Switzerland.

79. Doyle and Spradbrow, 1990, p. 181.

80. Miller and Williams, 1990, p. 104.

81. UNIDO, 1984, p. 27.

82. Doyle and Spradbrow, 1990, p. 182.

83. World Bank, 1991a, p. 13.

84. Trigo and Jaffe, 1990, p. 49.

85. Statement by Dr Luiz Pereira da Silva, Unit de Parasitologie experimentale, Institut Pasteur, France, quoted in Sorj et al., eds, 1989, p. 12.

Chapter 10

Diagnostics:
A Bridge to Vaccines and Therapeutics

In considering biotechnology policy for developing countries, it is important to note that development of a MAb-based diagnostics industry and associated expertise can also facilitate both vaccine and therapeutics development over the medium and long term. Additionally, the cash flow resulting from diagnostics production may be indispensable for financing advances in these and other areas of biotechnology. In the history of the biotechnology industry in developed countries, some firms seem to have been saved by their decision to develop a diagnostics capability:

> Two stages can be distinguished in the typical relationships between dedicated biotechnology enterprises (DBEs) and large established companies (LECs). In the first, the research and development stage, LECs supply financing in exchange for research results. In the second, the production/marketing distribution stage, LECs supply financing in exchange for rights to exploit DBE's patents and know how… Some [DBEs] have been taken over by LECs, others have gone bankrupt and others streamlined operations and/or merged. A few are becoming increasingly self-supporting through product sales, licensing and research contracts, often starting first by quickly developing products such as diagnostic kits.[1]

A bridge to the vaccines industry: subunit and anti-id vaccines

The development of efficient and cheap vaccines against major human diseases in developing countries – malaria, cholera, leprosy, typhoid fever, amoebiasis, AIDS, tuberculosis – as well as vaccines affecting animals there, remains a major challenge to biotechnology in those countries. Valuable work in these fields goes on in a number of countries, such as India, Colombia, Argentina and Brazil. Monoclonal antibodies (MAbs) are playing a major role in helping researchers worldwide to identify and separate out antigens capable of becoming a basis for subunit vaccines as well as for a new type of vaccine, called an anti-id.

MAbs have been instrumental in identifying the specific antigenic determinants or protein segments of the pathogen which would become the essential part of the subunit vaccine. In turn, an anti-id MAb, particularly one of mouse origin, will elicit a strong immune response; an anti-id approach is useful when a protective antigen cannot readily be produced in commercial quantities by recombinant DNA or chemical methods, because, for instance, it is a glycolipid – that is, a non-protein; a glycolipid is a type of complex carbohydrate in which sugars are linked to lipids (fats). (Annex 4 describes subunit and anti-id vaccines.)

Monoclonal antibodies as therapeutics

In principle, experience gained from developing and producing MAbs for use in diagnostic kits and imaging agents can be most useful if a decision is subsequently made to develop MAbs as therapeutic agents. When MAbs were first discovered, great excitement was generated about their possible use as "magic bullets" to destroy unwanted cells, such as cancer cells, either directly or by coupling cytotoxic agents (radioisotopes or toxins) to MAbs, which would then direct the agents to the diseased cells, without harming normal tissue.

It was not until the late 1980s, however, that progress in developing MAb-based therapeutics was made. Two of the major problems initially encountered were the patient's own resistance, which quickly built up against repeated administration of (rodent-derived) MAbs, and, in the case of MAb-based therapeutics against cancer, the lack of capacity to identify specific and unique marker proteins on malignant tumors to distinguish the cancerous tissue from normal body tissue. (A further elaboration of these problems, and consideration of recent technical advances achieved to overcome these obstacles are to be found in Annex 5.)

The 1990s

Research and technical advances in MAb-based vaccines and therapeutic drugs continue; indeed they form one of the core activities of a substantial number of DBFs and research institutes headquartered in industrialized countries. The commercial promise, and prominence, that MAb-based vaccines and MAb-based therapeutics hold within the biotechnology industry for the decade of the 1990s is considerable: one-third (46 out of 132) of all biotechnology medicines in human clinical trials in the USA in 1991 were MAb-based – MAb-based therapeutics representing the largest product category (out of sixteen categories).[2] This sizeable proportion held steady through March 1995, with MAb products accounting for 69 of the 243 biotech drugs and vaccines in clinical trials or awaiting approval in the USA.

In fact, since the Pharmaceutical Manufacturers Association (Washington DC) began conducting these surveys in 1989,

> monoclonal antibody products have continued to outnumber all other categories by a wide margin. Among the most versatile of biotechnology drugs, these "magic bullets" selectively bind to foreign organisms or specific cells. They can be used to diagnose and treat diseases. They can be made into homing devices that carry treatments to the disease site. While about half of the MAbs listed in this [1995] surgey target various cancers, MAbs are now in clinical trials for a wide variety of disorders, including rheumatoid arthritis, heart disease and AIDS.[3]

Companies in the USA and Europe are developing MAb-based therapeutics against a broad range of diseases, including AIDS, hepatitis, schistosomiasis, cytomegalovirus, herpes zoster, a variety of cancers, blood clots, several autoimmune diseases, and for the prevention of rejection of organ transplants.[4]

The prominent role that MAb-based vaccines and therapeutics are likely to play within the biotechnology industry strengthens the rationale for those developing countries sufficiently scientifically advanced to conduct new biotechnology research and industrial commercialization to give high priority to MAb development. Not only can it result quickly in diagnostic products which are most useful and ready for commercial sale, but it can also lead to development of biotechnology-based therapeutic (drug) and vaccine industries – potentially of enormous importance for developing countries.

Notes

1. Sercovich and Leopold, 1991, p. 48. See also Chapter 3 of this study.
2. PMA, 1992. The next two largest product categories were vaccines and interferons, with eighteen and sixteen products respectively.
3. PhRMA, 1995, p. 1. In 1995, after MAbs, the next largest product category was vaccines, with 43 products in development.
4. Brown, 1992; Coghlan, 1991a, p. 39; and PMA, 1992.

Conclusion

The major finding of this study is that one product line of biotechnology, monoclonal antibody-based diagnostics, is much easier to develop than other lines and is more viable within the resources available in developing countries for product development. The demand for these products is large and growing, capital requirements are relatively small, and product development times relatively short. The fields of application are human health care, agriculture – including animals, aquaculture and plants – and environmental monitoring. Furthermore, this line of diagnostics can serve as a stepping stone to, and basis for, the development of other biotechnology products in two ways: first, due to short product development times, it can generate relatively quickly the cash flow needed to help finance current operations and research requirements (thus reducing dependence on external capital); second, it is an integral part of the vaccine development process, for which the demand in developing countries is enormous. Additionally, monoclonal antibodies offer possibilities for development into therapeutic drugs by enhancing the body's natural immune system or by serving as a "magic bullet" to deliver cell-killing agents to diseased cells and tissues.

Another way in which scientifically more advanced developing countries may enter biotechnology despite its high cost of development is to undertake contract research for external biotechnology firms and institutions and other users of biotechnology research data (for example, pharmaceutical firms and government research institutes), mostly located in developed countries. Contract research has been used on a substantial scale by existing biotechnology firms in industrialized countries in the early phases of their development, enabling them to generate cash flow before they were able to place their products on the market.

Such contract research is encountered in several developing countries, mainly commissioned by institutions in developed countries.

A recent development has been the conclusion of bilateral arrangements between a developed and developing country under which co-operative and complementary biotechnology product ventures and sales have been organized and financed (the US–Thailand agreement of 1991). While it is too early to assess the impact of this arrangement, in principle it may lead to biotechnology development in developing countries advancing faster than would be the case otherwise, provided the interests of developing countries in pursuing their priorities in research and development are adequately protected.

Contract research and bilateral agreements may focus on diagnostics development. In such an approach, not only would cash be generated in early phases of biotechnology development, but skills and knowledge generated could, more directly and more rapidly than in other biotechnology sectors, serve the broader policy objectives in developing countries of improving the health care of their populations and promoting agricultural growth by domestic application of modern and cost-effective biotechnology techniques. Their priority for diagnostics development would be reinforced by contract research in this field and by bilateral agreements which would focus in particular on the creation of a domestic diagnostic industry.

Annex 1

Patents and Intellectual Property Rights

Given the time and expense needed to develop biotechnology products and processes, companies have been ardently seeking patent protection for their inventions. Securing a clear-cut patent for biotechnology products, has, however, proved extremely difficult, from the inception of new biotechnology, through the 1980s and continuing into 1996, resulting in an immense number of lawsuits. The issue has been fraught, in industrialized countries as well as on a global level, with confusion, controversy and debate over what exactly is patentable and subject to patent law.

Complexities of patent application in medical biotechnology

A patent is a legal right granted by a government to an inventor. The patent gives the inventor the right to exclude others from manufacturing, using or selling a patented product or process for a limited period of time, usually seventeen to twenty years, without the consent of the inventor. In return for the patent, the inventor must make full public disclosure of the invention.

Patents are designed to encourage invention by rewarding successful efforts and their backers with an incentive to risk time and money in R&D. The patent system also encourages public disclosure of technical information which may otherwise have remained secret, so that others are able to use it. The inducement in both cases is the potential for economic gain through exploitation of the patent right.

According to the laws applied in most countries, the four principal requirements for patentability are novelty, non-obviousness or inventiveness, practical utility or industrial applicability, and requirements concerning the specification of the patent – it must be disclosed to the public in sufficient detail to enable those of ordinary skill and experience in the field to follow the directions and obtain the promised results. The invention is defined in the claims which form part of the specification. Common forms of claims are directed to an apparatus or device, a process or product of manufacture, and a method of treatment, testing or use.[1]

Traditional pharmaceuticals, most of which were synthetic chemicals, were easy to define for patent purposes in terms of structure and function. These drugs were discrete chemical entities, easily distinguished by their atomic structures. Patents were awarded to companies that discovered unique chemical structures.

This has not proved to be the case with drugs produced by means of biotechnology. Patent litigation has been extensive, leading to uncertainty as to who has the rights to sell the products. The reasons for litigation include complex overlapping patent claims, the high value of the products involved, the relative newness of biotechnology and the rapid pace at which new discoveries continue to be made, and the fact that many companies are pursuing the same product. Unlike traditional pharmaceuticals, products of biotechnology are complex proteins that must maintain a certain three-dimensional structure, and in many cases acquire certain chemical modifications in order to function to their full potential. Thus, depending on the organism used to produce the protein, and the process used to purify it, two recombinant-DNA-derived versions with identical amino acid sequence could fold into three-dimensional structures with different levels of activity. This leads to the question of whether the patent on one protein product excludes the rights to patent all other versions.[2]

The non-obviousness requirement that inventions must meet to qualify for a patent pertains to the degree of difference between the invention and the "prior art". An invention that would have been obvious at the time it was made to a person with ordinary skill in the relevant field of technology is not patentable. The rapid development and the complexity of the biotechnology field make it difficult to determine, at a given point in time, what is ordinary skill or what is obvious. One of the fundamental questions the non-obviousness criterion raises is the following: once a protein is discovered, is it obvious to produce it subsequently using recombinant DNA (r-DNA) technology?[3]

Major disputed medical cases[4]

The non-obviousness criterion was at the heart of a patent battle between Genentech and the Wellcome Foundation of the UK. Genentech obtained a British patent on tissue plasminogen activator (TPA, a blood clot dissolver used for the treatment of heart attacks) in 1986. Wellcome, collaborating with the US DBF Genetics Institute to develop TPA, immediately sued to have the patent revoked because the company claimed that the use of recombinant DNA techniques to produce TPA was obvious to anyone with knowledge of biotechnology. Genentech sued Wellcome for infringement of its patent, claiming that the patent was valid because the unravelling of the genetic machinery needed to produce recombinant TPA was anything but obvious, despite knowledge of the existence of TPA. The British court ruled against Genentech's retaining exclusive marketing rights in Britain. The court held that the scope of claims on Genentech's patent were too broad and that the company had merely found one route to an end.

Companies are also grappling with the question as to what constitutes something different. If a company changes one or even several dozen amino acids out of several hundred, is the resulting protein "different" from the one protected with a patent? This is what was at issue in the *Genentech* v. *Wellcome and Genetics Institute* patent dispute over TPA in the USA. This time the court ruled in Genentech's favor.

Genentech, which had spent five years and $200 million developing TPA, had three patents on TPA when Britain's Wellcome developed a version that changed only one of TPA's 527 amino acids. Genetics Institute made changes in 82 amino acids in its version of TPA. The US court concluded that Wellcome's and Genetics Institute's drugs performed in approximately the same way to obtain essentially the same results as TPA, and thus these companies had infringed the Genentech patents.

Similarly, if one company has a patent on a genetically engineered drug for treating septic shock that uses antibodies derived from mouse cells, and another company also makes a drug that treats septic shock but with antibodies derived from human and mouse cells, would that consititute patent infringement? Xoma, which has the patent on the mouse-derived medicine, thinks that it does constitute infringement. Centocor, which developed the other product, disagrees, and the issue is being settled in court. The dispute is critical to both companies, which expect a $500 million market for the drug in the United States.

Another issue critical to the biotechnology industry is whether a recombinantly produced product infringes upon the natural product. This issue played a major part in the four-year legal dispute between Amgen and Genetics Institute for erythropoietin or EPO. EPO replicates the action of a hormone in the human kidney by triggering the production of red blood cells, enabling seriously anemic patients to avoid costly and dangerous blood transfusions. This product, with a potential US market of $400 million and a market outside the USA estimated at between $500 million and $1.2 billion, induced Amgen and Genetics Institute in the early 1980s to begin spending the first of more than $100 million each to develop EPO.

EPO is a naturally occurring hormone secreted by the human kidney. Genetics Institute isolated EPO from human urine, purified it and in 1987 received a patent for the resulting purified hormone. Genetics Institute claimed that its patent covered any form of EPO used to treat anemia, no matter what the source.

Genetics Institute, however, still lacked a product it could market commercially. EPO is found only in the urine of a certain class of anemic patients, and even the best purification techniques yield only a miniscule amount of the protein. Thus Genetics Institute raced to find a way to mass-produce EPO using r-DNA technology (the only way commercial quantities could be obtained), something which Amgen was already busy working on.

It will be recalled that to genetically engineer a protein, the scientist must find the gene containing the instructions for manufacturing the protein and a cell that will act as a protein factory. In the case of EPO, Amgen discovered the gene sequence necessary to reproduce EPO and received a patent on the sequence. Amgen also discovered that a Chinese hamster's ovary cell would reproduce EPO if injected with the EPO gene, and the company received a second patent on the use of the hamster cell as an EPO factory. Amgen was granted the patent covering the manufacture of EPO using r-DNA technology several months later than the Genetics Institute (purified product) patent was granted, and Amgen immediately sued Genetics Institute for patent infringement. Meanwhile Genetics Institute had continued its work and succeeded in mass-producing EPO for the market through recombinant means different to those of Amgen and filed its application for its recombinant method about thirteen months later than Amgen's application.

Amgen's position in the subsequent patent dispute was that, because it discovered the means to produce EPO in commercial quantities through r-DNA technology first, it deserved the patent protection. Genetics Institute argued, however, that its patent covered all EPO used for treating anemia. Supporters of Amgen argue that patent laws should create an incentive to use recombinant DNA technology to produce drugs in commercial quantities, as patents are designed to encourage innovations which benefit society. Genetics Institute's supporters say that such an interpretation – attempting to differentiate between two identical products simply on the grounds that one is produced in a preferable way – would distort the patent law.

The issue is central to the biotechnology industry, yet it was not resolved in the EPO case. The court issued a narrow ruling, avoiding the larger question of whether patents for naturally occurring purified proteins can block a product produced by recombinant DNA technology. In striking down Genetics Institute's patent in March 1991, the court cited a technical point. It asserted that the company's EPO was not in fact more pure than the EPO found in nature, and therefore the company's product had failed to do what its patent claimed, thereby rendering the patent invalid. Investors react quickly to the latest legal decisions. Following the court's ruling, Genetics Institute's stock plummeted $21.75 to $40.25; Amgen's shares closed up $12 at $113. Genetics Institute appealed the case to the US Supreme Court, and lost.

The debate over whether a naturally purified protein is the same as one produced by recombinant DNA technology has locked in controversy a number of other products. This was the issue at stake in the patent-infringement battle between Scripps Clinic and Research Foundation (US) and Genentech over a protein called Factor VIII. The protein, long known to be a key blood-clotting protein missing from the blood of hemophiliacs, was purified by scientists at Scripps Clinic, which holds the patent for the purified natural protein. Scripps Clinic sued Genentech, claiming that Scripps should receive a royalty on all manufactured forms of Factor VIII; Genentech argued that its recombinant version of Factor VIII does not infringe Scripps' patent claim: Genentech won.

Lawyers in medical biotechnology: a new growth industry?

There is a huge demand for patent attorneys who are experts in biotechnology, according to Irving Kayton, professor at George Washington University National Law Center. Hundreds of patent lawyers are taking courses to learn the new language and sciences associated with biotechnology patents. At least one firm, Pennie and Edmonds of New York, has hired people with doctorates in areas such as biochemical engineering and molecular biology, and then paid their way through law school. Others, such as the 140-lawyer Los Angeles firm of Irell and Manella, have merged with smaller firms that specialize in biotechnology.[5]

How the courts will interpret biotechnology patent claims and how well domestic companies protect patent rights abroad will be issues facing biotechnology companies for at least several years into the future, according to biotechnology analysts and patent attorneys and an October 1991 Office of Technology Assessment study. Uncertainty over patent rights will be costly and will influence the way many biotechnology companies structure their R&D strategy. Until precedents are set in court rulings, predicting the outcome of patent litigation will be extremely difficult.[6]

Complexities of patent protection in agriculture[7]

The issue of patents also arises in biotechnology applied to agriculture. In most developed countries two systems of protecting intellectual property applicable to plants and plant biotechnological innovations exist: the industrial patent (described in the first section, above) and the plant breeder's right (PBR). A plant breeder's right is a right granted by a government to plant breeders to exclude others from producing and selling propagating material (mostly seed) of a protected plant variety for a period of fifteen to twenty years.

For a plant variety to be eligible for PBR protection, it must be distinctive (that is, clearly distinguishable from other protected varieties), homogeneous or uniform (that is, its characteristics are uniform) and stable (that is, its characteristics remain unchanged after repeated reproduction or propagation).

The scope of protection offered is different under the two systems. First, the rights conferred under PBR extend only to commercial manufacture and marketing of propagating material at the production stage of the variety. Thus, farmers who have bought seeds from a plant breeder (that is, a seed company or other entity or person producing a new plant variety) are free to retain a portion of their protected variety crops and seeds for resowing the following year (or next production cycle) on their own farms. The farmer is thus not required to pay again for the use of the seed – this is referred to as the "farmer's privilege". Under patent laws, however, such a payment is mandatory. Farmers would therefore have to pay a royalty on each new generation of seed, which in practice means payment of annual royalties. Second, under the so-called "breeder's exemption", the utilization of a variety for purposes of creating new varieties, or for the marketing and commercialization of such new varieties, does not require authorization or payment to the breeder of the original variety. This is not the case for patented inventions if they are considered dependent on prior patents, in which case royalties would have to be paid.

Since 1985, genes, plant parts, plants, plant varieties, and processes for developing new varieties and hybrids have all been considered patentable under general patent law in the USA. During the 1980s the drive to patent plant material spread to other industrialized countries. In Japan, for example, the Patent Office granted patents on two plant varieties in the 1980s. A jurisdictional dispute in 1985, however, resulted in an agreement whereby plant varieties *per se* are to be protected under the Seed and Seedlings Law, while processes for developing these varieties can be patented.

In Europe there has been a storm of controversy concerning the patenting of genetically engineered plants and animals. The patent laws of European countries are national in origin and effect, but the laws became to a large extent harmonized under the European Patent Convention (EPC) of 1973. Patent applications can still be filed through national offices, but the majority currently go to the supranational European Patent Office (EPO) based in Munich. European patent laws are affected by EC measures which become national law or which harmonize national law in the member states if approved by the European Council.

The European Patent Convention, in force since 1977, states that patents cannot be granted on plants or animal varieties or essentially biological processes for the production of plants and animals; this does not apply to microbiological processes or the products thereof. Applying this ruling to biotechnology has posed problems, however. In 1989 the EPO examiners rejected a European Patent application for a transgenic mouse (a transgenic plant or animal is a plant or animal which contains a foreign gene) submitted by two Harvard Medical School scientists. The mouse, which has a cancer-causing gene or "oncogene" inserted into it, develops tumors within a few months of birth. This is very helpful to cancer researchers, and it had already received a patent in the

USA in 1988. The EPO rejected the patent on the grounds that it was an animal "variety". The EPO examiners were overruled in 1990 by the EPO appeals board. When the convention was written, "variety" could only have described animals produced by a breeding program; a recombinant DNA technology variety did not exist. The appeals board felt that the term was not meant to exclude all animals from patenting. With that decided, the next issue was one of morality. The examiners were asked to decide whether the mouse's suffering outweighed its potential benefit to medical research. In October 1991, the EPO decided in favor of cancer research, and that the mouse could be patented. At the same time, however, it gave a ruling against a French application for a mouse which had various genes for hair and wool added, rendering it a model system for research into hair growth. The creature's *raison d'être* was judged to be too trivial to be morally justifiable.

Furthermore, while the EPC states that "plant varieties" are not patentable, this does not necessarily mean that plant varieties are free of all patent rights. The EPO has considered that where the invention is applicable to modifying plants of any kind, the plants thus modified are of a higher classification than a "plant variety", and have granted patents on plants. However, what exactly constitutes a variety has been open to interpretation. For example, in 1990 the Belgian DBF Plant Genetic Systems (PGS) obtained a patent on a method to produce herbicide-resistant plants, which covered all plants and seed resulting from the method. Greenpeace opposed the patent, and during the dispute PGS withdrew six claims related to seeds and plants which had been granted in 1990. Then, in February 1995, the EPO's highest appeal board rejected the earlier decision by the EPO on the grounds that the examples provided by PGS were deemed to concern plant varieties.

Uncertainties concerning animal and plant patents continue. In 1988, the Directorate-General for Industrial Affairs (DG-III) of the Commission of the European Community submitted a proposal aimed at harmonizing and enlarging patent protection in biotechnology inventions in member states. In the draft directive on the Legal Protection of Biotechnological Inventions, plants and animals and the progeny of these plants and animals would be patentable subject matter. After years of heated debate, it was rejected in March 1995. The USA's first animal patent on the Harvard oncogenic mouse in 1988 resulted in broad public debate on various economic, social, governmental and ethical issues concerning the patenting of animals. Due to the controversy, the US government imposed a moratorium on the approval of animal patents until December 1992, and the issue remains contentious.

The debate on proprietary rights for living material is intense, and many legal and ethical issues remain to be resolved. The move to reinforce patent protection for biotechnological inventions has pitted chemical and biotechnology companies against plant breeders and animal farmers. It has also provoked a North–South debate on the issue of property rights to genetic resources.

Farmers' rights

Most of our crop plants evolved in the tropics, and most of their different varieties are still found there. Those varieties constitute the genetic repertoire available to the species. In developing new varieties, the plants used as the sources of genes have often been developed by small farmers in developing countries, who reap no reward. Thus, developing countries, in whose territories are to be found the bulk of *in situ* plant genetic resources, have expressed resentment against the notion that laboratory-created products of biotechnology should be the subject of property rights, while the genetic resources or raw materials of the process represent the fruit of the labor of generations of farmers in their countries, and are gathered freely without payment. Developing countries maintain that the rights of their farmers and plant-genetic conservationists should also be recognized. For this purpose, "farmers' rights" (not to be confused with "farmer's privilege", referred to in the previous section) have been proposed as a counterpart to patents and plant breeders' rights. International recognition of this right would imply a reward to farmers in developing countries for their efforts in producing and maintaining genetic diversity. They would receive compensatory payment for the traditional farming of varieties that peasant farmers have selected, characterized and bred, thus conserving and improving wild plants and local varieties. The concrete legal mechanisms and procedures for putting the "farmers' rights" concept into practice is an ongoing debate.[8] Western powers have taken a cautious attitude towards this concept.

The international dimension and GATT

In developing countries protection for intellectual property is usually limited, particularly for food and medicine. India, for example, forbids the patenting of agriculture or horticulture; any process for the medicinal, surgical, curative, prophylactic or other treatment of human beings; or any process for the similar treatment of animals or plants to render them free of disease or to increase their economic value or that of their products; or any substance intended for use, or capable of being used, as food, medicine or drug. Furthermore, "medicine or drug" includes insecticides, fungicides, herbicides and all other substances intended to be used for the protection of plants.[9] Similarly, in Brazil, patents are not allowed on products or processes for production of foodstuffs, or chemical/pharmaceutical substances.[10]

Such laws illustrate a general pattern in developing countries. The rationale for these patent exclusions is that food and medicine are too vital, are "basic needs", and people in developing countries should not be vulnerable to the monopoly pricing associated with patents.

Industrialized countries (particularly the USA) have been arguing that their goods should have the same protection in the developing world as they do elsewhere. They are prepared to press hard for protection where "piracy" is possible. For example, the USA ordered trade sanctions against Brazil in 1988 for that country's refusal to provide patent protection to US pharmaceutical and chemical manufacturers. The US contended that Brazil was permitting unauthorized copying of pharmaceutical products and processes that were invented by US firms. The sanctions, which involved imposing punitive tariffs on selected Brazilian imports at an aggregate value of US$200 million were the response to a petition under Section 301 of the Trade Act, filed by the US Pharmaceutical Manufacturers' Association (PMA). The PMA said that Brazil's refusal to respect patents had cost American pharmaceutical manufacturers $160 million in lost sales since 1979.[11]

In 1991 Brazil drafted changes in its patent laws, calling for patent protection for pharmaceutical products and processes as well as for biotechnological products. In June 1990, two days after Brazil announced that it would give patent protection to both pharmaceutical products and processes, the USA lifted its retaliatory tariffs on Brazilian imports.[12] Similarly, a US threat to impose trade sanctions against Chile led that country to pass a law in 1990 recognizing pharmaceutical patents.[13]

More generally, intellectual property protection was one of the major issues at the Uruguay Round of multilateral trade negotiations, launched in 1986 under the auspices of the General Agreement on Tariffs and Trade (GATT). The issue was discussed in the negotiating group of

Trade-Related Aspects of Intellectual Property (TRIPS), one of the key fifteen negotiating groups in the Uruguay Round.

The industrialized countries advocated a harmonization and strengthening of intellectual property rights, including reduction in the scope of exclusions for patents, expanding their duration, and abolishing compulsory licensing.[14] Developing countries argued that this would greatly increase the royalties paid to Western multinational companies, strengthen their monopoly power, and curb the development of local Third World technology. Developed countries countered by claiming that stronger protection would boost foreign investment and technology transfer by reducing companies' fear of theft of knowledge and processes resulting from the fruit of their research and expenditure.

The result of the TRIPS negotiations was a 34-page draft of December 1991, encompassing all forms of intellectual property, that was intended to strengthen and harmonize standards of protection and provide for effective enforcement at national and international levels. Among the main features is the protection of patents for twenty years, regardless of place of invention or whether products are imported or produced locally. The main permitted exclusions would relate to animal and plant inventions and biotechnological processes for their production. However, the exclusion does not apply to medical products and processes derived from biotechnology, although there is a temporary exemption (see below). There would be strict limits on compulsory licensing of patented products by governments, now used for pharmaceuticals in both industrialized and developing countries.

These rules would have to be implemented in national legislation by the 102 member countries of GATT, observing the basic fair-trade precepts of national treatment (equal treatment for domestic and foreign right-holders) and non-discrimination between trading partners. A council on TRIPS would supervise operation of the accord, along with GATT and the envisaged General Agreement on Trade in Services under the umbrella of the proposed Multilateral Trade Organization (MTO).

Although the TRIPS council would be separate from GATT, intellectual property disputes would be subject to the MTO's integrated disputes-settlement machinery. In principle, therefore, countries could find themselves subject to reprisals on goods traded for breaches of the intellectual property accords. On the other hand, the GATT accord would require all signatories to abide by the MTO's disputes procedures, which would curb, for example, recourse by the USA to the "Section 301" provisions of its Trade Act to secure concessions.

The very poorest countries, defined by the UN as "least developed", such as Burundi and Bangladesh, have an extra ten years or more to implement the accord, according to the December 1991 draft. Most developing countries, such as India and Thailand, have been given five years to effect implementation, and the industrialized nations one year. In areas like pharmaceuticals where no patent protection exists (presumably including biotechnology drugs), developing countries (presumably including India and Thailand) have ten years to put legislation into effect.[15] In December 1993, the Uruguay Round successfully concluded, and the TRIPS draft began to be translated effectively into national law of GATT member states. The MTO was launched in January 1995.

Notes

1. US Congress, 1984, p. 385; ICDA, 1989, p. 7.
2. US Congress, 1988b, p. 182.
3. *Ibid.*; US Congress, 1984, p. 387.
4. The disputes described in this section are discussed in: Baum, 1987; *The Economist* 1988a; *The Economist*, 1987c; Gladwell, 1988b; Rundle, 1991; and Sugawara, 1991.
5. *New York Times*, 1987a, p. D5.
6. Sugawara, 1991, p. H7; US Congress, 1991, p. 223. Disputes over patent rights have continued unabated. For example, in 1995 a dispute started between Schering and Biogen over beta interferon – the first drug available to treat multiple sclerosis, worth 323 million Deutschmarks in US sales in 1994. Biogen inserts the gene into Chinese hamster ovary cells, and Schering into bacteria: each company claims that its process patent covers its adversary's production process.
7. Information for this section was derived from: ACOST 1990, p. 3; Mackenzie, 1991; UNCTAD, 1991; Watts, 1991; Van Wijk, 1990, 1995; Andrews, 1993, p. A1; Bisbee, 1995.
8. UNCTAD, 1991, pp. 16–17; Mackenzie, 1991; RAFI, 1994; Ten Kate, 1995; Sanchéz and Juma, 1994.
9. Evenson and Putman, 1990, p. 337.
10. Van Wijk, 1991.
11. Roberts, 1988; Auerbach, 1988.
12. Van Wijk, 1991.
13. Durr, 1990.
14. Under compulsory licensing, the government requires the patent-holder to license her/his product or process to a domestic producer, often at a royalty rate determined by the government.
15. Williams, 1992.

Annex 2

DNA Hybridization Probe Technology and PCR

DNA hybridization probe technology relies on detecting the actual DNA of a disease-producing organism. To understand how a gene probe works and what it is, a brief comment on the structure of DNA as well as hybridization is necessary.

DNA structure

The DNA molecule consists in part of an invariant "backbone" made up of two coiled strands of repeating sugar (deoxyribose) phosphate components. These two strands are in a double helix shape, much like a spiral staircase. Each sugar has attached to it one of four chemical bases. These four bases – adenine (A), guanine (G), cytosine (C) and thymine (T) – in certain combinations form bridges across and linking the two backbones, analogous to the stairs of a spiral staircase. The chemical structure of the four bases is such that an A must pair with a T, in either order (A–T or T–A); and a C must pair with a G, in either order. The partner base pairs are referred to as "complementary" base pairs, and the strands of the DNA molecule as "complementary" strands. Thus, given a sequence of bases on one strand of a DNA molecule, for example A–T–A–C–G–T, one can deduce the complementary sequence, in this example T–A–T–G–C–A, which must be attached to the other strand of the DNA molecule.

DNA hybridization

If the DNA molecule is exposed to near boiling temperatures, it will "unzip" – by breaking the bonds between the base pairs – and the DNA molecule will change from its double stranded normal state to two single strands. This process is referred to as denaturation. If the complementary strands are subsequently exposed to cooler temperatures, the single strands will bind together again, or renature, through their complementary base pairs. This reforming of the native double-stranded DNA is also referred to as hybridization. The separate DNA strands must have exact or nearly exact complementary base sequences for hybridization to occur; thus a given DNA strand can hybridize only with its corresponding complementary strand.

Probes in research

DNA hybridization is a powerful tool in molecular biology. Radioactive phosphorous is usually incorporated into one of the DNA strands, which is the "probe" that enables the hybridization process to be visualized, using the radioactive label, with x-ray film. DNA hybridization is used, for example, to select and isolate for further study particular DNA sequences from an entire genome, and also to determine where certain base sequences are located on chromosomes. Labeled single stranded DNA probes have been instrumental in helping to uncover what is known about how, when and where organisms translate genetic base sequences into proteins.

Probes as diagnostics: problems encountered

Apart from the usefulness of these methods in understanding genetic structure and function, DNA probes are used for diagnosis in clinical medicine. Scientists are able to isolate and reproduce (clone) characteristic DNA segments from a known pathogenic organism, label the DNA radioactively and then denature the DNA from its normal double-stranded state to a single-stranded state; this labeled single-stranded DNA from a known pathogen is what constitutes the gene probe. A sample of body fluid for which one wants to detect the presence of the pathogen is then exposed to denaturing conditions. Finally, the probe (containing single-stranded DNA) and the sample (containing single-stranded DNA) are exposed to renaturing conditions. The presence of the pathogen is then determined by whether or not the labeled probe and sample DNA will hybridize together to form the stable double-stranded DNA; hybridization can only occur if the probe has base pairs complementary to the DNA contained in the sample. After washing the reaction to flush out unbound, non-hybridized DNA, hybridization can be detected by radioactivity emitted from the labeled probe DNA, complementarily bound to the pathogenic DNA. If hybridization takes place, it means that the pathogen is present in the patient's sample.

Through most of the 1980s, however, obstacles remained which confined DNA probe technology to research laboratories, preventing their use as diagnostics in hospital and independent clinical laboratories, where methodologies must be streamlined for general use, and where much larger markets exist.

To be useful in a hospital, a test must be quick, easy and safe to perform; it must be sensitive enough to detect fewer organisms than cause a disease; and it must be specific – that is, avoid false positives. DNA probes are highly specific, as each pathogen has its own unique genetic material. However, even by the turn of the 1990s the technology was still in its infancy as a practical diagnostic application.[1]

Tests were complicated to run, frequently requiring tedious sample preparation, numerous wash steps and long incubation times (up to several days); they were difficult to automate and needed x-ray film to read the final result. Furthermore, the radioactive phosphorous employed in most of the tests as labels was expensive and raised safety problems, rendering them inconvenient to handle and dispose of. Also, since radioactive phosphorous loses its radioactive strength rapidly, it was practical to label only only small batches of probes with radioactivity at any given time, thereby complicating the manufacturing process.[2]

Strategies to overcome problems

By the latter part of the 1980s, however, strategies began to emerge to overcome these obstacles that prevented more widespread use of DNA probes as diagnostics in clinical laboratories. Molecular biologists began to develop different, non-radioactive labeling methods. These included, for example, identifying hybridization (of the probe with the pathogenic DNA) by color changes or the generation of visible glows (luminescence), a technique employed in immunoassays. These types of tests could produce results in several hours.[3] However, these labeling methods were often less sensitive than radioactive labels, and methods were devised to overcome this problem.

Polymerase chain reaction to increase probe sensitivity

One approach to making DNA probe tests more sensitive involves using the polymerase chain reaction (PCR), initially devised in the mid-

1980s and by the early 1990s hailed as one of the most important advances in molecular genetics since genetic engineering.[4] It is being applied in many areas of molecular genetic research[5] and has unleashed new opportunities for diagnosis using DNA probes.

PCR is a technique whereby a specified DNA sequence of interest is reproduced exponentially. It involves the use of two DNA probes, which bracket or flank the ends of the DNA of interest – the "target" DNA – adding the enzyme DNA polymerase and the four chemical bases constituting DNA, namely A, C, T and G. The reaction mixture is then exposed to denaturation and renaturation temperature conditions. This constitutes one "cycle", whose duration averages eight minutes[6] and results in a doubling of the amount of target DNA initially present. The cycle is repeated a number of times, depending on how much DNA one wants to reproduce. After n cycles 2^n molecules will be reproduced; after twenty cycles there will be over one million molecules of targeted DNA from one original DNA molecule. In the late 1980s, the raising and lowering of temperature in the PCR process became automated.

The significance of PCR in conjunction with DNA probes for diagnosis

For diagnosis it is important to note that the specific DNA sequence that is exponentially reproduced by PCR is determined by the flanking DNA probes, made specifically to be complementary to the base sequences flanking the target DNA; under proper conditions, only the DNA that lies between the bracketing probes is reproduced. Thus, if one was trying to detect a virus in a blood sample, for example, the probes would be made specific to the viral DNA; and only if the virus was present in the sample would the viral DNA be exponentially reproduced.

The significance of PCR used in conjunction with DNA probes is that it permits an unprecedented degree of sensitivity in diagnosis. For example, some leukemic and lymphomic cancers arise from a piece of one chromosome being switched and exchanged (that is, translocated) with a piece of another chromosome that involves known genes. Follicular lymphoma, for instance, results from a translocation between chromosomes fourteen and eighteen (humans possess twenty-three pairs of chromosomes). Conventional analysis of these cancer cells permitted detection if the translocations were present at concentrations of one in one hundred normal cells, so that a patient judged cancer-free could still harbor significant numbers of cancer cells. In contrast, probes in conjunction with PCR are capable of detecting as few as one cancer cell in one million normal cells, thus providing a test up to 10,000 times as sensitive to the oncologist.[7]

Problems encountered with PCR

PCR is not, however, fail-safe. "It's a great technology, with lots of potential. But if you get sloppy and don't take certain precautions, you get false positives everywhere", states J. Richards, director of business development at the US DBF Gene-Trak Systems (Framingham, Massachusetts).[8] An unforseen and unwelcome corollary of the extraordinary amplification power of PCR is that minor contamination of the starting materials can lead to serious consequences, with unwanted, untargeted DNA being reproduced. This can also occur as a result of the probe annealing to DNA sequences that differ slightly from the target sequences. As materials from one cycle are reused in subsequent cycles, one ends up with both unwanted and targeted DNA being reproduced, leading to as much as a 30 per cent rate of false positive readings.[9] Methods are being developed, however, to counteract these problems and new amplification techniques are also emerging.[10]

Some researchers have also expressed concern about some of the practical implications of PCR's ability to detect the presence of disease-bearing genes long before symptoms appear. Although this quality is clearly advantageous in many circumstances, PCR might amplify the DNA of microorganisms present at subclinical levels, leading to an incorrect diagnosis of active infection. For example, some yeast cells are usually present in the female reproductive tract. Only when they become unusually prevalent do symptoms of a yeast infection appear which warrant and necessitate pharmaceutical intervention.[11] As Dr R. Yolkon of the Johns Hopkins Hospital (Maryland) pediatrics department observes, "The key question is what are we going to do with all this increased sensitivity? Will we diagnose more people who are sick, or will we find out that everyone is carrying small amounts of virus and [actually] do more harm than good?"[12] The two major areas for which diagnostic probes are being developed are infectious and genetic diseases.

Probes for human infectious diseases

Several probes that identify and differentiate among species of bacteria that cause diarrheal diseases and different strains of human papilloma viruses – linked to genital warts and cervical cancer – have already been developed. Other infectious diseases for which probes have been developed include the herpes virus, the bacteria which cause tuberculosis, and the commonly sexually transmitted infection chlamydia.[13] PCR and other DNA amplification techniques being developed promise to make these probe tests even more sensitive and hence increase their utility as a diagnostic.[14]

Once the glitches in using DNA probes and PCR (and other DNA amplification technologies) described previously are overcome, probe diagnostics will likely begin to compete with immunoassays, which use monoclonal antibodies for diagnosis of infectious diseases. Ultimately, the relative strengths of each will have to be assessed on an individual product per disease basis. In some cases, however, the two types of assay can provide complementary information. A notable example occurs in AIDS testing, where an ELISA (enzyme-linked immunoabsorbent assay) can provide data on a patient's immune state, indicating the extent of damage being done to a person's immune system, while a DNA probe that binds to the human immunodeficiency virus (HIV) can determine whether and to what extent the viral genome is present.[15]

Probes for infectious diseases in agriculture

DNA probe tests in combination with PCR also show promise in the diagnosis of infectious diseases occurring in plants and animals. The first such probe test kit, to be used in conjunction with PCR, approved in the USA in the early 1990s was for detection of *Mycobacterium paratuberculosis* (Johne's disease), an acute gastrointestinal disease in cattle. Prior to the test, the disease could be diagnosed only by culturing the suspect sample in the laboratory and waiting the required ten to fourteen weeks for the test results. During that period, cattle who were infected would often lose weight, produce less milk and become increasingly ill. The PCR-probe test yields results in two days, thereby providing a substantial improvement in diagnosis.[16]

Probes for genetic diseases

The second major thrust of DNA probe use in diagnosis is that for genetic or inherited diseases. There are some 3,500–4,000 inherited diseases, such as sickle cell anemia, which are known to be caused by mutations in a single gene (although the same gene can be mutated in different ways in different people). Most of these diseases are extremely rare. However, some genetic diseases are more common: for example, the most prevalent genetic disease amongst Caucasians is cystic fibrosis, where the proportion of carriers in affected populations is between 1 in 20 and 1 in 30,[17] resulting in about 1 in 2,500 newborn Caucasians in the USA suffering from the disease;[18] in sub-Saharan Africa between 1 and 2 per cent of all infants are born with sickle cell disease, and the vast majority die in their first two years from anemia or infections.[19]

With advances in molecular biology and gene amplification techniques, the ability to locate and analyze those single genes that, if defective, can cause a genetic disease increased greatly, particularly since the end of the 1980s. This has resulted in new diagnostic tests becoming available, based on gene probes which detect the defective gene. The principal users of much of the new testing are pregnant women and other family members who are concerned about the future health of unborn children.[20]

To understand the notion of symptomless carrier parents being able to produce a child with full-blown disease, and hence the need for and use of genetic and prenatal testing, a few concepts must be explained. Virtually all the cells in the human body contain forty-six DNA-containing chromosomes. The only exceptions are sperm and egg cells, which contain half that number (non-sex chromosomes are called autosomes). Each individual will have inherited twenty-three of their chromosomes from their mother (via an egg cell) and twenty-three from their father (via a sperm cell), or twenty-three pairs of chromosomes. Thus, all the genes on chromosomes come in two versions, one inherited from each parent.

In a few cases, a single abnormal gene from one parent is sufficient to cause disease, and the gene is said to be dominant, the disease autosomal dominant. Much more frequently in genetic diseases, a child must inherit a defective gene from both parents in order for the disease to manifest itself. In this case the genes involved are termed recessive, the disorder autosomal recessive. Healthy, symptomless persons who have just one defective recessive gene are called carriers. They do not suffer from the disease but could pass it on to their children.

Such diseases as thalassemia, sickle cell anemia, cystic fibrosis and phenylketonuria are examples of autosomal recessive diseases which can be transmitted by symptomless carriers who inherited the trait from their parents. The mutant genes for autosomal recessive diseases may be quite common in the population. It has been estimated that, in Africa and Asia, between 1 and 25 per cent of most populations are carriers of one of these disorders.[21] If a carrier and a noncarrier have children, some of the children will be carriers, some not, but none will have the disease. However, if both parents are carriers, on average one in four of their children will inherit the defective gene from each of the parents, which will result in the child having the full-blown disease; or, put another way, there is a one-in-four chance that a child of parents who are both carriers will be affected by the disease in question; and there is a one-in-two chance that the child will be a carrier of the disease.

In the case of single-gene-inherited diseases, once the causative defective gene giving rise to the diseases has been identified, diagnostic tests based on gene probes and DNA amplification procedures can be and have been developed to test carriers (prospective parents, from blood samples) and to perform prenatal diagnosis to detect the disease in fetal cells. The genes responsible for a variety of single-gene diseases are known, including those for cystic fibrosis, Duchenne's muscular dystrophy, sickle cell anemia, Lesch-Nyhan's syndrome, hemophilia and fragile X syndrome (the most common cause of mental retardation in the USA, affecting 1 in 2,500 newborn males and 1 in 2,000 newborn females).[22] However, the vast majority of diseases caused by a defect in a single gene cannot be diagnosed with gene probes because scientists have not yet determined which gene (if defective) gives rise to the disease; thus gene probes cannot be made for the defective gene. In such cases researchers may draw on other approaches based on genetic linkage.

Linkage analysis

Researchers have known since the early 1900s that certain genes tend to be inherited as a group. These genes are said to be "linked", as they are physically close to each other on a chromosome. If scientists cannot locate the disease-causing gene in families known to harbor an inherited disease, then one of the things they can do is find a gene that is linked to it, and which can be located. Such neighboring genes can be used as "markers" to look for the presence or absence of the gene the researchers wish to study. Linkage is determined by relying on family studies to trace the inheritance of the marker and faulty gene through several generations. A marker must be polymorphic; that is, it must exist in different forms so that the chromosome carrying the mutant gene can be distinguished from the chromosome with the normal gene, by the form of the marker it also carries. Until recently, however, few marker genes for genetic diseases had been found. This situation changed dramatically with the discovery of restriction fragment length polymorphisms (RFLPs).

Restriction fragment length polymorphisms as markers for linkage analysis

To understand the term "restriction fragment length polymorphism", one first needs to know what restriction enzymes are. Restriction enzymes are naturally occurring enzymes from bacteria which act like molecular scissors and chop the long strands of DNA into smaller fragments. Each kind of restriction enzyme (there are hundreds) recognizes a particular and different sequence of between four and six bases and cuts the DNA at precisely these points. For example, the restriction enzyme called Bg/II cuts DNA at the following specific sequence, to yield fragments as shown:[23]

```
... A ↓ G A T C   T ...  ⇒  ... A              G A T C T ...
... T   C T A G ↓ A ...      ... T C T A G           A ...
```

These sequences will occur at various points throughout the DNA, yielding smaller fragments of DNA of varying sizes, depending on how many bases intervene before the next sequence the enzyme recognizes appears on the DNA. It has been discovered that there are regions of our DNA which do not code for proteins and which can contain harmless base pair changes. Although the base changes are innocuous, they may occur within the base sequence that the restriction enzyme recognizes, so that the enzyme will no longer cut the DNA at that site; alternatively, the base change could have the effect of creating a new cutting site along the DNA strand. For example, in the figure above showing where the restriction enzyme Bg/II cuts, if the base pair G–C was substituted for the first A–T base pair, Bg/II would no longer cut the DNA strand at the site shown (and would cut the DNA at the site it next encountered along the DNA containing the specified base sequence). When this occurs, different sized DNA fragments are produced upon exposure to the enzyme (compared to when no base pair change occurred at the restriction enzyme cutting site), and the site where a base change occurs which alters a restriction enzyme cutting site is called a restriction fragment length polymorphism (RFLP).

The RFLP is inherited just like any other gene. When a given restriction enzyme site is present on the chromosome inherited from one parent but absent from the paired chromosome inherited from the other parent, a shorter fragment is produced from the chromosome with the site, and a longer fragment from the chromosome without the site, when the chromosomes are exposed to the restriction enzyme. It is now possible to distinguish the two chromosomes in such an individual on the basis of this RFLP. Probes can easily be made to the RFLPs, and the individual chromosomes can be followed as they pass from generation to generation by tracing, with probes, the inheritance of the marker fragments (extremely old DNA samples can be tested without posing any special difficulties); and, indirectly, the gene which if defective causes disease can also be followed, as the location of that gene is linked (close to) the marker. By 1992, the combination of probes to known defective genes and linkage analysis using probes with RFLPs, sometimes with PCR or other gene amplification techniques, could be used to detect symptomless carriers or for prenatal screening for over two hundred inherited diseases.[24] This combination of analysis is also an integral part of the "DNA fingerprinting" used in paternity testing and in forensic science to help determine the identity of the perpetrator of a crime among several suspected persons.[25]

Problems with DNA-based tests for widespread use in diagnosis of genetic diseases

The combination of genetic probes and linkage analysis (with or without gene amplification techniques) falls under the heading of DNA-based tests. The carrying out of these tests requires specialized training and the ability to perform complex procedures. Furthermore, researchers are finding that the specific nature of a test must be tailored to the peculiarities of the gene involved. "Variety and nongeneralizability about gene structure and mutational patterns seem to be the rule in going from analysis of one human genetic disorder to another,"[26] so that these tests are unsuitable for routine application. Moreover, the tests are not 100 per cent accurate and are costly.[27] If and when these tests achieve widespread use remains a matter of speculation.

The difficulty with diagnosis of polygenic and multifactorial disorders by DNA-based tests

The most common diseases that afflict us are not single gene disorders; rather, they result either from mutations in any of a number of different genes (polygenic disorders) or the interactions of environmental factors with multiple genes (multifactorial disorders). Coronary heart disease, autoimmune disease, Alzheimer's, alcoholism and psychiatric illness are all examples of multifactorial diseases. This group of disorders is extremely difficult to analyze because of the complexity of factors involved. Neverthleless, as more and more genes are located on the human genome, the outcome may be the development of predictive tests for polygenic and multifactorial disorders, although variable environmental factors will confound the predictive power of tests for the latter group of disorders.[28]

While DNA-probe-based tests hold much promise for the future, by the beginning of the 1990s glitches preventing their widespread routine use in laboratories were only just being overcome – by mid-1992, it is doubtful if even 5 per cent of US diagnostic laboratories were using these tests;[29] in other countries the proportion would be even less. Based on the experience of industrialized countries thus far, probe diagnostics does not appear suitable as a field of entry for biotechnology development in developing countries, in marked contrast to monoclonal antibody-based diagnostics.

Notes

1. Hoffman and Rosenberg, 1992, p. 9.
2. Fahrlander and Klausner, 1988, p. 1165; Baines, 1989, p. 49; US Congress, 1984, p. 148; Hoffman and Rosenberg, 1992, p. 9.
3. Andrews, 1990; Fahrlander and Klausner, 1988, p. 1167; Baines, 1989, p. 50.
4. Cookson and Lynch, 1992.
5. See, for example, Watson et al., 1992, ch. 6.
6. *Ibid.,* p. 82.
7. Chase, 1991b; and Watson et al., 1992, p. 89.
8. Lewis, 1990, p. 54.
9. Chase, 1991b; Watson et. al., 1992, p. 95.
10. Lewis, 1990, p. 54, Chase, 1991b; Watson et. al., 1992.
11. Lewis, 1990.
12. Chase, 1991b.
13. Klausner, 1988; *Genetic Engineering and Biotechnology Monitor,* September 1990;

Enzo Biochem Inc., 1991a and 1992; US Congress, 1984, p. 84.
14. Lewis, 1992; Watson et. al., 1992, p. 90; Chase, 1991b.
15. Fahrlander and Klausner, 1988, pp. 1165–6.
16. Fox, 1992, p. 7.
17. Dodge, 1988, p. 17.
18. Glaser, 1992, p. 20.
19. Bulyzhenkov and Modell, 1988, p. 20.
20. Fox and van Brunt, 1990, p. 903.
21. Bulyzhenkov and Modell, 1988, p. 21.
22. Glaser, 1992, p. 20.
23. Watson et al., 1992, p. 519.
24. *Ibid.,* p. 539.
25. Neufeld and Colman, 1990, pp. 20, 22; Lowry and Wells, 1991.
26. Fox and van Brunt, 1990, p. 904.
27. For example, a test to identify couples who carry the cystic fibrosis defective gene costs on average $170 per test and enables detection of 85–95 per cent of carriers. Stevens, 1992, p. 84; Glaser, 1992, p. 20.
28. Watson et al., 1992, pp. 532–3.
29. Hoffman and Rosenberg, 1992, p. 9. Firm figures for later years are not available. However, in 1994 the DNA testing market for inherited diseases in the USA was a modest $8 million, although it is regarded as a fledgling industry poised to take off. Industry analysts foresee a $500 million market for genetic testing in the next decade (Brownlee et al., 1994, p. 65).

Annex 3

Applying Biotechnology to Agriculture in Developing Countries: Summary

The present situation

The slow application of biotechnology in the agriculture of developed countries, discussed in Chapter 2, was accompanied by an even less satisfactory performance in developing countries, although for different reasons. According to many observers, including World Bank consultants, agricultural biotechnology in the early 1990s is essentially a commercial industry dominated by private companies operating for profit. Given the large front-end costs of such biotechnology research, industrialized countries provide the only profitable markets, at present, for agricultural biotechnology. Consequently, the focus of current research efforts centers on the crops and livestock of the temperate zones. Some trickle-down of biotechnology to the technical problems of developing countries will occur; but, in the absence of major new initiatives, its impact on these problems is likely to be small.[1]

> In 1990 the leading 30 American agrochemical, animal health and agricultural biotechnology companies spent nearly $400 million on food research and development, but only one-tenth as much on food problems in the developing world... Let's admit that the primary beneficiary of biotechnology research and development is not the developing world but the food industry, which badly needs products that can compete in today's fiercely competitive food marketing system.[2]

A United Nations Conference on Trade and Development (UNCTAD) 1991 study on the trade and development aspects of agricultural bio-technology concurs, with this view: "A vastly larger effort [than the present one] will be required of developing countries and the inter-national community on ... crops before biotechnology can be expected to come even close to achieving its potential in raising the productivity of agriculture."[3]

One important factor in the slow progress of agricultural applications in developing countries has been stagnation and decline in agricultural research. Faced with mounting national debts and severe budget constraints, many countries have found it increasingly difficult to maintain the level of investment in agricultural research precisely at a time when research budgets should be increasing.[4] Slowdown in research notwithstanding, several countries in Latin America have developed excellent undergraduate and graduate programs in the biological sciences. As the crisis continues, and no meaningful employment is available for students within their own countries, the likelihood of their migration to the USA will be stronger in the years ahead.[5]

The widening North–South gap

Mr Barker, a World Bank consultant, has drawn attention to the danger of a widening gap in technological progress opening up between the North and the South under present circumstances:

> New biotechnologies appear to offer a wide range of potential benefits to the developing countries. However, because these technologies are knowledge-intensive and location-specific, a considerable amount of investment will be needed to facilitate technology transfer to the developing countries. Although the private sector will play an increasingly important role, much of this investment must be made by the public sector if benefits are to be widely distributed across societies. Although in absolute terms the benefits of biotechnology will extend broadly, it seems almost inevitable that the gap in technological progress will widen not only between the industrialised and developing countries, but also between the more technologically advanced and the less technologically advanced countries in the Third World.[6]

Professor Junne has indicated another aspect of the danger of a widening gap, to which the application of biotechnology may contribute: the possibility of an early concentration of technological efforts on export commodities, mainly produced by developing countries, leading to excessive supply, declining prices and an associated deterioration in the terms of trade.[7] This possibility seems likely to be realized in the case of cocoa. According to UNCTAD's 1991 study,

> the importance of *cacao* for both the food and the specialty chemicals industry makes it one of the crops targeted by developed market-economy research

efforts... The single most important research programme aiming at the clonal propagation of high-yield plants is probably that of Pennsylvania State University in the US, supported by the American Cocoa Research Institute and the Chocolate Manufacturers' Association of the United States. Similar research is also pursued in other industrialised countries. Moreover, several exporting countries, such as the Cote d'Ivoire, Ghana and Costa Rica are also undertaking research on cacao plant improvement.[8]

In fact, the world cocoa economy was barely emerging from a crisis of overproduction, resulting from excessive investment in cocoa growing, partly financed from external sources. World production of cocoa grew by 10 per cent a year through the latter part of the 1980s, an increase mainly due to a massive planting of high-yielding varieties in the 1970s, when prices were up. This production explosion meant that prices fell from 1984 to 1988 by 50 per cent and since then by a further 18 per cent in 1989.[9] If the proposed biotechnology "solutions" (for instance, the development and application of micropropagation) prove fruitful, average yields could even go up from the current 500–1,000 kg/ha to an average of 3,400 kg/ha, leading to a new drop in prices.[10]

Policy suggestions

The World Bank and its consultants have made three proposals as to how to cope with the lags in agricultural applications of biotechnology in developing countries:

1. Establish a special biotechnology research program for commodities of interest only to developing countries – "orphan" commodities.

2. Involve the major agro-biotechnology companies of the industrialized countries in identifying and implementing biotechnology applications through investment in the more advanced developing countries (about ten in total), with the assistance of loans from the World Bank and other development lenders.

3. Encourage other less advanced developing countries to concentrate on upgrading the teaching of biological sciences and strengthening more traditional biological research, for example, plant breeding as a necessary prerequisite for the use of bio-technology (a World Bank proposal); and grant support, donated by developed countries or international agencies, which would be used by agro-biotechnology companies of the industrialized countries to develop, on contract,

biotechnology products for these less advanced countries (consultants proposal).

One can only support the "orphan" commodities program proposal, which reads:

> The poorer countries need grant funds to finance innovative collaborative research programs. To meet this need research consortia involving several donor countries and agencies would be established to promote research on the specific problems of the "orphan commodities" which are important only in the Developing World and which are largely ignored in the biotechnology programs financed in industrialized countries.[11]

No specific commodity coverage of the "orphan" group is given in the Bank paper; one of the Bank's consultants lists, as examples, cassava and banana/plantain;[12] another, cassava, sorghum, millet, grain legumes (especially pigeon peas and cowpeas) and plantain.[13]

Concerning proposals (1) and (2), the expectation that private agro-biotechnology companies will play a major role in biotechnology agricultural development in developing countries, either as private investors under patent protection in more advanced countries or on grant-supported contract in less advanced countries, will have to prove its worth in specific cases. Two problems can be anticipated:

1. The specificity of problems in individual developing countries may be such as to reduce much of the comparative advantage that the industrialized country companies may have acquired under their domestic climatic soil, diet, market and other conditions. For example, the OECD's Development Center biotechnology study on maize, covering Brazil, Indonesia, Mexico and Thailand, arrived at the conclusion that

> evidence from the country studies highlights the complexity and magnitude of the task of providing genetically improved maize varieties and high-quality seed for a diversity of production and agro-ecological conditions. Not only are production conditions more heterogenous and less standardized than those of industrialized country producers; a large share of cultivation is in rainfed areas, [and] on small holdings, so that a variety which performs well in one location may perform poorly nearby.[14]

Furthermore, and perhaps even more significant:

> The emphasis on quality modification and on varieties conforming to very specific quality and nutritional specifications which characterize the new

biotechnologies, is a response to preoccupations and to production and market conditions where product differentiation is increasingly important. In contrast, in developing countries yield-enhancement and broad adaptability are the major objectives of research.[15]

Finally, it is unlikely that private interests would meet the technology needs of all producers in any of the four countries. The OECD report concludes:

> In all cases, there are particular problem areas either for research or technology diffusion where there are no obvious short-term profits to be made, but where the government has a particular responsibility. These include, for example, the characterization of local genetic resources and the diffusion of improved seed to small-scale subsistence farmers. There is a continuing need for public research effort and for government intervention in the maize system.[16]

2. Company research in the developed countries may prove extremely costly. This has certainly proven to be the case in medical research (see Chapter 5), and there are signs that high costs are encountered in agriculture. According to a 1991 report, "Latin American nations are debating whether to spend more money on biotechnology research to enhance agriculture or boost harvests by more traditional means."[17] Referring to patent protection, an UNCTAD study notes that

> large plant protection firms which have already acquired a substantial inventory of original genetic lines would be able to secure a dominant market position at the expense of more numerous and less powerful seed companies. What this would do to biotechnological innovation in general is not clear. However, the higher returns to companies in the sector could be translated into higher costs to users of the innovations, especially developing countries not linked to R&D networks, and to farmers who could be paying more for seed.[18]

If, on examination of the specific offers of agricultural biotechnology development on the part of private international companies to individual developing countries or country groups, it is found that this route has limited scope, then the solution will have to be sought in expanding public research and development, financed partly domestically and partly from abroad, on terms that are as "soft" as possible, and hiring the needed expertise where it can be found. In cases where such "soft" foreign financing is extended, it may be accompanied by the condition that a country which benefits from it must share the results of research with neighboring low-income countries.[19]

As described in Chapter 2, there has been widespread consumer resistance in developed countries to new foods produced by genetic engineering. The extent to which this would occur in developing countries is not known. On the one hand, there is a tremendous need and demand for additional food in many developing countries. On the other hand, people adhering to religious dietary laws, for example, may be averse to fish, fowl, fruit or grain that has been transformed by a gene that produces an animal protein. (This would also apply in the case of such people in industrialized countries.) Thus cultural, religious, ethical and other reasons for consumer resistance may operate to curb demand for new bioengineered foods. Short of an extensive survey of consumer attitudes in developing countries, an examination of consumer acceptability of new food technologies introduced in the past in selected developing countries with large markets might shed light on possible consumer reaction to new bioengineered foods.

Notes

1. Bromby et al., 1990, pp. 432–3; Ellis, 1992.
2. Nestle, 1992.
3. UNCTAD, 1991, p. 24.
4. Barker, 1990, p. 304. For the overall public-finance situation in developing countries in the 1980s, see Chapter 7.
5. Orrego, 1989, p. 49.
6. Barker, 1990, p. 304.
7. Junne, 1987, p. 87.
8. UNCTAD, 1991, p. 24.
9. In the last quarter of 1989, the price was driven below US$l,000/ton. At its peak in 1977, the price was $5,467/ton.
10. *Biotechnology and Development Monitor*, June 1991, p. 21.
11. World Bank, 1991a, p. ix.
12. Persley, 1990, p. 442.
13. Barker, 1990, p. 304.
14. Brenner, 1990, p. 2.
15. *Ibid.*, p. 3.
16. *Ibid.*, p. 4.
17. As reported in UNIDO's *Genetic Engineering and Biotechnology Monitor*, December 1991, p. 6. The US agricultural TNC Monsanto is reported to have spent a hefty $500 million to develop its highly contoversial genetically engineered milk-yield-enhancing hormone, BST, which increases milk production in dairy cows by 10–25 per cent (Maitland, 1994).
18. UNCTAD, 1991, p. 18.
19. Buttel, 1990, p. 320.

Annex 4

Subunit and Anti-id Vaccines

Subunit vaccines

Prior to the advent of new biotechnology, most vaccines consisted of organisms (or closely related organisms) that cause the disease that the vaccine is supposed to prevent. The pathogens would be grown in cell culture in the laboratory and would then either be attenuated – that is, weakened by various means such that they would remain infectious enough to stimulate immunity without causing the disease – or killed (inactivated) by heat, formalin or other methods without destroying the pathogen's ability to stimulate immunity. These nonvirulent pathogens would then be injected into the person receiving vaccination, and ideally the recipient would respond by producing antibodies and memory B cells which would protect the recipient against the live pathogen, should it be encountered again in the future.

Although killed and attenuated vaccines represent one of the highest achievements of medicine, problems nevertheless persist. One of the most serious is that killed or attenuated vaccines contain the complete genetic material of the pathogen, and if it is not killed or attenuated completely, the vaccine itself may be capable of causing the disease it is intended to prevent.

To overcome this problem, as well as some others posed by killed and attenuated vaccines, subunit vaccines – which contain only portions of the pathogen – are being developed. The basis of subunit vaccines is identification of the part of the pathogen – bacteria, virus or parasite – which is responsible for eliciting an antibody response that will confer immunity; a whole pathogen contains many proteins, most of which are not involved in eliciting antibodies that confer protective immunity.

MAbs have been instrumental in identifying the specific antigenic determinants or protein segments of the pathogen which would become the essential part of the subunit vaccine. If, for example, one or several of many MAb preparations made against a particular parasite can be shown to prevent infection by that parasite in experimental models, one can use the successful MAb(s) to "fish out" the antigenic determinant(s). This strategy includes "the identification of antigens, useful in manufacturing a vaccine carried by the malaria parasite *Plasmodium falpicarum*. Monoclonal antibodies have been constructed against these antigens and are being used to isolate and recover individual targeted antigens so these, in turn, may be cloned and studied."[1]

> Recent human experimentation [has] further encouraged the hope that a vaccine for the sporozoite form of the Plasmodium may now be obtained. Similarly, thanks to the genetic engineering techniques, it could be possible to obtain the production of antigens (and therefore possibly of vaccines) for the other forms of the life cycle of Plasmodium...[2]

Similarly, MAbs are being used to isolate and characterize schistosome (the parasitic worm that causes schistosomiasis) protective antigens for schistosomiasis vaccine development.[3] MAbs are also playing a crucial role in the selection and identification of antigenic components to be incorporated in vaccines for fertility regulation,[4] as well as for a number of viral and bacterial diseases.[5]

Anti-id vaccines

MAbs are the essential component in a new type of vaccine called an "anti-idiotype" or "anti-id" for short, which is generally used to make therapeutic vaccines – that is, to boost the immune systems of patients already afflicted with the disease in question. Anti-id vaccines are based on anti-idiotypic monoclonal antibody technology. An anti-idiotypic monoclonal acts as a surrogate antigen. It is produced by, first, making a protective MAb against the disease-causing antigen; and then, making a second MAb against the first MAb – that is, in effect, producing an anti-antibody, which is termed an anti-idiotypic antibody. Since the binding site of the first MAb is specific and complementary to the antigen (analogous to a negative image of the antigen), the second MAb, being complementary to the first (analogous to a negative-negative or positive image), in effect mimics the antigen and serves as the "antigen" to be incorporated into the vaccine to stimulate production of the original protective antibody in the patient.

As a vaccine, an anti-id is useful when the mimicked antigen does not naturally elicit a strong immune response because it is too small or similar to self; an anti-id MAb, particularly one of mouse origin, will elicit a strong immune response. An anti-id approach is also useful when a protective antigen cannot readily be produced in commercial quantities by recombinant DNA or chemical methods, because, for instance, it is a glycolipid (that is, a non-protein: a glycolipid is a type of complex carbohydrate in which sugars are linked to lipids [fats]). Using MAb technology, companies can readily produce commercial quantities of anti-id antibodies which could serve as a surrogate or mimicked glycolipid.[6]

Anti-ids form one of a handful of therapeutic vaccine approaches to cancer, designed to boost the immune systems of patients already afflicted with the disease. This would avoid the deleterious side effects of chemotherapy and radiation as well as providing the means to react early to recurrence of the cancer.

> Some companies are trying to increase the effect of antigens – mainly complex fats – that normally would provoke weak immune responses. The concept is complicated, but basically researchers use mice to manufacture synthetic versions of tumor-associated antigens. These anti-ids, as they are called, may arouse more of an immune response than the original substance, partially because they are more foreign.[7]

Anti-id vaccines are being tested, for example, in post-surgery malignant-melanoma patients. The first line of therapy for malignant melanoma, an often fatal form of skin cancer, is the surgical removal of tumors. However, invasive tumors metastasize, leading to recurrence of incurable disease in a significant percentage of patients. The therapeutic vaccines are designed to stimulate the patient's immune system to produce antibodies against malignant-melanoma cells, to prevent the spread of the disease to the other parts of the body.[8] An anti-idiotypic antibody vaccine used to immunize experimental mice against subsequent infection with *Schistosoma mansoni* (one of the three major species of the schistosome worm causing schistosomiasis in humans) did confer protection and "indicates the feasibility of this approach to vaccination [for schistosomiasis in humans]".[9]

Notes

1. UNIDO, 1984, p. 22.
2. International Center, 1992, p. 3.
3. Mahmoud, 1989, p. 141.
4. Griffin, 1988, pp. 177–98.
5. Bloom and Jacobs, 1989, pp. 160–62; and US Congress, 1984, pp. 136–7.
6. Spalding, 1992b.
7. Freundlich, 1992, p. 42.
8. IDEC, 1991, pp. 10, 11.
9. Mahmoud, 1989, p. 141.

Annex 5

Monoclonal Antibodies as Therapeutics: Past Problems and Recent Technical Advances

Problems encountered with MAbs used as therapeutics

Hypersensitivity reactions

It was not until the end of the 1980s that progress was made in the development of MAb-based therapeutics. As promising results were issuing from company laboratories – for example, with radioisotopes coupled to MAbs against lymphoma and colon cancer in the mid-1980s – one large problem remained: as exciting as they seemed, most of the MAbs could be used in a patient only once or twice. When MAbs derived from rodents[1] are injected into humans the human immune system will recognize them as foreign proteins and launch a counter-attack of antibodies. After one or two exposures to a rodent antibody, the human body is primed (through its memory B cells) to destroy rapidly any further incursions of the rodent protein. Thus, in repeated treatments many of the antibodies would be destroyed before reaching their targets, or could provoke hypersensitive allergic reactions. This problem is of little importance for diagnostic uses (in *in vivo* imaging), where the radioisotope-tagged antibodies are only used for a short period of time. But it represented a major obstacle for cancer therapy, where repeated treatments could be necessary, and where therapy calls for the cancer-killing monoclonals to circulate long enough to detect and destroy hidden pockets of cancer cells.

Lack of unique markers

Another major problem encountered with MAb-based therapies for cancer was that there had been a serious shortage of distinctive "marker" proteins which distinguish the tumor well enough to make it a clear target for the MAb therapeutic, and some of the early candidate drugs cross-reacted unexpectedly with normal tissues.

Recent technical advances in overcoming obstacles encountered with MAb-based therapeutics

Engineered antibodies

In efforts to overcome hypersensitive or allergic reactions to rodent-based MAbs used as therapeutics, so called "engineered" antibodies began to be developed in the late 1980s. Pioneering work in this area was carried out by US DBFs and researchers at the UK's Medical Research Council (MRC) Laboratory for Molecular Biology. One strategy of the antibody engineers is to "humanize" the rodent MAbs by producing a chimeric MAb, which is part human and part rodent: an approach which reduces the likelihood that human recipients will reject or react against the treatment.

Physically, an antibody resembles a three-dimensional "Y". The tips of the two arms contain the binding sites, molecular cups that are custom-designed to fit over the target (invading) protein. The remaining part of the two arms and the trunk of the antibody are what flags other parts of the immune system to attack and destroy the target foreign invader. A remarkable feature of antibodies is that the trunk and the part of the arms not involved in the binding of all human antibodies are pretty much the same and biochemically constant, while the cup-like binding sites can be varied to fit over almost any conceivable protein target, analagous to fingers coming together to "pinch" the antigen.

Researchers have exploited this facet of antibody structure, and in seminal experiments carried out in 1988, Gary Winter and colleagues at the MRC Laboratory (Cambridge) succeeded in transplanting (using genetic engineering techniques) the variable binding regions from a rat monoclonal – designed to bind the proteins contained in lymphoma cancer cells (a malignancy of white blood cells) and trigger the immune system to destroy the cells – onto the constant part of a human antibody. The chimeric antibody was then successfully used in treating two lymphoma patients for whom chemotherapy and radiation had failed to wipe out the circulating white blood cells.[2] The British researchers turned their chimeric antibody over to the UK drug company Wellcome PLC for scale-up production and for testing in large clinical trials, which were proceeding in Autumn 1992. The chimeric antibody contains only 1 per cent rodent material and does not provoke any adverse reactions.[3] Chimeric antibodies are also going through clinical trials in the USA for treatment of myeloid leukemia; breast, colon, lung and ovarian cancers; as well as for the autoimmune disorders, rheumatoid arthritis and multiple sclerosis.[4] Autoimmune diseases result when the immune system mistakes self molecules as foreign, and mistakenly starts attacking its own tissue(s). The MAbs in these diseases are designed to attack and neutralize the T-cells which are carrying out the inadvertent self-destruction.[5]

MAbs as cruise missiles

Another strategy being employed to avoid the immune reaction to rodent MAbs is to make them smaller, so – like a cruise missile – they can sneak into the body without being detected by the immune system's defenses. Thus, some companies are slicing their mouse or rat MAbs into smaller fragments, which retain their ability to bind to diseased cells while possessing greatly reduced bulk. These fragments, which contain the binding sites, would be small enough not to provoke an immune reaction and would perhaps be small enough to penetrate deep into solid tumors, which whole antibodies have difficulty in doing.[6]

Better markers

Steadily, since the 1980s, researchers have discovered more and more distinctive "marker" proteins to distinguish cancerous tumors well enough to make the cancer a clear target for the MAb therapeutic, "and once a diagnostic antibody against a distinctive marker has been made, it can often be developed into a drug."[7] Dr P. Abrams, president and CEO of the US DBF NeoRx – which specializes in MAb-based imaging and therapy targeted against cancers – underscores this by stating that he views the imaging and therapeutic research as "biphasic", in which the company's imaging products have laid the groundwork for the development of MAb-guided radiotherapeutic agents.[8]

Other advances achieved

Other advances achieved in the 1980s and 1990s include the development of more effective radioisotopes and toxins, improved methods of attaching them to MAbs, and improved ways of delivering doses to diseased cells.[9]

Notes

1. See Chapter 9, note 9 for a description of the basic method for producing monoclonal antibodies.
2. Bishop, 1989b, p. 7.
3. Cookson, 1992.
4. PMA, 1992, p. 6; Morrow, 1995, p. 24 (Dr Morrow was reporting on The Tenth International conference on Monoclonal Anibody Immunoconjugates for Cancer, held in March 1995 in San Diego, California).

In the summer of 1995, patients were being enrolled for Phase II trials of a chimeric MAb for cytomegalovirus (CMV) retinitis in AIDS patients. The disease is a progressive infection of the retina that often leads to blindness if not successfully treated. As people with AIDS are living longer, the incidence of the disease is increasing. Clinical investigators estimate that at least 20 per cent, and possibly as much as 40 per cent, of the AIDS population will develop CMV retinitis. At the same time, Phase II trials were also under way for a chimeric MAb for treating inflammatory bowel disease, where inflammation of parts of the intestine results in chronic conditions of diarrhea and abdominal pain, and poor food absorption. Approximately one million people worldwide have this disease; the currently available treatments have a limited effect on the intensity and duration of symptoms.

5. Bishop, 1989c, p. 8; Steinman and Conlon, 1995.
6. Coghlan, 1991a, pp. 35, 37; Bishop, 1989b, p. 7; Griffith, 1994.
7. Quotation from Cookson, 1992; Pfeiffer, 1995.
8. SCRIP, 1992.
9. Perera, 1988; Coghlan, 1991a, p. 39; Cookson, 1992; Abrams, 1993; Goldenberg, 1994; Morrow, 1995, p. 24; Johannes, 1996.

References

Abrams, Paul. 1993. "Have Monoclonals Fulfilled Their Promise?". *Bio/Technology*, February: 156–7.

ACOST (Advisory Council on Science and Technology) 1990. *Developments in Biotechnology*. London: HMSO.

Alper, Joseph. 1995. "Has Consolidation Finally Commenced?". *Biotechnology*, January: 10–11.

Amgen. 1995. *Annual Report*.

Andrews, Edmund 1990. "A Diagnostic Technique Uses Enzymes and Light". *New York Times*, 22 December: D2.

—— 1993. "US Resumes Granting Patents on Genetically Altered Animals". *New York Times*, 3 February: A1f.

Auerbach, Stuart. 1988. "Reagan Orders Sanctions Against Brazil on Trade". *Washington Post*, 23 July.

Baines, William. 1989. "Disease, DNA and Diagnosis". *New Scientist*, 6 May: 48–51.

Barker, R. 1990. "Socio-economic Impact". In Gabrielle Persley, ed., *Agricultural Biotechnology: Opportunities for Industrial Development*. Wallingford: CAB International: 299–310.

Barnum, Alex. 1989. "Biotech Firm Postpones Plans To Go Public". *Washington Post*, 14 November.

Batchelor, Charles. 1989. "Raising Finance: The Biggest Hurdle". *Financial Times*, 5 June.

—— 1990. "Struggle to Open Up the Money Bags". *Financial Times*, 9 July.

—— 1991. "Seven in Ten Venture Capitalists Prefer Manufacturing". *Financial Times*, 15 January.

Baum, Rudy. 1987. "Biotech Industry Moving Pharmaceutical Products to Market". *Chemical and Engineering News*, 20 July: 11–32.

Bialey, Harvey. 1992. "Bio/Afrique; An Experiment in Commercial Biotechnology Development in Africa". Prepared for *Bio/Technology*.

Bifani, Pablo. 1988. "Biotechnology: Overview and Developments in Latin America". In Inter American Development Bank. *Economic and Social Progress in Latin America 1988 Report*: 195–283.

Biotechnology and Development Monitor. 1990. (Joint publication of the Directorate General International Cooperation of the Ministry of Foreign Affairs, The Hague and the University of Amsterdam) "IITA: Biotechnology for the African Smallholder". December: 18–19.

————— 1991a. "Biotechnology Policy and Research in China". March: 11–15.
————— 1991b. "World Bank Bio-policy in the Making". June: 20–21.
Bisbee, Chester. 1995. "Defeat of European Draft Directive Clouds Animal Patenting Issue". *Genetic Engineering News*, 15 April: 1f.
Bishop, Jerry. 1989a. "Engineered Antibodies Show Great Promise in Fighting Cancer". *Wall Street Journal*, 11 July: 1f.
————— 1989b. "A Host of Other Ailments are Major Targets for 'Magic Bullets'". *Wall Street Journal*, 11 July: 7.
————— 1989c. "'Antibody Bullets' Aimed at a Variety of Ailments". *Asian Wall Street Journal*, 18 July: 8.
Bloom, Barry and William Jacobs. 1989. "New Strategies for Leprosy and Tuberculosis and for Development of Bacillus Calmette-Guerin into a Multivaccine Vehicle". In Barry Bloom and Anthony Cerami, eds, *Biomedical Science and the Third World*. New York: New York Academy of Sciences: 155–71.
Bock, Richard. 1991. "Wall $treet BioBeat". *Genetic Engineering News*, January: 23.
Brenner, Carlienne. 1990. "Summary and Recommendations of the OECD Development Center Study". In *Biotechnology and Developing Country Agriculture: The Case of Maize*. CD/R(90) 13. Paris: OECD, October.
Bristol-Myers Squibb Company. 1990. *Annual Report 1990*.
Bromby, P., A. Pritchard and G. Persley. 1990. "Issues for the World Bank". In Gabrielle Persley, ed., *Agricultural Biotechnology: Opportunities for Industrial Development*. Wallingford: CAB International: 429–36.
Brown, Phyllidia. 1992. "The Parasite that Exploits the Immune System". *New Scientist*, 25 April: 14.
Brownlee, Shannon, Gareth Cook and Viva Hardigg. 1994. "Tinkering with Testing". *US News and World Report*, August: 59–67.
Brummer, Alex. 1995. Playing it Long with Pharmaceuticals". *Guardian*, 27 January: 11.
Buderi, Robert. 1991. "A Tighter Focus for R&D". *Business Week*, 2 December: 80–84.
Bulyzhenkov, Victor and Bernadette Modell. 1988. "Hereditary Diseases are Preventable". *World Health* (Geneva: WHO), October: 20–21.
Burrill, Steve. 1988. "Biotechnology in 1989: Commercializing an Industry". *Bio/Technology*, October.
————— 1990. "Perspectives on Biobusiness 90: Entering a Changing Environment". *Bio/Technology*, October: 915–17.
Burrill, Steve and K. Lee. 1991. *Biotech 92: Promise to Reality*. San Francisco: Ernst & Young.
————— 1992. *Biotech 93: Accelerating Commercialization*. San Francisco: Ernst & Young: 35.
————— 1993. *Biotech 94: Long-Term Value, Short-Term Hurdles*. San Francisco: Ernst & Young: 63.
————— 1994. *Biotech 95: Reform, Restructure, Renewal*. Palo Alto: Ernst & Young: 28.
————— 1995. *Biotech 96: Pursuing Sustainability*. Palo Alto: Ernst & Young: 74.
Buttel, F. 1990. "Sociological Impact". In Gabrielle Persley, ed., *Agricultural Biotechnology: Opportunities for Industrial Development*. Wallingford: CAB International: 311–21.
Bylinsky, Gene. 1995. "Who Will Feed the Startups?". *Fortune*, 26 June: 78–82.
Capron, André and J. Grzych. 1983. "Making Hybridomas Work for Us". *World Health* (Geneva: WHO), November: 18–21.
Carty, Peter. 1995. "A Very Demanding Exercise". *Financial Times*, 18 May: VIII.
Centocor News Release. 1991. 26 November.

Chase, Marilyn. 1990. "Genentech's TPA Prospers, But Eminase Challenge Nears". *Wall Street Journal Europe*, 11 January: 8.

——— 1991a. "Cetus and Chiron, Pioneers in Biotech, Agree to Merge". *Wall Street Journal Europe*, 23: July 3.

——— 1991b. "Gene Amplification is Dramatically Altering the Way Many Disorders are Diagnosed". *Wall Street Journal*, 31 October: 4.

——— 1993. "Genentech Drug's Sales Sour After Release of Heart Study". *Wall Street Journal Europe*, 3–4 September: 3.

Chase, Marilyn and John Lublin. 1990. "Genentech's Sale of Stake to Roche Reaffirms Potential of Biotechnology". *Wall Street Journal Europe*, 5 February.

Clarke, Lucy. 1995. "New Drugs in the Pipeline". *Financial Times*, 27 November: III.

Coghlan, Andy. 1991a. "A Second Chance for Antibodies". *New Scientist*, 9 February: 34–9.

——— 1991b. "Dutch Lack Appetite for Genetically 'Altered Foods'". *New Scientist*, 17 August.

Cookson, Clive. 1991. "Hopes Centre on Control, Not Cure". *Financial Times*, 8 January: 14

——— 1992. "Fighting the War with Magic Bullets." *Financial Times*, 17 September: 12.

——— 1996. "The Gene of Distress". *Financial Times*, 23 January: 10.

Cookson, Clive and Jenny Lynch. 1992. "A Chain Reaction". *Financial Times*, 2 October: 13.

Copmann, T. 1989. "PMA Analysis Tracks Trends in Biotechnology Research". In Pharmaceuticals Manufacturers Association (PMA), *Biotech Medicines in Development 1989 Survey*. Washington DC: PMA.

——— 1990. "PMA Patent Analysis Track Four Year Trends in Biotechnology Research". In PMA, *Biotech Medicines in Development 1990 Survey*. Washington DC: PMA.

Coy, Peter. 1994. "WHAT'S THE WORD IN THE LAB? COLLABORATE". *Business Week*, 27 June: 44–5.

Crawford, Mark. 1986. "Biotech Market Changing Rapidly". *Science* 231, 3 January: 12–14.

Curran, John. 1987. "Will Biotech's Boom Go Bust?". *Fortune*, 6 July: 75–6.

Dailami, Mansoor and Michael Atkin. 1990. "Stock Markets in Developing Countries". Policy Research and External Affairs Working Papers of the World Bank and IFC. WPS 515. October.

Daly, Peter. 1985. *The Biotechnology Business: A Strategic Analysis*. London: Francis Pinter.

Davis, William, Travis McGuire and Lane Perryman. 1982. "Biomedical and Biological Application of Monoclonal Antibody Technology in Developing Countries". In National Research Council, Board on Science and Technology for International Development. *Priorities in Biotechnology Research for International Development*. Proceedings of a workshop, Washington DC, 26–30 July. Washington DC: National Academic Press: 179–207.

De Palma, Angelo. 1990. "Survey Finds Strategic Partnering as the Key Issue for Biotech Industry Executives". *Genetic Engineering News*, November/December: 1f.

Dibner, Mark. 1985. "Biotechnology in Pharmaceuticals: The Japanese Challenge". *Science* 229, September: 1230–35.

——— 1986. "Biotechnology in Europe". *Science* 232, 13 June: 1367–72.

Dodge, John. 1988. "Cystic Fibrosis". *World Health*, October: 17–19.

Doyle, J. and P. Spradbrow. 1990. "Animal Health". In Gabrielle Persley, ed., *Agricultural Biotechnology: Opportunities for Industrial Development.* Wallingford: CAB International: 176–86.

Dramik, Mary. 1992. "Environmental Testing Becomes a Vital Growth Sector for Biotechnology Industry". *Genetic Engineering News*, March: 11f.

Durr, Barbara. 1990. "Chile Surrenders to US Threat on Pharmaceutical Patents". *Financial Times*, 1 February.

The Economist. 1985. "The Bugs Business". 23 November: 41.

—— 1986a. "Biotechnology's Hype and Hubris". 19 April: 92–3.

—— 1986b. "Good News from Arcadia for the Old". 22 November: 89–90.

—— 1987a. "The Drug Industry Brings on the Boffins". 24 January: 79–80.

—— 1987b. "Medicine's Home Front". 6 June: 92–3.

—— 1987c. "Patently Outdated". 18 July: 19.

—— 1988a. "Biotechnology Survey". 30 April.

—— 1988b. "Genentech's Style". 14 May.

—— 1989. "The Money Guzzling Genius of Biotechnology". 13 May: 69–70.

—— 1990. "The Doctor's Dilemma". 27 January: 75–6.

—— 1991a. "Trials and Tribulations". 16 March: 88.

—— 1991b. "Priceless Medicines". 26 October: 14–15.

—— 1994a. "Capitalist Cultures". 14 May: 78.

—— 1994b. "Panic in the Petrie Dish". 23 July: 57–8.

——1995a. "Unshackled: A Survey of Biotechnology and Genetics". 25 February.

—— 1995b "Bugged If I Know". 18 March 1995: 73–4.

—— 1995c. "Unseemly Couplings". 13 May: 78–9.

—— 1995d. "Plant Workers". 6 May: 87–8.

—— 1995e. "Alien Culture: Biotechnology in Japan". 18 November: 87.

Ellis, James. 1992. "Can Biotech Put Bread on Third World Tables?". *Business Week*, 14 December: 100.

Enzo Biochem Inc. (New York). 1991a. News Release of 12 February.

—— 1991b. Press Release, 25 February.

—— 1992. Third Quarter Report to Shareholders Fiscal.

Erikson, Deborah. 1992. "Doomsday Diagnostic?". *Scientific American*, August: 99.

Ernst, David and Diana Mackie. 1988. "Fighting the Financing Frenzy: What Next for Biotechnology Companies?". *Bio/Technology*, 16 May: 495–501.

Evenson, R. and J. Putman. 1990. "Intellectual Property Management". In Gabrielle Persley, ed., *Agricultural Biotechnology: Opportunities for Industrial Development.* Wallingford: CAB International: 332–66.

Fahrlander, Paul and Arthur Klausner. 1988. "Amplifying DNA Probe Signals: A 'Christmas Tree' Approach". *Bio/technology*, October: 1165–8.

Financial Times. 1991. "Largest Clinical Heart Attack Study Favours Older Drug". 4 March: 3.

—— 1992. "Cancer Drug Gains Approval". 20 March.

—— 1996. "Emerging Markets". 22 January: 14.

Fisher, Lawrence. 1989. "Biotech Firms Born of Disease of Elderly". *International Herald Tribune*, 24 August.

—— 1990. "Venture Capital's Assault on the Genetic Code". *New York Times*, 7 October: F5.

—— 1993a. "New Standard for Drug Makers: Proving the Cure is Worth the Cost". *New York Times*, 18 January: A1ff.

—— 1993b. "Campbell Delays Plans on Biotech Tomatoes". *New York Times*, 12 December: D4.

Fishlock, David. 1988a. "Biotechnology Companies 'Find Finance a Problem'". *Financial Times*, 20 April.

—— 1988b. "Biotechnology: Investors and Enthusiasts". *Financial Times*, 27 May: I.

—— 1988c. "Ventures That May Appeal to the Heart of the City". *Financial Times*, 27 May: II.

—— 1989. "Time Span of Success". *Financial Times*, Survey: Biotechnology, 12 May.

Fowler, Cary, Eva Lachovics, Pat Mooney and Hope Shand. 1988a. "Regulating the 'Super Natural'". *Development Dialogue* 1–2: 212–24.

—— 1988b. "The Lords of Life: Corporate Control and the New Biosciences". *Development Dialogue* 1–2, 1988b: 179–93.

Fox, Jeffrey. 1990. "Antibodies Against Sepsis". *Bio/Technology*, 8 December: 1240–41.

Fox, Jeffrey and Jennifer van Brunt. 1990. "Towards Understanding Human Genetic Diseases". *Bio/Technology*, October: 903–9.

Fox, Sandra. 1992. "PCR Increasingly Employed in Agriculture and Veterinary Biotechnology". *Genetic Engineering News*, 1 June: 6f.

Freudenheim, Milt. 1988a. "Mail-Order Drug Sales Booming". *New York Times*, 27 February.

—— 1988b. "Drug Makers Try Biotech Partners". *New York Times*, 30 September: D1f.

—— 1989. "Price Revolt Spreading on Prescription Drugs". *New York Times*, 14 November: D1f.

Freundlich, Naomi. 1992. "A Shot in the Arm for the Fight Against Cancer". *Business Week*, 12 October: 40–42.

Fujimura, Robert. 1988. *Biotechnology in Japan*. US Department of Commerce. International Trade Administration. Washington DC: US DOC.

Fukui, S. 1990. "Current Status in R&D of Biotechnology and Bioindustry". *Genetic Engineering and Biotechnology Monitor*, September: 10–11.

Furgusun, Anne. 1988. "Biotech's Baby Blues". *Management Today*, January: 55–60.

Gamlin, Linda. 1988a. "The Human Immune System". Part One. *New Scientist*, Inside Science No. 7, 10 March.

—— 1988b. "The Human Immune System". Part Two. *New Scientist*, Inside Science No. 8, 24 March.

Gangal, S. 1987. "Application of Monoclonal Antibodies in Infectious Diseases". In *Biotechnology in Tropical Crop Improvement*. Proceedings of the International Biotechnology Workshop, 12–15 January, ICRISAT Center, India: 51–6.

Gannes, Stuart. 1987. "The Big Boys are Joining the Biotech Party". *Fortune*, 6 July: 44–9.

Gebhart, Fred. 1989. "Biotechnology's Shining Star Tries to Remove Some Tarnish". *Genetic Engineering News*, January: 1f.

—— 1990. "Industry Considers the Roche–Genentech Deal a Major Vote of Confidence for Biotechnology". *Genetic Engineering News*, March: 1f.

Genetic Engineering and Biotechnology Monitor (UNIDO). 1990. "New HPV Identification Test". September: 26.

Genetic Engineering News. 1989. "FDA Approves Alpha Interferon for KS Treatment". January: 32.

—— 1991a. "Report from President's Council Gives a Strong Boost to Biotechnology". April: 3.

—— 1991b. "US Survey Finds Bioexecutives Well Paid". May: 23.

———— 1992. "Thailand Launches Technology Commercialization Program with the US". January: 13.

———— 1993. "Sales of Monoclonal Antibodies Predicted to Rise to $3.8 Billion by 1988". August: 3.

Gill, David (Director, Capital Markets Department, International Finance Corporation [IFC], Washington DC) 1981. "Venture Capital Investment – IFC's Strategy". Paper presented at the First International Seminar on Venture Capital. São Paolo and Rio de Janeiro, 1–2 September.

———— 1984. "The Strategic Role of Venture Capital in the Development Process". Paper presented at the Venture Capital Conference. Lisbon, 25–27 May.

Gladwell, Malcolm. 1988a. "Medicare Stance May Limit Use of Heart Drug". *Washington Post*, 6 March: H1f.

———— 1988b. "New Wonder Drugs Pose Patent Questions". *Washington Post*, 5 August: A1f.

Glaser, Vicki. 1992. "Human Genetic Testing: The Technology, the Companies and the Issues". *Genetic Engineering News*, 15 May: 20f.

Goldenberg, David. 1994. "Radiolabeled Antibodies". *Scientific American & Medicine*, March–April: 64–73.

Gourlay, Richard. 1993. "Biotech Babies Find a Life-giving Source". *Financial Times*, 2 July: 15.

Goy, Patricia and John Duesing. 1995. "From Pots to Plots: Genetically Modified Plants on Trial". *Bio/Technology*, May 1995: 454–8.

Graff, G. and J. Winton. 1987. "Biotechnology Growing Greener at Last". *Chemical Week*, 30 September: 20–37.

Green, Daniel. 1994. "Economists in the Salesforce". *Financial Times*, 24 March: 9.

———— 1994a. "Red, White and Better All Over". *Financial Times*, 27 May: 12.

———— 1994b. "Clinical Trails Encourage British Bio". *Financial Times*, 17 June: 28.

———— 1995. "Growth in Global Drugs Sales at Three-year High". *Financial Times*, 6 December: 5.

———— 1996. "Pharmaceutical Groups Finish the Year on a High". *Financial Times*, 8 January: 21.

Griffin, P. 1988. "Vaccines for Fertility Regulation". In E. Diczfaluses, P. Griffin and J. Khana, eds, *Research in Human Reproduction Biennial Report 1986–1987*. Geneva: WHO: 177–98.

Griffith, Victoria. 1994. "Back on Track". *Financial Times*, 14 January: 16.

Griffiths, David and Geoffrey Hall. 1993. "Biosensors – What Real Progress Is Being Made?". *Trends in Biotechnology*, April: 122–30.

Gupta, Udayan. 1989. "Watching and Waiting". *Wall Street Journal*, supplement, 13 November: R32.

Hacking, Andrew. 1986. *Economic Aspects of Biotechnology*. Cambridge: Cambridge University Press.

Hamilton, Joan. 1993. "Biotech: An Industry Crowded with Players Faces an Ugly Reckoning". *Business Week*, 26 September: 66–70.

Hamilton, Joan and James Ellis. 1992. "A Storm is Brewing Down the Farm". *Business Week*, 14 December: 98–101.

Hinden, Stan. 1992. "Health Care Funds: Ailing Now, but Regulation Could Make Them Sicker". *Washington Post*, 13 May: G3.

Hodgson, John. 1990. "Why Ethics and Biotechnology Collide". *Scientific European*, April: 24–7.

Hoffman, David and Stewart Rosenberg. 1992. "The Impact of Biotechnology on the In-Vitro Diagnostics Medical Market". *Genetic Engineering News*, 15 June: 8–9.

Houlder, Vanessa. 1995. "Movement on Arthritis Front". *Financial Times*, 16 November: 14.

Husbands, Robert and David Dichter. 1989. "Venture Capital for the Third World". *Development and Cooperation* (Bonn), No. 2/89: 15–16.

IBA (Industrial Biotechnology Association). 1988. "Biotechnology at Work: Diagnostics". Washington DC: IBA.

ICC Information Group. 1988. *Biotechnology Products, Keynote Report, an Industry Sector Overview.* London.

International Center for Genetic Engineering and Biotechnology. 1992. *Activity Report.* Part II. Vienna, February.

ICDA (International Coalition for Development Action). 1989. *Patenting Life Forms in Europe.* Proceedings of an International Conference at the European Parliament. Barcelona: ICDA Seeds Campaign.

IDEC Pharmaceuticals Corporation. 1991. Annual Report 1991.

IFC (International Finance Corporations). 1980. "Venture Capital Activities in Selected Countries". Papers presented at conference Entrepreneurship in the 1980s. Association of Canadian Venture Capital Companies, Toronto, 6–7 March.

———— 1986. *Some Considerations in Establishing a Venture Capital Company.* Washington DC: IFC.

———— 1990a. *Emerging Markets Data Base.* 3rd Quarter 1990. Washington DC: IFC.

———— 1990b. *Emerging Stock Markets Factbook 1990.* Washington DC: IFC.

———— 1991. *Annual Report 1991.* Washington DC: IFC.

IMF (International Monetary Fund). 1992. *World Economic Outlook.* Washington DC: IMF.

Jacob, Miriam. 1989. "India's Immunology Institute Exhibits a Broad Range of Scientific Skills". *Genetic Engineering News*, February: 16–17.

James, C. and G. Persley. 1990. "Role of the Private Sector". In Gabrielle Persley, *Agricultural Biotechnology: Opportunities for Industrial Development.* Wallingford: CAB International: 367–77.

Johannes, Laura. 1996. "'Magic-Bullet' Drugs Making a Recovery". *Wall Street Journal*, 1 February: 4.

Jonquières, Guy. 1996. "Bank Warns over Boom in Commodities". *Financial Times*, 16 January: 5.

Junne, Gerd. 1989. "Avenues for Future Social Sciences Research on Impact of Biotechnology". *Society for International Development: Seeds of Change* 4: 86–90.

Kaplan, Victoria. 1989. "Latin America Provides Quality Contributions to Biotechnology Research". *Genetic Engineering News*, February: 18f.

Katz Miller, Susan. 1992. "Ethics Lobby Forces Rethink on Growth Hormones". *New Scientist*, 15 August: 9.

Kehoe, Louise. 1989. "Pendulum Is Set to Swing Back". *Financial Times*, 12 May: 34.

Keough, Michele and Aager Sharmel. 1995. "Sales of US Biopharmaceutical Products Expected to Triple by 2004". *Genetic Engineering News*, 15 March: 6.

Klausner, Arthur. 1988. "FDA Approves 'Second Generation' Gene Probe". *Bio/Technology*, February: 119.

Koenig, Peggy. 1989. "Monoclonal Antibody Companies Set Sights on Potential $6 Billion Market". *Genetic Engineering News*, April: 5f.

Kolata, Gina. 1993. "Mysterious Epidemic of Furtive Liver Virus". *New York Times*, 19 January: C1f.

Koning, Wim. 1994. "Recombinant Reproduction". *Bio/Technology*, October: 988–92.

Kumar, Nagesh. 1987. "Biotechnology in India." *Development: Seeds of Change* (Rome) 4: 51–56.

Lancaster, Hal. 1984. "Efforts to Develop Monoclonal Antibodies Progress Slowly, and Enthusiasm Wanes". *Wall Street Journal*, 22 May: 18.

Lewis, Ricki. 1990. "Competitors Take on PCR for a Share of Diagnostics Market". *Genetic Engineering News*, November/December: 1f.

——— 1992. "Competitors are Alive and Well and Moving Rapidly Towards Commercialization". *Genetic Engineering News*, 1 June: 1f.

Lowell, Christina and David Witrock. 1989. "Employee Stock Ownership: A Key Ingredient for Biotech Company Success". *Genetic Engineering News*, April: 37.

Lowenstein, Roger. 1990. "Genentech's Pact with Roche Irks Holders Who Feel It Limits Profits". *Wall Street Journal*, 16 February.

Lowry, Pauline and Susan Wells. 1991. "Genetic Fingerprinting". *New Scientist*, Inside Science No. 52, 16 November.

Lucas, Pieter, Alfred Muller and Bill Pike. 1995. *European Biotech 95: Gathering Momentum*. London: Ernst & Young.

Lynn, Matthew. 1993. "Biotech Grows on Market". *The Times*, 20 June: 6.

Mackenzie, Deborah. 1990. "Jumping Genes Confound German Scientists". *New Scientist*, 15 December.

——— 1991. "The West Pays Up for Third World Seeds". *New Scientist*, 11 May: 18–19.

Mackler, Bruce. 1990. "GEN's 10 Most Important Pieces of Legislation". *Genetic Engineering News*, January: 26f.

Maguire, Maria. 1987. "Making Provision for Ageing Populations". *The OECD Observer*, October/November: 4–9.

Mahmoud, Adel. 1989. "Strategies for Vaccine Development: Schistosomiasis". In Barry Bloom, and Anthony Cerami, eds, *Biomedical Science and the Third World*. New York: New York Academy of Sciences: 136–44.

Maitland, Alison. 1994. "Monsanto Seeks to Allay European Fears about Its Milk Yield-boosting Hormone". *Financial Times*, 21 July: 26.

Marsh, Hilary. 1988. *Attitudes of UK Venture Capitalists to Biotechnology Investments*. London: The Association for the Advancement of British Biotechnology.

Marsh, Peter. 1987a. "Drug that Leads Race against AIDS". *Financial Times*, 16 July: 7.

——— 1987b. "D-I-Y Tests on the Way". *Financial Times*, 1 October.

——— 1987c. "Biotech Companies Risk Being Exploited". *Financial Times*, 20 November.

——— 1988. "Attacking the Heart of the Market". *Financial Times*, 7 April.

——— 1989. "Role for Small Teams". *Financial Times*, 6 November: 28.

Marsh, Peter and James Buchan. 1989. "Prospects Undimmed by Slow Progress". *Financial Times*, 10 October.

Martin, Carole. 1989. "Japan Views Biotechnology as a Critical Industry for the 21st Century". *Genetic Engineering News*, February: 10f.

Maurice, John. 1991. "Cancer Will Overwhelm the Third World". *New Scientist*, 14 December: 9.

Merrill Lynch Research Comment. 1990. 28 November.

Miller, Linda. 1987. "The Commercial Development of Biotechnology – A Four Part History". *Paine Webber Biotechnology Monthly*, February.

Miller, S. and R. Williams. 1990. "Agricultural Diagnostics". In Gabrielle Persley, ed., *Agricultural Biotechnology: Opportunities for Industrial Development*. Wallingford: CAB International: pp. 87–107.

Le Monde. 1992. "SIDA: La DDC est autorisée aux Etats-Unis" (AIDS: DDC is approved in the USA). 24 June: 10.

Montagnon, Peter. 1990. "The Return of the Food Mountain". *Financial Times*, 9 November.

Moore, Stephen. 1991. "Two Swedish Drug Firms Hope to Gain Sales in the US from Heart-drug Battle". *Wall Street Journal Europe*, 4 April.

Morrow, John. 1995. "Positive Results of Immunotherapy Trials Boost the Enthusiasm for Mab Technology". *Genetic Engineering News*, 15 April: 1f.

Murray, James. 1986. "The First $4 Billion is the Hardest". *Bio/Technology*, April: 293–6.

National Research Council (Washington DC). 1982. Board on Science and Technology for International Development. *Priorities in Biotechnology Research for International Development*. Proceedings of a workshop, Washington DC, 26–30 July. Washington DC: National Academy Press.

—— 1984. Board on Agriculture. *Genetic Engineering of Plants*. National Academy Press: Washington DC.

Nestle, Marion. 1992. "Food Biotechnology: Truth in Advertising". *Bio/Technology*, September: 1056.

Neufeld, Peter and Neville Colman. 1990. "When Science Takes the Witness Stand". *Scientific American*, May: 18–25.

Newman, A. 1990. "Bigger Biotech Firms Outshine Others: Nasdaq Index Off 1.9; VeriFone Plunges". *Wall Street Journal*, 19 September: C6.

Newmark, Peter. 1988. "Diagnostics Unification". *Bio/Technology*, February: 117.

—— 1988. "New Survey: UK Manpower Shortage". *Bio/Technology*, May.

New Scientist. 1994. "Taking Stock of Science". 12 February: 3.

New York Times. 1987a. "Patents Disputed in Biotechnology". 9 March: 1f.

—— 1987b. "Scientists See Biotech Battle". 23 June.

—— 1989. "Amgen to Give Drug to Needy". 10 November.

Nimgade, Ashok. 1990. "East European Biotech Offers its Own Type of Peace Dividends to Partners in the West". *Genetic Engineering News*, September: 4.

OECD (Organization for Economic Cooperation and Development). 1985. *The Pharmaceutical Industry: Trade Related Issues*. Paris: OECD.

—— 1988. *Biotechnology and the Changing Role of Government*. Paris: OECD.

—— 1989. *Biotechnology: Economic and Wider Impacts*. Paris: OECD.

Okie, Susan. 1988. "Children Reach for New Heights in Study of Growth Hormone". *Washington Post*, 31 October: A1f.

—— 1991. "Cheapest Heart Drug is Best". *International Herald Tribune*, 4 March.

Olson, Steve. 1986. *Biotechnology: An Industry Comes of Age*. Washington DC: National Academy Press.

Orrego, C. 1989. *Excellence Under Adversity: The Life Sciences and Biotechnology in Latin America*. Washington DC: Interciencia Association.

Osborn, June. 1986. "The Aids Epidemic: An Overview of the Science". *Issues in Science and Technology*, Winter: 40–55.

Ozorio, P. 1988. "Heart Attacks: Developing in Developing Countries". *World Health*, October: 26–7.

Perera, Judith. 1988. "Refining the Accuracy of the Cancer Bullet". *South*, January: 86.

Persley, Gabrielle, ed., 1990a. *Agricultural Biotechnology: Opportunities for Industrial Development.* Wallingford: CAB International. This is a companion volume of articles to the World Bank's study, *Agricultural Biotechnology: The Next "Green Revolution"?*. Washington DC: World Bank.

———— 1990b. "Issues for International Development Agencies". In Gabrielle Persley, ed., *Agricultural Biotechnology: Opportunities for Industrial Development.* Wallingford: CAB International: 439–43.

Pfeiffer, Naomi. 1995. "Companies Report Progress in Possible Monoclonal Therapies". *Genetic Engineering News*, November: 1f.

PMA (Pharmaceutical Manufacturers' Association). 1990a. *Biotechnology Medicines in Development 1990 Survey.* Washington DC: PMA.

———— 1990b. *In Development: AIDS Medicines.* Washington DC: PMA.

———— 1991. *Biotechnology Medicines in Development 1991 Survey.* Washington DC: PMA.

———— 1993. *Biotechnology Medicines in Development 1993 Survey.* Washington DC: PMA.

PhRMA (Pharmaceutical Research and Manufactureres of America – formerly PMA). 1995. *Biotechnology Medicines in Development 1995 Survey.* Washington DC: PhRMA.

———— 1995a. *AIDS Medicines in Development 1995 Survey.* Washington DC: PhRMA.

Pollack, Andrew. 1985. "Marketing of Biotechnology: New Products Appearing". *New York Times*, 12 August: D1f.

———— 1988. "The Price of 'Miracles': Out of Reach". *International Herald Tribune*, 12 February.

———— 1989. "Firms Focus on Detecting Disease". *International Herald Tribune*, 29 August.

Protein Design Labs (California). 1995. Press Release, 18 July.

RAFI (Rural Advancement Foundation International, Ottawa). 1994. *Conserving Indigenous Knowledge.* New York: UNDP.

Relchlin, Igor. 1989. "Fast-Maturing Market". *Financial Times*, 30 November: VII.

Reuben, B. and H. Wittcoff. 1989. *Pharmaceutical Chemicals in Perspective.* New York: John Wiley and Sons.

Roberts, Steven. 1988. "US Sets Brazil Curbs Over Patent Piracy". *New York Times*, 23 July.

Rodger, Ian. 1989. "Why Japan's 'Copiers' Have Got the Creative Urge". *Financial Times*, 12 May.

Roitt, Ivan. 1991. *Essential Immunology.* Oxford: Blackwell Scientific Publications.

Rundle, Rhonda. 1989. "Venture Capitalists Bail Out of Biovest". *Asian Wall Street Journal*, 29 September: 18.

———— 1991. "Amgen Takes Rights for Biotech Drug in Surprise Win Over Genetics Institute". *Wall Street Journal Europe*, 7 March: 3.

———— 1994. "Biotech Firms Suffer Severe Lack of Cash". *Wall Street Journal Europe*, 7 April: 4.

———— 1995. "Some Investors Question Pay of Biotech Executives". *Wall Street Journal Europe*, 29 March: 9.

Sanchéz, Vicente and Calestous Juma, eds. 1994. *Biodiplomacy: Genetic Resources and International Relations.* Nairobi: African Centre for Technology Studies.

Schlender, Brenton. 1988. "Ciba Geigy Invests in Biotechnology, Buying 7.9% of Chiron for $20 Million". *Wall Street Journal*, 15 November.

Schneider, Keith. 1987. "Gene Altered Bacteria Released Outdoors in a Historic Experiment". *New York Times*, 25 April: 1f.

Schoon, Nicholas. 1996. "Alarm over Genetic Science 'Complacency'". *Independent*, 26 January: 6.

Schrage, Michael. 1984. "Kits for Performing Health Tests at Home Gaining in Popularity". *International Herald Tribune*, 13 September: 6.

————. 1990. *Washington Post*, 30 November.

Schropp, Carola. 1995. "European Bioindustry Shows Signs of Renewed Momentum". Genetic Engineering News, 1 May: 31.

SCRIP (Surrey, UK). 1992. "NeoRx Moves into Therapeutic Phase". 21 August.

Sercovich, Francisco and Marion Leopold. 1991. *Developing Countries and the New Biotechnology: Marketing Entry and Industrial Policy*. Ottawa: International Development Research Center.

Sharon, Nathan and Halina Lis. 1993. "Carbohydrates in Cell Recognition". *Scientific American*, January: 82–9.

Sharp, Margaret. 1985. *The New Biotechnology: European Governments in Search of a Strategy*. Sussex European Paper No. 15. Sussex: University of Sussex.

Shmergel, Gabriel. 1986. "Technology Transfer: Biotechnology Industry Perspective". *Technology in Society* 8: 233–6.

Simpson, Karl. 1989. "BioEurope". *Genetic Engineering News*, February: 6f.

————. 1990. "BioEurope". *Genetic Engineering News*, January: 10–11.

Sorj, Bernardo, Mark Kantley and Karl Simpson, eds. 1989. *Biotechnology in Europe and Latin America*. Dordrecht: Kluwer Academic Publishers.

Spalding, B. 1988. "Biotech Steps Closer to Profitability". *Chemical Week*, 21 September: 37.

————. 1992a. "37 Biotech Firms Raise $1.3 Billion". *Bio/Technology*, May: 481.

————. 1992b. "New Firms Pursue Anti-Ids". *Bio/Technology*, September: 950.

————. 1992c. "Institutions Increase Ownership". *Bio/Technology*, September: 951.

————. 1993. "1992 Financing Nets $2 Billion". *Bio/Technology*, February: 149.

Spencer, Vernon and David Kirk. 1994. "UK Boasts Europe's Biggest Sector". *Bio/Technology*, October: 958–9.

Steinman, Lawrence and Paul Conlon. 1995. "Designing Rational Therapies for Multiple Sclerosis". *Bio/Technology*, February: 118–20.

Stevens, Carol. 1986. "From Bugs to Drugs". *Newsweek*, 29 September.

————. 1992. "Save Your Life". *The Washingtonian*, December: 81–8.

Stewart, J. 1988. "Analysing Cost and Timing of the Biopharmaceutical Development Process". *Genetic Engineering News*, November/December: 58–61.

Sugawara, Sandra. 1991. "Drug Patent Race Heads to the Bench". *Washington Post*, 15 September: H7–8.

Templeton. 1988. *Annual Report*. St Petersburg, Florida, USA.

Ten Kate, Kerry. 1995. "Biodiversity Prospecting Partnerships". *Biotechnology and Development Monitor*, December: 16–21.

Treble, J. 1982. "Scale-up of Hybridoma Business Ventures: Investment Requirements and Perspectives". *Genetic Engineering News*, July/August.

Trigo, Eduardo and Walter Jaffe. 1990. "Biosafety Regulations in Developing Countries". *Genetic Engineering and Biotechnology Monitor* (UNIDO) November: 46–52.

United Nations. 1989. *Monthly Bulletin of Statistics*. January.

UNCTAD (United Nations Conference on Trade and Development). 1989. *Trade and Development Report 1989*. Geneva: UNCTAD.

————. 1991. *Trade and Development Aspects and Implications of New and Emerging Technologies: The Case of Biotechnology*. TD/B/C.6/154. Geneva: UNCTAD.

UNCTC (United Nations Centre On Transnational Corporations). 1988. *Transnational Corporations in Biotechnology*. ST/CTC/61. New York: UN.

UNIDO (United Nations Industrial Development Organization). 1984. *Biotechnology and the Developing Countries: Applications to the Pharmaceutical Industry and Agriculture*. Vienna: UNIDO.

———— 1988. *Genetic Engineering and Biotechnology Monitor* 1988 IV: 12.

———— 1990. *An International Approach to Biotechnology Safety*. Vienna: UNIDO.

United States. 1991. The President's Council on Competitiveness. *Report on Biotechnology Policy*. Washington DC: Office of the Vice President.

US Bureau of the Census. 1988. *Statistical Abstract of the United States*.

———— 1990. *Statistical Abstract of the United States*.

US Congress. OTA (Office of Technology Assessment). 1984. *Commercial Biotechnology – An International Analysis*. Washington DC: GPO.

———— OTA. 1985. *Status of Research and Related Technology for Tropical Diseases*. Washington DC: GPO.

———— OTA. 1987. *New Developments in Biotechnology: Ownership of Human Tissues and Cells*. Washington DC: GPO.

———— OTA. 1988a. *New Developments in Biotechnology. Field Testing Engineered Organisms: Genetic and Ecological Issues*. Springfield, Va.: National Technical Information Service.

———— OTA. 1988b. *New Developments in Biotechnology: US Investment in Biotechnology*. Washington DC: GPO.

———— OTA. 1991. *Biotechnology in a Global Economy*. Washington DC: GPO.

US DOC (US Department of Commerce). 1988. *US Industrial Outlook 1988*. Washington DC: GPO.

———— 1989. *US Industrial Outlook 1989*. Washington DC: GPO.

———— 1991. *US Industrial Outlook 1991*. Washington DC: GPO.

———— 1992. *US Industrial Outlook 1992*. Washington DC: GPO.

Van Kleef, Bas and Broer Scholtens. 1988. "Risico in biotechnologie zijn nog niet te overzien" (Risks in Biotechnology Are Still Incalculable). *Volkskrant* (Amsterdam), 17 September: 35.

Van Wijk, Jeroen 1990. "Intellectual Property Protection for Plants". *Biotechnology and Development Monitor*, September: 3–7.

———— 1991. "Brazil to Recognize Biotechnology Patents". *Biotechnology and Development Monitor*, September: 18.

———— 1995. "Broad Technology Patents Hamper Innovation". *Biotechnology and Development Monitor*, December: 15–17.

Volkskrant (Amsterdam). 1991. "Genetechnologische veldproeven vragen om maatschappelijk debat" (Gene Technology Field Tests Ask for Society Debate). 10 August: 17.

Wagstyl, Stefan. 1994. "Small is Successful in a Liberalised India". *Financial Times*, 24 February: 4.

Wald, Salomon. 1989. "The Biotechnological Revolution". *The OECD Observer*, February/March: 16–20.

Waldholz, Michael. 1991. "Nova Phamaceuticals Potent Drugs for Arthritis That May Reduce Side Effects". *Wall Street Journal*, 18–19 January: 10.

———— 1992. "New Discoveries Dim Drug Makers' Hopes for Quick AIDS Cure". *Wall Street Journal*, 26 May: A1f.

Wallich, Paul. 1995. "The Many Costs of Drug Testing". *Scientific American*, March: 32.

Wall Street Journal Europe. 1989. "Biotech Firms Join Hands with Drug Manufacturers". 6 October.

———— 1990. "Genentech's Pact with Roche Irks Holders Who Feel It Limits Profits". 16 February.

—— 1991a. "The AIDS Hoax". Editorial. 22–23 March: 6.

—— 1991b. "Biotechnology Paid Executives Better Than Other Industries". 4 April: 4.

Watson, J., M. Gilman, J. Witkowski and M. Zoller. 1992. *Recombinant DNA*. New York: Scientific American Books.

Watts, Susan. 1990. "Have We the Stomach for Engineered Food?". *New Scientist*, 3 November: 24–5.

—— 1991. "A Matter of Life and Patents". *New Scientist*, 12 January: 56–61.

Whelan, Susan. 1989. "World Cancer Patterns". *World Health*, June: 25–7.

Williams, Frances. 1992. "US Criticism Baffles Backers of Patent Rights Draft". *Financial Times*, 22 January: 4.

Whitten, M. and J. Oakeshott. 1990. "Biocontrol of Insects and Weeds". In Gabrielle Persley, ed., *Agricultural Biotechnology: Opportunities for Industrial Development*. Wallingford: CAB International: 123–42.

WHO (World Health Organization). 1983. *World Health*. November issue, "Immunology". Geneva: WHO.

—— 1995. Press Office. "AIDS". *In Point of Fact* No. 86, May.

Wiggins, Steven. 1987. *The Cost of Developing a New Drug*. Washington DC: Pharmaceutical Manufacturers Association.

World Bank. 1988. *World Development Report 1988*. New York: Oxford University Press.

—— 1989a. *World Development Report 1989*. New York: Oxford University Press.

—— 1989b. *Biotechnology in Agriculture 1989*. Washington DC: World Bank.

—— 1990a. *World Development Report 1990*. New York: Oxford University Press.

—— 1990b. *Report on Adjustment Lending II: Policies for the Recovery of Growth*. Washington DC: World Bank.

—— 1991a. *Agricultural Biotechnology: The Next "Green Revolution"?*. World Bank Technical Paper Number 133. Prepared by the Agricultural and Rural Development Department, World Bank, Australian Center for International Agricultural Research, Australian International Development Assistance Bureau and the International Service for National Agricultural Research (The Hague). Washington DC: World Bank.

—— 1991b. *Global Economic Prospects and the Developing Countries*. Washington DC: World Bank.

—— 1991c. *World Bank News*, 7 February.

Wysocki, Jr., B. 1988. "Japanese Now Target Another Field the US Leads: Biotechnology". *Wall Street Journal*, 17 December: 1f.

Xenova Group PLC. 1994. Annual Report: 11.

Yanchinski, Stephanie. 1987. "Boom and Bust in the Bio Business". *New Scientist*, 22 January: 44–7.

Yuan, Robert. 1987. US Department of Commerce (US DOC). International Trade Administration (ITA). *Biotechnology in Western Europe*. Washington DC: US DOC.

—— 1988. US DOC. ITA. *Biotechnology in South Korea, Singapore and Taiwan*. Springfield, Va.: National Technical Information Service.

—— 1995. "South Korea: A Developing Industrial Power, Part II". *Genetic Engineering News*, 1 November: 12.

Zagor, Karen. 1989. "Lower Returns and Quick Party". *Financial Times*, 30 November.

—— 1991. "Amgen Set to Entrance the Medicine Men". *Financial Times*, 8 March.

Index